SPEAKING AMERICAN: A HISTORY OF ENGLISH IN THE UNITED STATES

Speaking American:
A History of English in the
United States

Richard W. Bailey

OXFORD
UNIVERSITY PRESS

OXFORD
UNIVERSITY PRESS

Oxford University Press, Inc., publishes works that further
Oxford University's objective of excellence
in research, scholarship, and education.

Oxford   New York
Auckland   Cape Town   Dar es Salaam   Hong Kong   Karachi
Kuala Lumpur   Madrid   Melbourne   Mexico City   Nairobi
New Delhi   Shanghai   Taipei   Toronto

With offices in
Argentina   Austria   Brazil   Chile   Czech Republic   France   Greece
Guatemala   Hungary   Italy   Japan   Poland   Portugal   Singapore
South Korea   Switzerland   Thailand   Turkey   Ukraine   Vietnam

Published by Oxford University Press, Inc.
198 Madison Avenue, New York, New York 10016

www.oup.com

Oxford is a registered trademark of Oxford University Press.

Library of Congress Cataloging-in-Publication Data

ISBN 978-0-19-517934-7

9 8 7 6 5 4 3 2 1

Printed in the United States of America
on acid-free paper

For
Oceana Yi Huttar Bailey

But there is no "story" of English, or of any language. Rather, there are many stories, many perspectives, many points of view. And it is the same with language as a whole.

David Crystal, *Just a Phrase: My Life in Language* (2009, 15)

Contents

Editorial Note

THIS BOOK IS, sadly, being published posthumously. Richard W. Bailey died on April 2, 2011, surrounded by friends and family. Professor Bailey had been struggling with serious health issues for four years, after a near fatal car accident in 2007. But he was determined to finish this book designed to tell the history of American English in an entirely original way, drawing on the kinds of archival treasures for which Professor Bailey was known. He submitted the full manuscript of the book to Oxford University Press the day after Christmas 2010.

The book readers will find here remains very faithful to the manuscript that Professor Bailey submitted to the Press. In editing the manuscript, there were times when we wished we could consult with him to resolve an ambiguous passage or ensure that the wording of a claim was accurate. Where we felt confident that we understood his intentions, we slightly altered wording for clarity; in other places, we left potential ambiguity unresolved, relying on readers to interpret the passage in context. We left the organization largely untouched, only moving some lengthy parenthetical material into footnotes.

We wish Professor Bailey were alive to see this book in print, and we hope that readers will enjoy learning from this rich source of historical material about the development of speaking American.

Preface

AMERICAN ENGLISH HAS often been seen, particularly in Britain, as an imperfect language, mainly derived from the survival of expressions that have become archaic in England, borrowings from other languages encountered here in North America, or even errors and mistakes that Americans didn't know enough to correct. But American English, from the beginning, began to take its own course, shaped by the new landscape and the various human languages found in it. Early in the seventeenth century, English observers noticed that words like *maize* and *canoe* had become English words and were valuable additions to the language. From that time forward, American expressions were recognized even if they were sometimes demeaned.

The history of American English does not consist, however, of what Britons (and anglophiles) thought about the language, but of the language itself as it evolved over four centuries. Most attention in the past has centered on New England, largely because the written records are most abundant there. Other places were also prominent and influential in shaping the evolution of the language, as this book details.

Chesapeake Bay provided the first settlements for English speakers. St. Mary's, in present-day Maryland, was an important outpost, as were the settlements along the James River in present-day Virginia. Being destined to these places was usually a death sentence with disease and starvation taking a huge toll on the migrants. English took a tenacious hold, however, and began the process of Americanization there.

Boston and its satellites exerted their influence beginning in the 1650s. The most zealous of the Puritans were giving way to a new generation more tolerant, if only slightly, than their forebears. Still, Quakers could be sentenced to death or expulsion for linguistic crimes, particularly for failing to give deference to authority. Both English settlers and Native Americans became bilingual, with consequent borrowings into native New England languages and English—for instance, *netop* 'friend.' Massachusetts settlers, in the third and fourth generation since the *Mayflower*, became more recognizably American.

Charleston, South Carolina presented a very different influence in the development of American English. While it was legally owned by a London corporation, the cultural and political shape of the colony came from Barbados, where a slave-based economy had established itself before 1700. In Barbados, a form of the Atlantic creole of English was used, and spread from there to Charleston. Shipping and trade connected Charleston to West Africa and the Caribbean, where a myriad of languages were spoken. Among the first cultural institutions for English-speaking culture—for instance, a theater and a library—were established there, but the language habits of the grandees were shaped by the practice of sending young men to England for school and university education. The result was class stratification with important differences between the wealthy who had been to England and those who had remained in the colony. Settlements in the up country were established by migrants from the northern colonies, with a major representation of Protestants from northern Ireland. Charleston found itself linguistically encircled but nonetheless satisfied by the linguistic culture there.

In 1750, Philadelphia became the major American city and later the first capital of the new United States. Germans were an important part of Pennsylvania, and they established and maintained institutions favoring their language. Some English speakers, principally Benjamin Franklin, organized efforts to discourage the use of German in public life. Like Charleston, Philadelphia played an important role in international trade with consequent linguistic influences on English. It was the natural place for the delegates from the colonies to meet to adopt the Declaration of Independence and the Constitution. In the 1790s, however, the yellow fever epidemic and the transfer of the capital to Washington did much to diminish Philadelphia's influence.

Early in the nineteenth century, the Louisiana Purchase brought great tracts of land into the United States, and New Orleans was the entry point for much of the development that took place there, particularly when the steamboat made it possible to travel from there up the Mississippi, Missouri, and Ohio rivers. Thus St. Louis and Cincinnati became satellites of New Orleans, and two major American dialects emerged. One was "southern" and linked the places connected to New Orleans. The other was "northern" and was connected to the East Coast, running from New York through the Erie Canal and westward into the Great Lakes, where Cleveland, Detroit, and Chicago became centers of heavy industry.

Though New York had long been a major city, its great period of growth and influence began in 1850 when it became the entry point for millions of European immigrants arriving at either Castle Garden or Ellis Island. Though many soon went west, some remained and their presence transformed American English. Fortunately for the historical record, many took an interest in the way New Yorkers talked, what Walt Whitman called "the blab of the pave" (1982, 33).

By 1900, the center of gravity for English shifted to Chicago, where transportation and communications spread the influence of a particular kind of English throughout the heartland of the country. The idea of changing English for the better also became popular and various means of effecting change were put into play to improve it.

In 1950, the explosive growth of California began. Aerospace, cybernetics, and the entertainment industry all affected the shape of American English. Los Angeles created ways of talking that were more influential than any prior efforts to improve the language. Before long, teenage girls from across the land were speaking in "Valley Girl," and urban youth were mimicking the Crips and the Bloods.

All of these developments have taken English a long way from the English spoken by immigrants who arrived in the seventeenth and eighteenth centuries. Once America achieved independence, we no longer welcomed convicts from Britain who had been shipped here in colonial times. Consequently, the British exported their criminals to Australia, and thereafter there was no substantial organized immigration from England, though large numbers of Irish fleeing the famine of the 1840s arrived in Boston and New York. British English voices were seldom heard face-to-face. In 1849, the Astor Place Riot in New York settled the matter by asking the question of whether the city should support English or American in performances of Shakespeare. Violence on behalf of American prevailed.

Speaking American tells the history of our language from the perspective of eight centers of influence, all of which have affected the present shape of the language. I hope it will inspire the telling of other stories of American English.

Acknowledgments

MOST REFERENCE LIBRARIANS reply with a perplexed look when asked, "What do you have that would help me understand how English was spoken around here in 1775?" Somehow this topic is seldom covered in catalogues, and the language is less well studied than other matters of intellectual history.

For attempting to answer such questions, I am grateful to reference specialists at the Maryland Historical Society, the Boston Public Library, the South Carolina Historical Society, the Historical Society of Pennsylvania, the New Orleans Public Library and the Historic New Orleans Collection, the New York Public Library, the Newberry Library (Chicago), the Huntington Library (Los Angeles), and the Margaret Herrick Library at the Academy of Motion Picture Arts and Sciences (Beverly Hills). I also relied on the invaluable collections of the University of Michigan Library and of the Clements Library (Ann Arbor).

Dates supplied to show the first use of expressions come mainly from the *Oxford English Dictionary*.

An earlier version of chapter 5 appeared in *American Speech* in an issue commemorating the bicentennial of the Louisiana Purchase. I am grateful to Connie Eble, then editor of *American Speech,* for encouraging me to submit it.

Individuals who encouraged me in this project include Judy Avery, Barbara Beaton, Anne Curzan, Ives Goddard, and Ernesto Medina. Erin McKean and Peter Ohlin of Oxford University Press were also helpful at the first and last stages of composing *Speaking American.*

Above all, I am grateful to my wife, the Reverend Julia Huttar Bailey, for technical support and, especially, for nurture.

R. W. B.

SPEAKING AMERICAN: A HISTORY OF ENGLISH IN THE UNITED STATES

1   Introduction

"THE LAND WAS ours before we were the land's." So begins Robert Frost's sonnet "The Gift Outright." In it he tells how the immigrants to North America, including those who came across the land bridge where the Bering Strait now is, adapted themselves to the landscape. We became the land's by living in it and, above all, by naming it—conjuring in the names a new reality.

As soon as words begin to be used, they begin to change, and so the history of a language develops and changes. Expressions jostle together in new ways in a new place and the language becomes new.

Dictionaries and printing may capture a moment in the life of a word, and purists hope to keep it in the same state as it was recorded in documents. Early in the eighteenth century, English writers thought that the language might be *fixed* for eternity, and Jonathan Swift wrote a proposal explaining how that goal might be achieved. Swift was, however, wrong. All the king's men could not bring language to perfection and keep it that way.

A generation later, Samuel Johnson declared that English could not be fixed in place. Change was inevitable. Dictionary makers ever since

Johnson have accepted this idea and attempted to capture fleeting innovations and drifting senses without living in a dream world of stability and perfection.

At the pinnacle of Elizabethan England, English came to America and began to settle in.

In 1643, Roger Williams published (in London) a major work of scholarship: *A Key into the Language of America*. His account described the language he heard from Native Americans in Rhode Island, and he knew that other varieties of that language were spoken in other parts of the continent. For him, "the language" was a rich collection of dialects and languages, and his book was a key to opening a part of it. Williams introduced words from Algonquian into English, but his sketch was part of a larger project to open the complexities of North American languages to European intellectuals.

In almost all contacts resulting in borrowings into English, we depend upon bilinguals and intermediaries. A word apparently coined in America for such persons was *linkister* (1649), a felicitous combination of *link* and *linguister*. Because such persons provided invaluable services—apart from enhancing the variety of English—they are sometimes remembered by name.

Among the earliest of the European linkisters was Alonso de Molina, a Spaniard who arrived in Mexico with Cortés. A young man, he found Aztec friends of his own age and soon became fluent in their language (later known to philology as Nahuatl). Molina found his vocation as a Franciscan, and in 1555 published the first dictionary in the Western Hemisphere: *Vocabvlario en lengua mexicana: Castellana y Mexicana*. In 1571, an enlarged edition appeared. It was designed to further missionary efforts, but it had the unintended effect of bringing words into Spanish which subsequently drifted into English.

The word *mesquite*, a thorny tree of the desert lands of Mexico and the southwestern United States, provides another example of the migration route from the Caribbean basin to English. In Molina's 1571 dictionary it appears as *mizquitl* and became part of the vocabulary in Spanish associated with the New World. In 1572, in the great anthology of travel writing published by Richard Hakluyt, it emerged in English as *mesquiquez*. Thence, the word went underground, only to surface again in Meriwether Lewis's 1806 botanical report to the U.S. Congress on his travels in the west with William Clark.

When *mesquite* entered English, it was a word within a rich and complex language of Middle America. Because the tree was common and yielded an edible pod, *mesquite* became an important part of Spanish-Nahuatl bilingualism before it appeared in both Spanish and English discourse about plants, shorn of its nuances and associations.

Alaska shows yet another circuitous route into and around English. Its origin in the Aleut language is *aláxsxaq*: 'the object toward which the action of the sea is directed.' Like other borrowed words, it lost its context and relation to other terms for topographical features, as well as its phonetic complexity, when it was borrowed into Russian as *Alaksu*. With the purchase of the huge tract of land by the United States in 1867, the form *Alaska* came into English and, because the exotic name was attractive to people, it was used as a town name in Minnesota and Wisconsin, both places distant from the action of the sea (Bright 2004). In 1909 it appeared in *baked Alaska*, a dessert in which quickly baked meringue encases a blob of frozen ice cream. Nowadays, there's a book about a hitherto unknown fish: The *Alaskan Barracuda*. It is, of course, a campaign biography of a politician hailing from Alaska.

When do words like these become English?

Whatever yearning still exists among purists for fixing the language, it remains fluid. *Mesquite* arrives, vanishes, and reappears. *Alaska* begins as a thing ('the object toward which the action of the sea is directed') and then becomes a place. But its history does not stop there, and compounding yields *Alaska candy* 'strips of smoked salmon,' *Alaska cotton* 'a species of grass growing in Alaskan wetlands,' *Alaska divorce* 'liberating oneself from marriage by murdering the spouse' (Tabbert 1991). English has only begun to spin the possibilities. There's no reason to imagine that the elaboration of words like these has come to an end.

Capturing a "state of the language" requires taking a sample of history at a particular time and place and describing, as best one can, the welter of voices speaking what speakers believe to be English. Overlying the portrait of the time may be opinions: for example, some kinds of English are broken, others standard. But they are all forms of English and all entitled to respect. Language does not speak with one voice; it is not created by brilliant individual innovators. It comes from people speaking to other people, old and young, and some of the speakers arrive in the community (as infants or immigrants) and others depart (by death or departure).

Writing a history of English in America involves addressing the historical record. For the distant past, there is too little evidence, and one must extract from fragments a portrait of the whole. Literates are privileged in those distant times; people whose speech was not recorded can barely be identified. For more recent eras, there is too much evidence, and one must select what seems most important from the cacophony of voices now not only seen but heard.

Writing a history of English in America involves adopting a perspective. In our new century, east of the Mississippi, northerners pride themselves on the "standardness" of their speech, while southerners embrace a set of speech values clustering around "pleasantness" (Preston 2004). History written from the northern point of view would celebrate propriety and precision. History written from the southern point of view would emphasize friendliness and family values.

To understand the whole of English in America, one must pick a viewpoint to see how things looked at a particular time and place—or better yet, many viewpoints, from different times and places.

Writing the history of English in America compels accepting that change is both inevitable and extremely rapid. In other nations, a distinction between city and country or between courtiers and churls has sometimes been uncritically accepted as a way of organizing observations about a language. This viewpoint has been reinforced by the celebration of people in "natural" settings, starting with Rousseau. Language on farms and villages retains ancient purity; language in urban centers and political capitals revels in novelty (which may be seen by observers as either good or bad) and invites corruption. The great theme of English in America, however, is rapid change wherever the language is spoken.

In *Democracy in America*, Alexis de Tocqueville recognized, during his short visit in 1830–31, that European ideas about capital and country were not useful here. Americans constantly yearned for change; they would not stay put. Europeans came to America with little capital and were stuck as laborers in the coastal cities; those already resident often acquired the money to finance the journey westward. Tocqueville wrote:

This double movement of emigration never stops; it begins deep in Europe, it continues over the great ocean, it follows across the solitudes of the New World. Millions of men advance at once toward the same point on the horizon: their language, their religion, their mores differ, their goal is common. They were told that fortune is to be found somewhere toward the west, and they go off in haste to meet it. (2000, 268–69)

Consequently, the coastal cities never coalesced as cultural centers influencing the language of their hinterlands. No standard English ever arose to render the other kinds of English "mere dialects" (though plenty of commentators have acted as if they had). Instead, a cluster of different kinds of English gained prestige and lost it, leaving behind a residue of usage that was subject to ridicule: the Brahmins of Boston, the belles of South Carolina, the burghers of old New York are now all forgotten or ignored.

There is no reason to suppose that the admired kinds of English in use today will fare differently.

Tocqueville's ideas about America have influenced our view of history, and they have influenced this book. Much of his thinking was deductive rather than empirical, and he contrasted *aristocracies* with *democracies*. Aristocratic languages yearned for precision and stability, democratic ones for exuberance and innovation. Since the American literary culture at the time of his visit was so fawningly dependent on England, the true democratic English had to be observed in speech. Americans would not comfortably accept rank, though they yearned for authority. Their search for authority in English is one theme of this book.

If we slice and dice the context, Tocqueville can be invoked to support almost any cultural idea, and so it is worth beginning precisely with his ideas about language to see the extent to which we are still persuaded by them.

Since the kind of work we do is the foundation of our prestige, Tocqueville believed that Americans would raise the status of lowly jobs by creating a learned and elegant vocabulary to describe them. The familiar English word *grave-digger* would not do for the new world. Something more exalted was required, and in 1810, Americans began to employ a new and specialized meaning for a long-established English word, *undertaker* 'a person who oversees the conduct of a funeral.' The same impulse toward respectability yielded a series of American terms: *funeral director* (1886), *mortician* (1895), *mortuary science* (1936), *memorial park* (1927). Foreign visitors, particularly those from Britain, have found something ridiculous in the American elaboration of words around death. For Evelyn Waugh, the English novelist, these topics were the subject of satire. Here is Waugh's fictional rendering of a sales pitch for laying corpses to rest in a California cemetery: "Normal disposal is by inhumement, entombment, inurnment or immurement, but many people just lately prefer insarcophagusment. That is very individual" (1948, 43). When American readers found these terms plausible (if not probable), Tocqueville's speculation was borne out.

Since few people in America had a profound knowledge of the classical languages, Tocqueville believed that the niceties of etymology would not be observed. Meanings in Greek or Latin would be wrenched from their roots; fragments of various languages would be put together without regard to rule. In this, too, he was right about American English, and a fondness for high-sounding words was (and is) a part of everyday life. Words in use during the time of his visit that illustrate etymological boisterousness: *bodaciously* 'completely' (1832); *slantdicular* (1832), a blend of *slanting* and *perpendicular*; *splendiferous* 'magnificent' (1843).

Americans were in love with the sound of English, and, at the time of Tocqueville's visit, one could hardly go wrong in seeking grandiloquence to ornament the speeches of important public occasions. Here is the renowned orator Edward Everett launching into his exposition of the meaning of the American Revolution on the occasion of the fiftieth anniversary of the battles at Lexington and Concord:

> ... the tall grass now waves in the trampled sally-port of some of the rural redoubts, that form a part of the simple lines of circumvallation, within which a half-armed American militia held the flower of the British army blockaded. ... (Everett 1825, 2)

Few in Everett's audience were likely to recognize *circumvallation*—it means 'surrounded by a rampart' and is first cited in the *OED* in 1655—but the American thirst for high-sounding vocabulary was satisfied by this speech whether listeners understood it or not.

Though not alone in English-speaking communities in seeking elegance in words, Americans became known especially for finding more genteel words to replace plain ones. A pudding made with corn became a staple food, first called *pone* (1612 < Virginia Algonquian *apones*), then *samp* (1643 < Narragansett *nasaump*), then *mush* (1671), then *hasty pudding* (already in use in English for a soup of other grains). More recently, this humble dish goes by the word borrowed from Italian, *polenta*. Other elegant words created or widely used in America include *rooster* (instead of British *cock*), *comfort station* (for *public toilet*), *limb* (for *leg*). Two British travelers whose visits came close to those of Tocqueville—Frances Trollope and Frederick Marryat—made special sport of American linguistic gentility.

High-sounding (even if ignorant) words seemed to Tocqueville particularly likely to arise in America, and he was persuaded that "generic terms and abstract words" (2000, 156) would also flourish here. Aristocratic peoples distrusted such expressions and were unwilling to think beyond inherited convictions about the similarities of things. Democratic peoples, in contrast, were fond of them because they were thinking not only of new things but of old things in a new way.

An empirical test for such a theory would be difficult to construct since every language has generic terms, abstract words, and the capacity to make new ones. All that can be said is that Americans like creating new doctrines and terms to go with them: *chiropractic* and *scientology*, for instance. And they have been enthusiastic borrowers (through adaptation or translation) of abstract terms from other languages. So *superego* and *id* come from Freud's German to English; *deconstruction* and *metaphoricity* arrive from Derrida's French; Chinese practices invite borrowings like *tao* and *feng shui*; Soviet political ideas provide *bourgeoisify* (from Lenin) and *racist* (from Trotsky). If Tocqueville was right that Americans are indifferent to etymology and indulgent about borrowing, then one might also cede that he was right about a fondness for abstractions, not requiring that they fit an established pattern but allowing generic terms to come into American English higgledy-piggledy.

Tocqueville imagined aristocracies to be linguistically static and fragmented: "It ordinarily happens in centuries of privilege that the exercise of almost all the arts becomes a privilege and that each profession is a world apart where not everyone is permitted to enter" (2000, 439). The result is "a sort of aristocratic jargon" (2000, 447). Democracies are just the opposite; learning can be diffused as widely and deeply as anyone might wish. There was scarcely a pioneer's cabin where books were not found, and Tocqueville read, for the first time, Shakespeare's *Henry V* in a *log-house* (this word was given in English in Tocqueville's French text) somewhere in the wilderness (2000, 445). Far from being oppressed by "aristocratic jargon," Americans could explore, as playfully as they liked, the pleasures of English and the wealth of the vernacular.

Thus it was in the early days of American independence that there arose a taste for fantastic words. In Britain, Maria Edgeworth and Walter Scott had put nonstandard voices on the printed page, and in America such experiments were even more likely and even more popular. Edgeworth's fiction explored status distinctions between British and Irish English speakers; Scott, persuaded that dialects in Scotland were rapidly vanishing, used the vernacular for historical flavor. In America, the use of innovative language was quite different. New images, and new words, were created to celebrate the boisterous life on the frontier: *rambunctious* 'exuberant' (1830), *catawampously* 'vigorously' (1834), *rip-roaring* 'spirited' (1834). The most prominent of the frontiersmen in the 1830s was Colonel David Crockett, a real person who was turned into a mythological giant employing fantastic language. From words attributed to him, the *Oxford English Dictionary* gives *back-out* 'withdraw' (1836), *banter* 'challenge to a race' (1836), and *blizzard* 'a sharp blow' (1834). Here's the *OED*'s illustrative sentence from "Crockett" for *jam-up* 'thoroughly' (1835): "[Andrew Jackson] went jam up for war; but the cabinet got him down to half heat." President Jackson, himself a southerner who moved west to Tennessee with little formal education, embodied pride in the *rough and ready* (the phrase an Americanism of 1843). Tocqueville viewed him as a president of "violent character and middling capacity" (2000, 265), but one who spoke a democratic English.

The foundation for an ideological American English began shortly after the Revolution, and its most articulate spokesman was the quarrelsome Noah Webster. In July 1788, he proclaimed an organization called the "Philological Society of New York," and, in a parade celebrating the ratification of the U.S. Constitution, he marched with a banner proclaiming "federal language" and displaying below that headline a crest densely illustrated with heraldic and allegorical symbols devoted to the independence of the English of America (Read 1934, 133).

By the time of Tocqueville's visit, Webster had become far less enthusiastic about signs of separation between British and American English. In his magnificent 1828 dictionary, Webster noted that *creek* was not limited to an inlet from the sea (as in Britain) but was used in the United States for a small river. This sense, he wrote, was "not justified by etymology." So much for "federal language."

Yet if Webster's enthusiasm for a separation of the two kinds of English had diminished, others took up the cause with relish. Early in the nineteenth century, the United States struggled to become a postcolonial culture, to stand square against the colonial cringe that presumed any marked departure from the linguistic tastes of London would be a source of shame. As Tocqueville noted, however smitten with British tastes the literary classes might be, ordinary people were entirely indifferent to the cavils of British critics. As an anonymous author observed in 1836, "Some [Americans] are so entirely Britannic, as to receive every thing for legal tender in letters, which comes across the water.... Others are so patriotically republican, as to set about the task of nursing the countless brood of cis-Atlantic words, into literary respectability" ("Borealis" 1836, 110). The dialectic between the two parties created a new sense of English in America.

As would often be the case as kinds of English coalesced into images, popular culture provided a focus for what was to come. From the 1780s forward, there emerged the image of the American—often called *Brother Jonathan* or *Yankee*—in popular entertainment, both in print and on the stage. The language of these characters was often drawn from many sources already present in drama: the rustic bumpkin; the downright simple patriot; the comic and good-hearted character (see Jortner 2005).

Of particular interest among these plays is *The Yankey in England* by David Humphreys, an accomplished military officer and former diplomat when his play was published in 1815. Humphreys presented not one character but three to represent types of Americans: a well-educated New Englander, a man of the "second class," and Doolittle, the Yankee. In his preface, Humphreys explained that at the time of the Declaration of Independence, English had become copious and refined, and that education since then had only improved it: "From this state of things, it is naturally to be concluded, that the English language is not generally spoken any where with greater purity than in many parts of America" (1815, 12). Doolittle, he noted, may be "a subject of risibility on account of his dialect, pronunciation, and manners" (15), but he has many good qualities—as the play amply demonstrates. It is not so much the particular features of Doolittle's speech that are of interest, but the fact that a virtuous character could be represented with ridiculous English. Humphreys even appended a glossary to explain the Yankeeisms employed in the play (103–10; see Mathews 1926). He took particular pride in a performance of his play in his hometown of Humphreysville, Connecticut, in which the youth acting Doolittle performed in "his usual dialect and pronunciation," not as a comic figure but a representative of his class expressed "in conformity with the best English standard" (111). The notion that American English was better than British English—more *pure*, more *uniform*—has continued to vex British observers to this day.

Tocqueville deduced that in aristocracies people were trapped in the rank to which they were born, and that, even should they should be deprived of property and position, their origins would still be apparent from their manners. (In making this observation, he doubtless had in mind the aristocrats of France displaced by the Revolution.) He observed: "In aristocratic peoples, the different classes are like vast precincts that cannot be left and cannot be entered" (577).

Democracies, constantly in motion and socially fluid, tended toward an unpredictable diversity of manners. In such societies, Tocqueville wrote, "a multitude of artificial and arbitrary classifications are created, with the aid of which each seeks to set himself apart out of fear of being carried away into the crowd" (578). Apart from appearances, nothing could be a better indicator of where Americans belonged than their language. Tocqueville speculated that democracies would be unable to form "a precise code in the case of social graces" (580), but he also imagined an energetic negotiation over just what social graces were most desirable.

In 1781, a Scots resident in the United States had coined the term *Americanism* to describe a distinctive usage (whether word or sense) found here. In so doing, he was drawing upon the term *Scotticism*, which had been in use in Britain at least since 1682. Gathering Americanisms became a recreation of the British literati, usually with the motive of urging American authors to avoid them or to hold up the English of the new nation to ridicule. British visitors before the Revolution had commonly praised the *purity* of American English or celebrated its freedom from local dialects over a huge territory. Afterward there was increasingly strident carping about "Americanisms" that continues to this day.

At the turn of the nineteenth century, pronouncing dictionaries began to be published in the United States. These included best-selling English works, the earliest of which was derived from the work of Thomas Sheridan and published in Wilmington in 1804; the immediate successor was by John Walker and published in Philadelphia in 1808. At first they were merely new editions of the dictionaries already appearing in London, and it would be some time before distinctively American works began to be produced. Nonetheless, the hunger for information about how words should be pronounced generated discussion about how words *were* pronounced, a discussion that became more vexed when the London fashion began to encourage speakers to insert sounds not in the American vernacular (like the [h]-sound in *heir* and *herb*) or to promote vowels that were wholly foreign to both tradition and to America (like extending the vowel of *father* to *grass* and *bath*). Still, American observers were reluctant to involve themselves in disputed questions of pronunciation. In his 1828 *Dictionary*, Webster limited himself to scattered observations such as: "The common pronunciation *cramberry* is erroneous."

Curiosity about pronunciations did not necessarily arise from social anxiety or a desire to mimic the speech of others. Here is a specimen from a letter written in Philadelphia in 1818. Writing to his wife in Boston, Horace Holley explained that his hostess was given to "a little genteel quizzing." (*Quiz* was quite a new word to English when he wrote; the sense here combines 'test' with 'amusement.')

> You will remember that the two words, which she detected in my pronunciation, as I mentioned them in a former letter, are *hev* for *have*, and *abzorb* for *absorb*. I detected her in *disconary* for *dictionary*, *agin* for *again*, *lezure* for *leisure*, and *recī-tă-tive* for *recitative*, i. e. *recitateeve*. (Holley 1818, 1)

Not long after this letter was written, many different pronunciations acquired a social stigma, and a conversation like this one soon would revolve around which of the variants was "right" and which "wrong." So, for instance, a writer of 1824 who published letters describing the speech habits of Americans up and down the Atlantic coast observed: "Until you leave home, you will not be aware how many provincial and fatherless and motherless heathenisms, are used in daily parle by *some* New Englanders; although they justly take pride in being more literate than most other states" (Knight 1824, 29).

Before the Civil War, varieties of American English were best heard in the Congress since each state sent representatives of its elite to Washington. Henry Clay of South Carolina sounded "strongly" southern, according to the secretary of the Senate. A representative from Virginia "seemed to delight in the African accent." Virginia's senator "would address 'Mr. Speakah,' and refer to the honorable member who had just had the 'flo'" (Forney 1873–81, 1:297). These observations were made in the 1850s, and soon sectional variety would erupt in sectarian violence.

Thus emerged the "multitude of artificial and arbitrary classifications" that Tocqueville anticipated as distinguishing marks of the American experiment in democracy.

Social nuance in English was one thing, variety in languages another. Recognizing the work of the American Philosophical Society (under the encouragement of Thomas Jefferson), Tocqueville acknowledged the recent recognition of the rich complexity of the indigenous languages of America: philologists "discovered for the first time that this idiom of a barbarous people was the product of a very complicated system of ideas and quite learned combinations" (2000, 678). Of course, Roger Williams had discerned exactly that two centuries earlier.

Tocqueville did not mention, however, that America was not demanding a rapid assimilation of other languages to English. In fact, his assumption that democracies would foster small groups of like-minded people, voluntarily formed and sustained by friendships, applied particularly to communities in which English was seldom used for important purposes. He must have noticed the flourishing German-speaking communities in Philadelphia and beyond, with their many newspapers and works of pleasure, improvement, and learning. In Utica, New York, a Welsh hymnal had been published in 1808, and in 1840 would begin in New York the long-running Welsh newspaper *Y Cenhardw Americanaidd*. Other magazines were published in Portuguese and French. Almanacs and similarly useful works appeared in Swedish and Spanish. Prayer books and religious texts appeared in a great variety of American languages including Ottawa (in Detroit) and Hawaiian (in Oahu).

Far from discouraging the use of languages other than English, political figures attempted to strengthen the nation by reaching out in other languages. In 1821, Vincente Rocafuerte published in Philadelphia a translation of works by Thomas Paine as well as Spanish versions of the Articles of Confederation and Constitution. His purpose was to persuade people in Central and South America of the desirability of American institutions of government. Works promoting immigration to the United States were published in European languages, here and abroad. While there were some complaints about communities where English was seldom spoken—famously, Benjamin Franklin's private complaints about German in 1753—on the whole, immigration was encouraged and languages other than English not discouraged.

In 1848, Jesse Chickering published a statistical account of immigrants to America since 1820 (Chickering 1848), and he showed that there had been steady growth as well as a spurt of newcomers starting in 1840. What was the impact of these immigrants? One reviewer noted that linguistic separation did not mean political division, and that all soon became Americans whatever language they might speak. Even those children born to immigrant fathers and mothers were "in every sense American" (Debow 1848, 247). The value added to national wealth, the reviewer said, was almost incalculable. And the settled immigrants acted as "a vast teaching class, dispersed over the whole country, advising the inexperienced and checking the rash among their countrymen" (248).

If Tocqueville had considered the matter, he would certainly have concluded that recent immigrants were as much Americans in their conduct and view of government as the long-settled citizens. While anxiety about foreign languages would eventually reach poisonous levels, these developments did not take place until after the Civil War.

In many respects Tocqueville's speculations about America provide a useful framework for considering the history of English in America. Rapid social change, restless movement of population, thirst for innovation, and struggles with issues of diversity and instability have all characterized our settlement history from the beginning. Those who seek stability in English seldom find it; those who wish for uniformity become laughingstocks; those who create variety find a ready market for the language of their imagination.

2 Chesapeake Bay, before 1650

THOUGH PRONE TO complaining about it, observers have regularly found something to praise about the English language. In a publication of 1619, a London schoolmaster, Alexander Gill, celebrated "the purity of our tongue." (*Purity* has meant a variety of things in talking about English, but it usually means that the language is relatively free of borrowed words.) The language would admit foreign words only "out of necessity," Gill thought, and America brought new necessities. Native American languages had given such expressions as *maiz* and *Kanoa*, the latter 'a boat hollowed out of a trunk of a tree by fire and flint-stones' (Gill 1972, 1:108–9). Both these words had reached English through Spanish more than half a century earlier. Still, Gill knew where they ultimately came from and he saw them (and their like) as ornaments to English rather than as impurities.

America came to English before the English came to America. A century behind Spain and Portugal in exploration, English people had a deep curiosity about the New World, and much of what they knew came at second and third hand. Asked to compile what was known about these distant lands, Pietro Martire d'Anghiera gathered reports and published them in

Spain as *De orbe novo* beginning in 1513. His title quoted Amerigo Vespucci, and from the phrase came the English expression *New World*. In 1555, Richard Eden translated *De orbe novo* and published it in London: *The Decades of the New Worlde or West India*. Eden's translation of this and other foreign works of navigation and discovery yielded nearly three hundred new words for the editors of the *Oxford English Dictionary*. Among those still familiar are *canoe, cacao, cacique* 'prince', *cassava, guava, hammock, iguana, maguey, manatee,* and *yucca. Hurricane,* another of Eden's words, shows the pattern of borrowing. It began in a West Indian language, Carib, as *huracan* and entered Spanish, Portuguese, French, and Dutch. The modern English form of the word was not, according to the *OED*, settled until about 1650.

Efforts to establish a presence in the New World were underfunded, tentative, and confused. Promotional literature intended to attract investment suggested that fabulous wealth in jewels and precious metals would be easy to pluck from the ground or from the inhabitants. Having already profited by piracy and plunder from Spanish ships, the English had a geopolitical goal: establish bases from which raids could be sent forth to attack shipping. Colonies might also be used to rid England of unwanted populations: religious dissidents, criminals, and the poor.

The first serious expeditions by the English had a strongly scientific bent. In 1585–86, Thomas Harriot, an astronomer and mathematician, visited Roanoke Island at the mouth of the Chesapeake. A remarkable genius, Harriot had gained some fluency in the Algonquian language of the region by working with two Native Americans who had been brought to London in 1584 and returned with Harriot to Virginia. Presumably, the language lessons continued on board ship, and Harriot made a note of the expression *Kecow hit tamen* 'What is it?' His report of his travels, published in 1588, showed a deep understanding and respect for the cultural practices of the people he encountered in Virginia. He drafted a phonetic alphabet which survives in manuscript: *An vniversall Alphabet conteyning six & thirty letters…first devised vpon occasion to seeke for fit letters to expresse the Virginian speche* (1590; see Salmon 1996, 151). Given the questions he asked, Harriot's lexicon consists mainly of nouns but there were many of them. Compared to Eden's translations, the words had little impact on English because the unfamiliar contours of the words had not been smoothed by the simplifications made in Spanish and Latin in Eden's words. English people knew how to borrow from Latin; they were not prepared to borrow firsthand from an Algonquian language.

Colonizing began almost immediately after Harriot's return to England. In 1587, a group of 117 men, women, and children established a settlement on an island near the mouth of the Chesapeake, but they were ill-prepared for supporting themselves. Some of them returned home to purchase supplies, but the relief expedition did not return until 1590. By that time, the colony had vanished, though curiosity about the fate of the settlers led to suppositions that they had joined Native Americans and moved to the forests of the interior. From time to time, later explorers came upon "white Indians" supposed to be survivors, or descendents, of these first colonists.

The first enduringly settled English people arrived in Chesapeake Bay and established themselves, tenuously, forty miles from what they called the Virginia Sea on Jamestown Island in 1607. There were 105 of them. By the end of the year, owing to famine and disease, only 38 were left. Not until 1618 did the population reach 600 people. In 1624, it had increased to 900; in 1624, it reached 1,275. This number was achieved only because 3,500 people had arrived in the intervening years (McFarlane 1992, 45). Most immigrants died of typhus or dysentery since they seem to have had no idea of how to separate drinking water from water sources used for human waste.

Just what sort of English these settlers brought to America is difficult to determine. Except for a few with sufficient capital to emigrate without contracting themselves to terms of indenture, most came from the south and southwest of England, so the distinctive northern dialects of the language were probably not influentially present (Horn 1994, 40, 42). Since the colony was stratified into "planters" and "servants," there must have been some hierarchy in the varieties of English spoken, but whatever norms existed would also have been battered by high mortality and the departure of those who could afford the return passage to England. Some of those who could not drifted into the forest and took up residence with the natives.

English was not neglected in planning for the new colonies. In 1622, John Brinsley published a grammar intended to lay a "sure foundation" for "good learning." He clearly explained his motive for doing so:

> Finally it hath bene, and is mine vnfained desire to all functions and places, and more particularly to euerie ruder place, as to the ignorant countrie of Wales, and more especially that poore Irish nation, with out louing countrie-men of *Virginia*, or where euer else, if it might please the Lord to cause the light to breake forth vpon them, which now sit in such palpable darknesse, and in the shadow of death, and wholly vnder the slauerie of Satan. To the end to make the way of knowledge more easie vnto them, not onely to the attaining of the Latine tongue, but also that hereby they may much more easily learne our English tongue, to helpe to reduce the barbarous to more ciuili-

tie, and so to plant Gods true religion there, that Iesus Christ may reigne amongst them. (Brinsley 1622, 15)

The ultimate end of this proposal was to bring Christianity to the "ignorant," but the means for doing so involved a foundation in the grammar of English, not only that Latin might be learned, but that languages other than English might be put aside. In Greek, *barbarism* referred to people who did not speak Greek. Brinsley used the word in just this sense except he meant that the *barbarians* were those who did not speak English. What he wanted to do was to promote *civility*—that is, civilized conduct that would emerge only after the "palpable darknesse" of other languages had been put aside and a knowledge of English gained.

In England, it was common to suppose that Native Americans were a people living in "palpable darknesse," but on the ground settlers discovered that the inhabitants had well-developed social structures and, most important, were able to prosper from the landscape in which they lived. Without the tradition of hospitality they encountered, the English settlers could not have survived, and to do so they had to identify the most powerful among the Native Americans and persuade them to help. One of Harriot's borrowed words came into English as *werowance*, which he explained as 'chief Lorde.' Subsequent writers defined the word as 'king' or 'commander.' That it had become an English word was apparent when, in 1615, Ralph Hamor described an expedition from Henrico (the second settlement after Jamestown) to visit Powhatan, the monarch most important to the survival of the English. Sent upriver by Thomas Dale (then governor of the colony), Hamor relayed that "there was two English sent vpon businesse to *Powhatan* from the English *Weroance*" (Hamor 1615, 38). Sending word, however, was complicated.[1]

In order to engage in useful negotiations with Native Americans, the Virginia settlers needed bilinguals to translate on their behalf. At first, they relied on gestures and signs, but some of the English must have learned a simplified Algonquian language, "pidgin Delaware," that was spoken up and down the Atlantic seaboard to facilitate communication among Native Americans speaking very different languages. John Smith's *Map of Virginia* (1612) contained examples of sentences in pidgin Delaware—for instance, one

---

1. Werowance Dale was a remarkable early figure in the expansion of the English empire. His first military service had been in the Netherlands, and he was then part of the force attempting to subdue the Irish. Dale's service in the Chesapeake colony (1611–16) included aggressive military action against Native Americans and severe punishments for colonists who stole from the common store of food. Some were tied to trees and starved to death. Dale then led an expedition to India and the East Indies where he battled against the Dutch, his former employers. He died in India in 1619.

translating into English as "Truely he is here. I doe not lie" (Goddard 2001, 72). In fact, many Europeans did not recognize that the language they had acquired was highly simplified and so were surprised when their friends began to speak in a far more elaborate and unintelligible form of their language. Some of the words introduced to English in Smith's accounts reveal their origin in pidgin: *moccasin* as *Mackasins* 'shoes' has the English plural *-s*. (The French borrowing of the same word from a more northerly Algonquian language was made plural in the French way, *Mekezin*.) (See Strachey 1999.)

Signs and gestures were limited, and the English determined to bridge the language gap by creating bilinguals. After only a month in Virginia, the colonists traded a thirteen-year-old boy, Thomas Savage, for a member of Powhatan's entourage, Namontacke, "his trusty servant, and one of a shrewd subtill capacity" (Smith 1612). The colonists thought he was a spy for Powhatan, and he likely was one. It was not necessarily a bad thing for Powhatan to discover that the English were improvident and incompetent.

Thomas Savage became an invaluable intermediary, able to act as a translator within a short time. Others, perhaps unwillingly, followed Savage's example: Henry Spelman, aged fourteen, who joined Powhatan's court in 1609, and shortly thereafter John Smith's page, Samuel Collier (see Kupperman 2000, 208–11; Axtell 2001, 47). Collier prospered but was unfortunately killed in 1622 by an English sentinel. He was memorialized in Smith's *Generall Historie of Virginia* as "one of the most ancientest [i.e., earliest] Planters, and very well acquainted with their language and habitation, humors [*sic*] and conditions, and Gouernor of a Towne, when the Watch was set going the round, vnfortunately by a Centinell that discharged his peece, [he] was slaine" (Smith 1624, 157).

Just how these young interpreters could be mistaken for Native Americans is not hard to see. Many Native Americans wore English clothing that they had acquired in trade, so appearance was not an unambiguous clue. Ralph Hamor reported having come upon one William Parker who had vanished from the settlement three years earlier. Parker had "growen so like both in complexion and habite to the *Indians*, that I onely knew him by his tongue to be an Englishman." Powhatan was not pleased to learn that Hamor and his companions expected to take Parker away with them: "You haue one of my daughters with you, and I am therewith well content, but you can no sooner see or know of any English mans being with me, but you must haue him away, or else breake peace and friendship...." (Hamor 1615, 44).

This daughter was Pocahontas (1595–1617). She appears in the historical record in April 1607 when she allegedly saved John Smith from execution by throwing herself over his body just before he was to be clubbed to death. This story is almost certainly fictionalized, for Smith did not include it in either of his two books about Virginia. Nonetheless, the scene has entered American folklore. In the middle of the nineteenth century, a touring burlesque troupe, the cross-dressing Wallace Sisters, performed an extraordinary version of the tale as imagined by John Brougham: *Po-ca-non-tas; An Original Aboriginal Erratic Operatic Semi-Civilized and Demi-Savage Extravaganza, being a Per-Version of Ye Trew and Wonderfulle Hystorie of Ye Rennownned Princesse, Po-ca-hontas*. In Brougham's play, Powhatan speaks in a broad Irish brogue (see Bailey 2003, 196–97). An equally fabulous treatment of the legend appeared in *Pocahontas*, an animated film released by Disney Studios in 1995. In real life, however, Pocahontas and her story hardly needed embellishment.

Pocahontas entered Jamestown as part of a delegation from Powhatan to the English settlers. She was at the time a girl of eleven or twelve, and soon she became a playmate of settler children and learned rudimentary English. At the same time, the colonists were learning pidgin Delaware: *Kekaten Pokanontas patiaquagh niugh tanks mantyens neer mawchick rawenock audowgh* 'Bid Pokahontas bring hither two little Baskets, and I will give her white Beads to make her a Chaine' (Smith 1986, 2:132).

Powhatan made Pocahontas, a favorite daughter, an intermediary as he supplied food to the town. However, in the autumn of 1609 relations between the English and the Native Americans deteriorated, and Pocahontas no longer visited. In 1613, she was deviously kidnapped by a ship's captain who held her hostage in negotiations to secure a peace. Powhatan agreed, returning prisoners and weapons to the struggling settlement in exchange for Pocahontas. Not long thereafter, though, her connections to the colony became more firmly fixed. In 1614, she was baptized by the Rev. Alexander Whitaker and given the weighty name of Rebecca, a reference to the Canaanite girl taken from her people to become the wife of Abraham's son Isaac. By leaving her culture for another far away, the biblical Rebecca became the mother of all Israel.

A man who was to have profound influence on the Chesapeake colonies, John Rolfe, became Pocahontas's husband later that year (see Vaughan 2004; Tilton 2004). Because of emphasis on the tale of Pocahontas's saving Smith, Rolfe's importance to the spread of English in America is often neglected. In fact, he saw opportunity where others found only despair.

Among the scientific observations made by Thomas Harriot in 1585–86 was that in Virginia could be found *uppówoc*:

There is an herbe which is sowed apart by itselfe & is called by the inhabitants Vppówoc: In the West Indies it hath diuers names, according to the seuerall places & countries where it growth and is vsed: The Spaniardes generally call it Tobacco. (Harriot 1590, 16)

Tobacco had come into common use in Europe, thanks to imports from the Caribbean. In 1604, James I of England decried the filthy habit of smoking it, but royal disapproval did little to discourage its use. Rolfe recognized that the species found in Virginia was bitter, and he contrived to import seeds or plants from the Caribbean islands. They flourished.

In 1614, just months after his marriage to Pocahontas, Rolfe sent four hogsheads of Virginia tobacco to England, where they found a ready market. Thus began the first of the English empires built on trade in narcotics.

If one were to choose an English word most representative of the first half of the seventeenth century, that word would be *tobacco*. Putting aside his father's distaste for the ill-effects of the burning weed, Charles I ordained that "foreign tobacco" be kept out of Britain and that the planters of Virginia and the "Summer Isles" (i.e., Bermuda) be given a monopoly in the trade (Charles I 1625).

In 1616, Rebecca and John Rolfe, with their infant son Thomas (1615–ca. 1657), left for England. Pocahontas was a celebrity, visited the court, sat for a portrait, and was received in society as an exotic princess. John Smith, whom she regarded as a father, wrote on her behalf to the queen, Elizabeth I. Pocahontas was, he declared, "the first Christian ever of that Nation, the first Virginian ever spoke English, or had a child in marriage by an Englishman" (quoted in Allen 2003, 314). In early 1617, the Rolfes prepared to return to Virginia, but as they were departing, Pocahontas fell ill and died. Thomas remained in England in the household of his uncle, while John returned to develop tobacco plantations. Then, in 1622, John Rolfe also died. When he reached adulthood, Thomas Rolfe returned to Virginia, took over his father's estates, and prospered. Just as was anticipated when his mother was baptized Rebecca, he became, in legend at least, the ancestor of many of the "first families of Virginia."

The year 1622 was not a good one for the colony. Powhatan had died and his successor launched what has been described as the "great assault." The object was to expel the foreigners from Virginia and, though the campaign did not succeed, the result was the death of more than 300 colonists. News of this attack reached England and did much to discourage further emigration. Desperate for new hands to work the fields, the promoters set out to greatly expand the practice of deporting the poor and the criminal. In 1618, a law had been enacted in London that resulted in poor children between eight and sixteen being deported, and after 1622 the number of such children greatly increased. A new crime arose: *spiriting* 'kidnapping' (1666), by which children were snatched from the London streets and sold abroad. Virtually every ship that arrived in the Chesapeake carried children to face the ordeal and perils of the New World. Recent archaeological work on graves yielded the somber fact that 40 percent buried there had died in their teens and another third in their twenties (Rountree 2005, 264 n. 28). Evidence from these young people's teeth revealed that most had suffered from malnutrition in early childhood. Life in the Chesapeake was (as a philosopher would later quip) nasty, brutish, and short.

Another important event for the development of English in America was the compelled migration in 1619 of the first West Africans sold into slavery on the mainland of North America. While the slave trade would greatly expand in later years, these first arrivals were treated badly but probably not worse than other "servants" of the colony, and no special notice was taken in law of African-descended slaves until the 1660s. In a report of the colony published in 1649, an anonymous author estimated that there were in Virginia "about fifteene thousand *English*, and of *Negroes* brought thither, three hundred good servants" (*Perfect Description* 1649, 1). No evidence of the speechways of these Africans seems to have survived from the period.

There are, however, examples of how Native Americans were supposed to speak. Here is a statement reported to have been made by a diplomat negotiating the end of hostilities with the English in the 1630s:

> The *Wicomesse* after a little pause, replyed: It is the manner amongst us *Indians*, that if any such like accident happen, wee doe redeeme the life of a man that is so slaine, with a 100 armes length of *Roarokee* (which is a sort of Beades that they make, and use for money) and since that you are heere strangers, and come into our Countrey, you should rather conforme your selues to the Customes of our Countrey, then impose yours upon us....(*Relation* 1635, 25–26)

Apart from two loan words—*wicomesse* 'a tribal name' and *roaroke* (< *roanoke* 'white beads')—there is little here that can be identified as anything but a highly formalized statement in seventeenth-century English. The subjunctive form *doe redeeme* was then typical of legal and persuasive language, as in this example from a London court record of 1632: "IT IS ORDERED THAT

MR Tr[easur]er do paye to Mʳ Drake in Chepside for sending a boy to Virginia" (quoted in Wright 2001, 250). This declaration shows the Native American in full command of a highly specialized style of English, but it is unlikely that he really spoke these words. Instead, the person presenting the speech depicted the *Wicomesse* as a fully competent adversary.

In the 1630s, the fortunes being made in the tobacco trade attracted others to the Chesapeake as a site for a colony. Despite strenuous opposition from the Virginians, in 1629, the English aristocrat Charles Calvert sought royal authority for a colony, and in 1632 a charter was granted to his son, by then his heir, authorizing the establishment of Maryland. In 1634, the first settlers arrived, soon joined by a second fleet bearing a Jesuit priest, Andrew White. An English Catholic, White wrote a vivid account of his first experience of the New World. To help in negotiations with the Native Americans, White and his companions engaged the services of Henry Fleet: "one of those who live in Virginia, a man especially welcome to the savages, fluent in the language, and acquainted with the region" (White 1995, 37; see also Cecil 1635, 4). Despite this praise, White was suspicious of Fleet's representations of religious doctrine: "we do not fully trust our Protestant interpreters" (41). The colony established itself in St. Mary's, a town north of Virginia in present-day Maryland.

Like Harriot a generation before him, White was deeply interested in the languages he encountered along the Chesapeake. He prepared a grammar and lexicon and translated the catechism into the Algonquian language of the northern Chesapeake. (None of these creations was printed.) To complete this work, White must have acquired some fluency in that language, and likely his helpers learned something about English at the same time. English began to take hold: "not long after, the young empress (as they call her at Pasataway [in Prince George's County]) was baptized in the town of St. Mary's and is being educated there, and is now a proficient in the English language" (White and Dalyrymple 1874, 82).

Relations between the Maryland colonists and Native Americans were far more harmonious than had been the case in Virginia, and the ways of planting and preparing tobacco for export were well understood by the English. Partly because Maryland allowed settlers to acquire land more quickly and more easily than had been the case in Virginia, the colony prospered. Though much is made of the fact that Roman Catholics were given full rights in Maryland, most settlers in the area were Protestants. While the Marylanders of these two versions of Christianity may have prospered together, Protestants from Virginia invaded in 1644 and burned

St. Mary's to the ground. White was shipped as a prisoner to London and not allowed to return. For the first time in the Chesapeake, English Americans were fighting against each other.

In 1644, there was another great assault by Powhatan's descendants on Jamestown and other settlements in Virginia. Quickly repulsed, the Native Americans withdrew to the west and south. The linguistic dialogue between them and the English had lasted nearly half a century. By 1650, it was no more.

For anything useful to be said about English in America in the first half of the seventeenth century, one needs to look at the special circumstances of life in the Chesapeake. Language contact between the English and others was limited. Native Americans were often hostile; Africans were too few to contribute much; the colonies of the Dutch and the Swedes higher up the Bay were small and separated from the English. As tobacco planting grew in importance, the planters lived at greater distances from Jamestown and Henrico. Since the ships that came to load tobacco arrived at the separated plantations in both Virginia and Maryland, civil life in the colonies was restricted. Only a few would travel any distance for reasons of government or commerce. Natural population increase was severely limited by the imbalance of men and women; in 1635, for every woman who left London for Virginia, there were six men (Horn 1994, 36). Certainly there must have been intermarriage between Native American women and Englishmen, or at least relationships that produced children. The arrival of English women, particularly when children began to be deported in large numbers, enhanced the development of a new kind of English in the Chesapeake. Of course, the death rate was alarmingly high, and the survivors must have been dispersed throughout the coastal regions.

Prestige varieties of English were represented, however, especially among the clergy. Alexander Whitaker, who baptized Pocahontas, had been educated at Eton and Trinity College, Cambridge. He was made priest in 1609 and went to Virginia in 1611. He did not live long: he was drowned in 1617 (Kupperman 2004). However brief his residence, he must have presented a model for an educated kind of English. According to a survey of Virginia published in 1649, there were eventually twenty churches "with Ministers to each" (*Perfect Description* 1649, 7). If this same anonymous enthusiast for Virginia is also right in projecting a population of 15,000 English by that time—the estimate is probably an exaggeration since the author was painting a rosy picture of the colony—these twenty churches probably had little influence on English. Schooling, too, must have been uncommon. What kind of English would have been spoken in those tumultuous times?

Lacking evidence, it is very difficult to know. But we can assume that English became more uniform in the Chesapeake than it had been at home since people of the middle and lower ranks of society were thrown together in desperate circumstances and then found themselves in settlements where distance and the need for strenuous labor kept them apart.

Linguistic historians often view the founders of a new settlement, particularly one isolated from the home country, as having a deep influence on the evolution of their language (known as the *founder principle*). In the case of the Chesapeake at this early period, it is difficult to imagine who the founders were and just what their influence might have been. To judge by the records of the Virginia company, many colonists stayed only briefly in the New World before returning to England and there giving testimony to the conditions they experienced (see Kingsbury 1906, 385–86). While recent historians have revised the view that Virginia was a colony in perpetual turmoil in the first half of the seventeenth century, there can be no doubt that there was great instability. More desirable kinds of tobacco—especially one called *sweetsents* (Horn 1994, 182)—could be more profitably grown on lands north of the tobacco coast on the James River, and migration within the colony naturally followed.

New farms were carved out of the forest as old ones became exhausted by successive crops of tobacco. There were few villages and nothing resembling a city. Whoever the elite may have been, they were unlikely to have been a readily identifiable group.

A second hypothesis proposes *colonial lag* to describe the tendency of varieties of English spoken at a distance from the metropolis not to participate in changes taking place there. Dialects at a distance, this idea alleges, tend to preserve older forms that disappear at home and thus to become archaic. Like the founder principle, this idea does little to illuminate conditions in the Chesapeake. A constant influx of new population, whether coming voluntarily or by deportation, suggests that the newcomers imparted the speechways of home to those who survived from earlier migrations. If anything, one might suppose that the linguistic circumstances of the colonies would show a greater extension and more rapid completion of changes afoot in London. At home, schooling, literacy, and the example of parents and educated persons (especially clergy) would all work to retard change. Abroad, English would become more American simply because it was more unconstrained.

3 Boston, 1650–1700

IN THE SECOND half of the seventeenth century, the colonies in Massachusetts still clustered around the arrival point in Plymouth but they grew increasingly diverse. Port towns, like New Bedford and Gloucester, looked eastward to the Atlantic and its fisheries; they attracted new settlers experienced in fishing, including migrants from Brittany and Normandy who brought linguistic diversity to the European-descended population. The generation of those who arrived in 1620 was succeeded by descendants and new arrivals, and the separatist communities of Puritans began to embrace more secular ways, particularly after the restoration of the Stuart monarchy in 1660—which, in both Britain and America, resulted in a lessening of enthusiasm for the ideas that had stimulated the original settlements around Massachusetts Bay. Puritan orthodoxy faded but remained powerful as new immigrants arrived with varied professions of Christianity.

Quakers found Massachusetts congenial, at least at first, but tolerance did not last long. The Puritans enacted a law to require deferential speaking: "And every person or persons whatsoever, that shall revile the office or person of Magistrates or Ministers, as is usual with the Quakers, such

Person or Persons shall be *Severely Whipt*, or pay the sum of *Five Pounds*" (Rawson 1660, 36). In 1660, the Puritans imprisoned some 3,000 Quakers because they refused to accept Puritan authority and submit to it. Those not willing to speak deferentially were banished with dire punishments promised should they return. Four Quakers were executed as part of this campaign, including Mary Dyer, who (like the others) rejected hierarchy, using the pronouns *thee, thou,* and *thy* instead of the gradations of status involved in using these pronouns in combination with *ye, you,* and *your* to distinguish degrees of respect. The Quakers were levelers; the Puritans were not.

In vocabulary, English was readily adapted to the New World. Some places were given (or retained) Native American names: *Nauset, Mashpee* (later anglicized to *Marshpee*), *Saugus*. Most settlers, however, applied the names of English towns and regions to the New World: *Boston, Essex, Plymouth*. The celebration of religious and civic virtues also found its place in the landscape. *Dedham* was at the outset called *Contentment*, and *Providence* endures as a name for the place where Quakers and others were exiled by the Puritans. Biblical names were common—for instance, *Mt. Pisgah* and *Sharon*. Personal names had a similarly uplifting flavor, particularly for women with names like *Patience* and *Prudence*. Always sensitive to language, the teenage Benjamin Franklin in the next century created *Silence Dogood* as a humorous character with a comic name. When New England Yankees became figures of fun in nineteenth-century humor, one could easily recognize the New England origins of Abijah Stone or Hosea Biglow from their names alone.

Puritans favored words of Germanic origin, associating terms borrowed from Latin-Romance sources with language not transparent to ordinary people. One such American usage was *selectman* (Massachusetts laws, 1646), an elected representative responsible for civic affairs in a town. Both on etymological grounds and in emphasizing the source of the authority of such persons, *selectman* was far better than *officer* or *councilor*. *Lecture-day* (for *Thursday*, 1677) made plain that people were expected to listen to sermons rather than conduct ordinary business. Though not a word original to America, a *fast-day* in the spring was ordained in New England and so called rather than employing words like *penitence* or *abstinence*. Similarly *outliver* (1675) was employed for a person who lived at a distance from settlements, perhaps in search of *settable* (1656) land— another New Englandism far more transparent than the established English word *arable*.

Innovations in the English of New England and the adaptation of the language to the new American reality are comparatively easy to discern given the massive documentary record that survives from the period. Nowhere in the English-speaking world at the end of the seventeenth century was literacy more common than in New England. Many men and women had quite limited skills, but the ideal of education was celebrated by all. In 1642, officials were required "to endeavour to teach, by themselves or others, their Children and Apprentices, so much learning, as may enable them perfectly to read the English tongue, and knowledge of the Capital laws: upon penalty of *twenty shillings* for each neglect therein" (Rawson 1672, 26). Thus literacy was diffused through the social hierarchy rather than being the accomplishment solely of the wealthy and powerful. Some of the impulse toward literacy has been associated with the Protestant emphasis on a personal encounter with holy texts and works of exegesis.[1] Other views of the data emphasize related phenomena, such as the rise of individualism and a growing sense of the need to adapt to new economic and social circumstances. Both of these stimulated the demand for literacy. Whatever the cause, however, New Englanders from the very beginning of settlement were copious producers of documents (see Lockridge 1981).

Lawyers were scarcely represented among the immigrants to New England, but notions of legal obligations were strong. There needed to be an apparatus for justice, and writing enabled decisions and transactions to be seen and remembered. Here is an extract from the presentments made by the Grand Inquest held at Plymouth in March 1654:

Imprimis, wee p[re]sent Willam Randall, and Elizabeth, his wife, of Scituate, for abusing the cunstable, Walter Hatch, in word and action, as by threats, and refusing to give securitie according to the warrant, and that when hee strained for the majestrates table, his wife tore the distress out of his hand, and hurt his hand soe as blood was sheed.

It., wee p[re]sent the same Willam Randall for selling stronge waters to an Indian.

It., wee p[re]sent James Gleghorne, and Abia Lambard, his now wife, of Barnstable, for carnall copulation before contraction....

It., we p[re]sent Joane, the wife of Obadiah Miller, of Taunton, for beating and reviling her husband, and egging her children to healp her,

---

1. Other regions of high literacy levels at the time included the north German states, Sweden, and Scotland, all places with strong Protestant institutions.

biding them knock him in the head, and wishing his victials might c[h]
oake him. (Shurtleff 1855, 75)

The first and last of these records report crimes that involve language: the
first recounts when the Randalls abuse the constable who attempts to
serve a legal paper (*distress*); the last includes such verbal actions as *reviling, egging, wishing*. Even the second and third are linguistic in nature: the
verbal transaction involving selling intoxicants charged against William
Randall, and the failure to execute a written contract that would make
premarital sexual relations acceptable within the law.[2]

The deep preoccupation with language in Massachusetts was connected
to a sense of hierarchy and the view that Massachusetts was a theocracy
(within a geographically distant monarchy). While the usual prohibitions
against blasphemy were common there and elsewhere in the Christian
world, the Puritans gave special attention to the fifth of the Ten Com-
mandments: "Honor thy father and thy mother." Silent obedience was an
ideal for children, but the commandment was elaborated into a doctrine
of "right speaking" that presumed that the clergy were surrogate parents
and thus empowered to govern the speaking of those of lesser status. Thus,
Anne Hutchinson was banished in 1637 for striving to address the male
ministers on equal terms, when, in their view, a woman was subordinate to
all men and thus required to keep silent. Laws against improper speaking
were adopted, and people of all sorts were brought to court. Some were
charged with offenses where capital punishment might have been imposed
upon them. Accusations resulting in "presentments for speech against authority" were at their peak from 1641 to 1680 (Kamensky 1997, 200).
These crimes were varied: children failing to speak respectfully to their
parents; servants using inappropriate language; women speaking at all
about matters of consequence in church and society. In the last years of the
century, these actions were still considered criminal but restitution might
be made in money instead of a public apology. (No one seems to have been
hanged for offensive speech, though some were sentenced to be executed.)

Concern for right speaking yields documentary evidence of what constituted wrong speaking. In midcentury, John Porter shocked the community by abusing his parents, calling his mother "the rankest sow in the

---

2. More than half the infants born in the period were illegitimate or conceived before the parents were married.
Very likely there was some other reason to vex the Gleghornes since their only reported fault was the failure to
execute and record a written contract declaring their intention to marry.

towne" and declaring his father "a thiefe." In 1664, he was tried and found guilty. His immediate punishment was to be whipped and imprisoned. Eventually, his case was forwarded to courts in England, but no satisfactory conclusion was reached, and John died in 1684 (Kamensky 1997, 103–11). Court records are filled with the minute particulars of speech that was entered into them during the course of public apologies and recantations.

These legal actions arose from the conviction that language was powerful and even magical, that harm could come to a person cursed or lowered to the state of an animal. The court records of Essex County from 1651 to 1680 show that 332 cases were brought as criminal presentments and 163 as civil proceedings. Criminal cases involved blasphemy and attacks on established authority; civil ones, threats and forms of assault on a person's character or livelihood. Animal names were particularly offensive, particularly ones involving dogs and pigs. The word *dog* was often accompanied by modifiers: *base, base Welch, black, foresworn, French*. These were used in verbal assaults on men. For women *sow* was a common term of abuse with modifiers: *base, bobtail, filthy, lying*. *Rogue* was a particularly productive term, by itself or with such words as *adulterous, base, cowardly, thievish*. For women, *witch* might be accompanied by *black-mouthed, old, spiteful, ugly*. Cursers might attack children, and terms that merited legal action for them included *dog, puncke, qu[e]ne*. (*Punk* and *queen* meant 'prostitute'; the words did not begin to refer to homosexuals until the twentieth century.) Ministers might bring someone to court for calling them *deceivers of the people*; magistrates found it offensive to be called *poopes* 'dolts.' In all, cases were brought over ninety-six different principal words which might be accompanied by eighty-nine modifiers. Nationality names became terms of abuse: *Indian curr, Jersey cheat* (from Jersey in the Channel Islands), *Scotch curr, French dog. Ishmaelite* was the seventeenth-century term for Muslims, and it too is among the catalogue of illegal words (St. George 1984). Those found guilty of such crimes of speech were, at the least, obliged to make public recantation and perhaps fined or imprisoned.

Because New Englanders were both literate and litigious, court records about such disputes reveal something about the way people talked. In 1661, Beatrice Canterbury of Salem was brought before the magistrates for slandering her son-in-law. One of her neighbors gave the following deposition:

[S]he heard her say to her daughter that her husband was both a rogue and a thief, her daughter sayd she must prove it[.] she sayd he was a thiefe for that he had stolen the best flower in her garden, & a rogue because he had brought her body to shame saying she did think the divel would picke his bones[.] this deponent sayd unto her she did not wel to speak so to her daughter agynst her husband. but you should do him the best good you can & give him good counsel for now he is your son: she sayd Cantebery's wife [i.e., Beatrice] answered that the divel shoul pick his bones before she would own him to be her son. (Quoted in St. George 1984, 277–78)

One should not presume that this is a precise transcript of what Canterbury said, though a high regard for minute detail in these crimes of speech meant that the neighbor was likely to have been scrupulous in what she reported. *Divel* 'devil' reflects a frequent variant pronunciation of the day, and the "devil would pick his bones" must have been a common curse in an age so profoundly convinced of witchcraft.

For the future of American English, contacts with Native Americans provided the most enduring effects. When Roger Williams published his great book in 1643, he called it *A Key to the Language of America*. He had endeavored to make himself fluent, and his work provides wonderful insights into relations between the two civilizations. That he called it "the Language of America" was significant, though in its subtitle he makes clear that he writes only of the language of New England. Of course, the diversity of languages was obvious to him, but he presented it to his readers as merely involving dialects (just as English dialects in Britain presented a challenge to travelers). By learning the *key* he provided, "a man may, by this *helpe,* converse with *thousands* of *Natives* all over the *Countrey*" (Williams 1997, A3v).

In order to understand the relationship between the English and Native Americans it is essential to realize that the English felt a strong kinship with them. Many regarded the newly encountered people as equal (and similar to) the European culture they brought with them. In 1650, Thomas Thorowgood wrote a book arguing that the natives were a lost tribe of Israel. When a second edition of *Jews in America* appeared in 1660, Thorowgood had a prefatory testimonial from John Eliot. Such speculation only advanced the ideas expounded by Thomas Morton a generation earlier pointing to resemblances between Native American languages and those of classical antiquity:

... & by continuance & conversation amongst them, I attaned to so much of their language, as by all probable conjecture may make the same manifest, for it hath been found by divers, and those of good judgement, that the Natives of this Country, doe use very many wordes both of Greeke and Latine, to the same signification that the Latins and Greekes have done... (Morton 2000, 14)

American settlers in the second half of the seventeenth century discovered that Native Americans spoke many languages. Among the most common lexical borrowings of the period were names for the languages and cultures of these people: *Montagnais* (1654), *Montauk* (1657), *Iroquois* (1666), *Cherokee* (1674), *Chickasaw* (1674), *Onondaga* (1674), *Natick* (1678), *Minisink* (1684), *Mascouten* (1698), *Osage* (1698), *Pawnee* (1698), *Conestoga* (1699), and *Yamansee* (1699). Of course, many of these languages were spoken far beyond the threshold of settlements in Massachusetts.

Bilingualism among the English colonists was probably not common, though some of them tired of the rigid society of Massachusetts, vanished into the wilderness, and took up Native American ways. A few were captives, and some of them chose to remain and embraced Indian languages. Others were adventurers.

Some knowledge of languages though seems to have been common if not widespread. Demaris Wescott Arnold (1621–1678) was the wife of the governor of Rhode Island who was the successor to Roger Williams. She was able to detect emissaries falsely claiming to be from Connecticut; they "could not put off the Narrowgansett tone" and so were recognized by her as imposters (Winthrop 1645, 6).

Balance in the ecology of language began to shift in favor of English. While the first half century of English settlement had been characterized by translators and by the use of one of the simplified pidgins, the second saw the increasing use of a pidgin (or perhaps creolized) English, particularly among the Native Americans. Early evidence of this pidgin occurs in a court record from a case in 1651. Connecticut had passed a law forbidding trade with the Dutch coasters sailing from New Amsterdam (modern-day New York) eastward along the New England shore. An English-speaking colonist, John Dyer, was ferrying people across the mouth of the Connecticut River and was engaged by three Native Americans to take them. The story continues:

[S]o hee [Dyer] brought them ouer, and when hee had turned the point into the North Coue, and came neare the vessels that rode there, the said Indians asked this deponent wch was the Dutch vessel, and hee tould y^m w^ch; then they asked this depondent whether the Dutchman had any coates: hee answered them, *tutta*; thene one of the Indians stood vp in the cannooe and called to the vessel and sayd, Way bee gon coates? Some answered, there was coates: then this deponent, tould the Indians, *Nux*; then they desired and hee sett them aboard, and this deponent tarried in the canoe: then Mr. Augustine, M^rch^t [Merchant], called to the skipper to shew the Indians some cloths, so the skipper and the Indians went downe into the hold, as hee supposed, amonge the cloth.... (Trumbull 1850, 1:219)

Here the evidence shows the use of pidgin with elements from both English and the languages of southern New England. *Tutta* 'I don't know; I can't say' and *Nux* 'yes' are from Massachusett. "Weaybee gon coates?" is pidgin: "Away be gone coats?" = "Do you have any coats?"

A subsequent example, from 1669, comes from the testimony of Edward James, who accused a Native American named Nimrod of attempted rape. Given the very high value placed on exactness of language in the courts at the time, this allegation seems to have passed from James's wife to her husband, who then presented it to the court. This chain of evidence suggests that both of the colonists were conversant with the pidgin English of southern New England:

Edmund James' complaint: that on Dec. 10, 1669, an Indian named Nimrod, with three other Indians, came to said James' house and without leave calling or knocking, his wife being at home alone, sat down by the fire to warm themselves. Nimrod became bold asking her the said Edmunds wife if she haue husband. she say yea. he said where he walke. she said little way fetch pigsack. Nimrod say you much ly, me great wake woods today. me no see pigsack. he no little wake [*sic*] he great way walke. come you give me meechin. Mee haue pudding. Mee haue meat wunnegin. she speake by by my husband come much hungry. he said your sannap be hangd me haue meechin. and so searching about the house for victaules but finding none drest he sate down again by the fire and began to speake partly in Indian and in broken English some baudy discourse about women which she began to understand and was sore afraid she standing knitting in the chimney corner with her back towards him, the other indians all the time laughing.... (Dow 1911–78, 4:230n)

Mary Mitchell, Edmund's wife, had been married just six months before, and she was very much frightened by this intrusion into her house. Fortunately for her, the other Native Americans "speaking in Indian" pulled Nimrod out the door, and they "tooke up theirs guns and hatchets and went away." In spite of her fears, Mary was able to speak pidgin, as shown by her answer to where her husband had gone: "little way fetch pigsack." Four usages in the extract come from Native American languages, including: *meechin* 'food' < *meechum* 'food'; *sannap* < *sanomp* 'adult male'; *wunnegin* 'good.' The most interesting of these is *pigsack* 'pigs': *pig* is a borrowing into pidgin from English with the Algonquian animate plural *-ak*. *Pigsack* is thus doubly plural, first with the English suffix *-s* and then with the Angonquian plural *-ak* (Goddard 1977, 40; Goddard [personal communication]). Other traits of pidgin appear in this report: generalized pronouns (e.g., *me* for *me* and *I*), simplified negative with *no*, omission of determiners (e.g., *a, some*), and reduplication (e.g., *by by* 'soon').

The effort that tipped the balance in favor of English was the attempt to convince Native Americans of the texts and principles of Christianity. After eight years of collaboration with a speaker of the Massachusett language, John Eliot published a complete translation of the Bible. It was generously supplied with loan words from English for culturally unfamiliar items like sheep and angels. Eliot hoped that Native Americans would become missionaries to their own people, using the catechisms and other religious texts he published. In support of this effort, he sought (and received) donations from English benefactors, and some of the works he published were directed at them. A few show the traces of the "broken English" he found typical of their speech, as he described in the following:

> Deacon Park propounded this Question. What is it in sin, why hee hateth it now more than before?
>
> Ans. his answer in broken English. I did love sin, but now not all one so, because I hear Gods Word, and that shewes mee, that which I loved is evil, and will bring mee to hell, therefore I love it not now. (Eliot 1660, 9)

Not much is "broken" about this English, and only "now not all one so" shows traces of pidgin. Eliot probably exaggerated the fluency of this speaker, Nishóhkou, in order not to distract attention from his repudiation of former sins.

The British audience for good news from New England was further encouraged by reports of Hiacoomes, a member of the Narragansetts, who appeared in 1643 at the mission under the direction of the Thomas Mayhews, father and son, on the island of Martha's Vineyard. Thomas Mayhew, Jr., taught Hiacoomes to read and write English, and he began to serve as an interpreter in Mayhew's work with Native Americans. Eventually, Hiacoomes became a missionary himself. The Mayhews were unusual in respecting the land and property rights of the Native Americans, and eventually Hiacoomes was ordained (by John Eliot) and in 1670 opened a church for the converts. As time went on, Hiacoomes played an increasingly important role in the affairs of the Christian Indians. The younger Mayhew was also unusual in seeking to empower them; he did not seek wealth and encouraged Native Americans to take charge of their own affairs. For example, Hiacoomes's son followed his father into the ministry. Escaping the tumult that soon would change the relations of English and Indians, Hiacoomes continued his work until his death in 1690. (See Standley 2000, s.v. Hiacoomes; Schultz 2000, s.v. Thomas Mayhew, Jr.)

On the mainland of Massachusetts and Rhode Island, the linguistic scene showed an imbalance, particularly in comparison to Martha's Vineyard. John Eliot was eager to bring Native Americans into the fold of Christianity. In 1651, he recorded for the first time the name "John Sosoman" as one of his assistants, and five years later he noted a payment of £30—a substantial sum—to three interpreters and schoolmasters: Sosaman, Monequason, and Job (Lepore 1994, 491). While hoping that educated English clergy would learn the local languages and carry out the work, he found few willing to do so. So the engagement of bilingual Native Americans was his only recourse, and he recognized that it was far more beneficial to his purposes to have them as missionaries. Eliot's colleague, Daniel Gookin, elaborated this point in a petition to English philanthropists in 1674. One method of encouraging bilingualism, he thought, was to put schools near Native American communities. Since "a schoolmaster will not be willing to leave English Society, and to live constantly among the Indians," these schools would draw children from their families for daily lessons and, at the same time, be given food and clothing (Gookin 1792, 79).

Gookin's other idea was that children might be brought into English families as servants and apprentices. Those acting as their employers would be required to teach them to read and write. Parents might be unwilling to cooperate with such a plan: "they are generally so indulgent to their children, that they are not easily persuaded to put them forth to the English" (1792, 79). However reasonable that reluctance seems in the twenty-first century, it would have seemed strange to a seventeenth-century audience. In England at the time, half the population was or had been "in service," and so common was this social practice that resistance to it must have seemed almost inexplicable.

Eliot was determined that Native Americans become Christians, and to do so fully they needed literacy in order to engage personally with the Bible. They might best do so, he thought, in "praying towns" where converts and their children would be removed from the influences of Native culture. At the same time, he argued, they might benefit from English ways in housing and clothing as well as acquiring skill in agriculture and the trades. In 1664, a census of the fourteen praying towns showed that (of 462 converts) 31 percent could read the Massachusett language, 16 percent could write in it, and 2 percent could read English (Lepore 1994, 492). These numbers show the remarkable success of Eliot's leadership in fostering literacy in the Massachusett language. Surviving documents written in Massachusett over the next century are numerous and varied; some are official and some personal. Unsurprisingly, literacy mirrored English practices—petitions to government officials, for instance—but they also show "many aspects of the precontact culture of the Indians" (Goddard 1994, 397; Goddard and Bragdon 1988).

John Sassamon, as his name is rendered by modern historians, is an emblematic figure illuminating the linguistic situation. Sassamon was a bilingual educated in English culture. He was likely to have been the child of a community devastated by imported diseases in 1633 and raised among the English. Yet he maintained his ties with Native Americans and was fluent, and eventually literate, in Massachusett. Assisting Eliot in the creation of the praying town in Natick, he remained a figure there at least through 1656. In 1662, he reappeared as a translator and counselor to Metacom—known to the English as King Philip. Metacom was the grandson of Massasoit, who had greeted and befriended the English colonists arriving in Massachusetts in 1620. Metacom resisted Eliot's repeated attempts to convert him, and he attracted Sassamon to his service as translator and go-between. Sassamon was thus a figure who did not belong. Both the Native Americans and the colonists distrusted him, and in 1674 he warned the English that Metacom was preparing for war. The colonists did not believe him; he was killed in March 1675 by three Native Americans who were subsequently betrayed, tried by both English and Native American courts, and then executed.

In June 1675, Native Americans allied with Metacom assailed Plymouth. Soon they found supporters in western Massachusetts and launched further attacks. By July 1676, twenty-five towns established by the colonists had been destroyed; a tenth of the European-descended population had been killed. Native American communities were even more devastated. After Metacom was assassinated in August 1676, the survivors were rounded up, their property rights were abrogated, and many were sold into slavery. Enraged colonists made no distinction between allies and enemies, so-called pagans and Christians.

Many colonists recorded the events of the war, but John Eliot did not. His dream of a bilingual New England with Christians everywhere was shattered. This shockingly violent conflict made for profound changes in the language ecology. Native Americans were evicted from their lands in many places. News of the war reached Britain and discouraged immigration. The economy went into decline, and not until the eighteenth century did the community begin to recover.

Before Metacom's rebellion, words from the languages of southern New England were borrowed into English. Some of these are traced by the *OED* to "Algonquin," a collective name for languages covering much of the Atlantic seaboard of North America. Among these are *wigwam* 'hut' (1628), *kantikoy* 'a dance' (1670), and *kinkajou* 'wolverine' (1672). More specific attributions to New England languages include *peag* 'wampum' (1649) from Massachusett, and from Narragansett *nocake* 'cornmeal' (1634), *papoose* 'child' (1634), and *squaw* 'woman' (1622). (In Massachusett *squa* 'young woman' was a word of neutral or positive connotations [Goddard 1997]; negative connotations developed much later.) In 1676, *sunck squaw* 'queen' was borrowed into English from Natick. These words are typical of the introduction of Native American words into the English of the colonists. After the rebellion (often called King Philip's War), the historical record shows few borrowings from these languages, not a surprising development in the wake of the widespread death and displacement on both sides that occurred during and after it.

In the Chesapeake, most surviving documents show the conventional forms of English that would have been used in England in the first half of the century. Part of the reason for this bias in the archives is that those able to write (or having a need to write) were educated, and the documents that survive are mostly official records of several kinds. Another part of the reason is that many of the papers that were written did not survive into the nineteenth century, when interest in colonial history began in earnest. High literacy rates in New England meant that more people were writing; there were more occasions requiring documentation; there was a great attention to preserving the past.

In this record of more standard written language, unconventional spellings allow insight into the way in which English was pronounced (Orbeck 1927). Most writers of the time would regard these as misspellings, but habits of speaking can be discerned in them. For instance, the use of [n] rather than [ŋ] was likely to have been even more common then than it is today: it results in spellings such as *stocken* 'stocking,' *accordenely*, *yearlin*, *gowen* 'going,' *riggin*, and *strenth*. This pronunciation is also apparent when writers improved their spelling by adding *g* where it was not conventionally used: *childring* 'children,' *oving* 'oven,' *suddingly* 'suddenly.' Vowel sounds in *sass* 'impudence' and *sassy* 'impudent' would eventually split off separate words from their originals, *sauce* and *saucy*. The distinction between *whoop* and *hoop* was increasingly lost, as shown in the 1775 title *The Yankies War Hoop* ("An American" 1775).

Final consonants were often omitted (as they are today): *nex* 'next,' *bes* 'best,' *threshall* 'threshold.' The collapse of initial [hw] and [w] is suggested by *whet* 'wet' and *where* 'were' (examples from Kytö 2004, 135).

The spelling *dafter* suggests *daughter* was pronounced to rhyme with *laughter*, though the most common spelling for the word was the modern one. Other competing spellings suggest variability in pronunciation. Examples from a body of late seventeenth-century New England documents produced such differences as these: *git(ting)* (10 instances) versus *get(ting)* (38); *divell* (125) versus *devil* (278); *parson*, *parsun* (14) versus *person* (378).

Far longer than in Britain, New Englanders retained the traditional pronunciation of words with the vowel of *fat*. According to William Dwight Whitney, describing in 1874 the English of the northeast in the mid-nineteenth century, this [æ] vowel had been preserved "until recently" in *calf* and *calm*, *ant* and *aunt*. The "new" pronunciations with [ɑ] in the second of these pairs was rarely heard, and when Whitney wrote, it had not yet begun to be appear in *chance*, *path*, *can't*, and similar words (Whitney 1874, 206).

The most interesting of these seventeenth-century pronunciations involves the pronunciation of *r* in the middle and at the ends of words. While the omission (or vocalization) of *r* is a prestige feature in modern British English, it was very much a rustic feature in seventeenth-century

England. In the evolution of *r*-less pronunciations, Boston led the English-speaking world in the development of norms that would later become important among opinion leaders in southeast England.

The process by which *r* becomes a vowel (or is omitted entirely) in the middle and ends of words started before settlement in America. The disappearance of *r* began in words where it appeared before *s*: *horse, parcell, worsted*. Words like these were sometimes spelled *hoss, passel, wosted*. In later American English, these pronunciations gave rise to separate meanings: *hoss* (as a term used for men with slightly mocking affection, *old hoss*) and *passel* (a collection of something, *a passel of trouble*). Weakened *r* spread in England during the seventeenth century, but observers seem to have regarded it as dialectal or simply a mistake. Only in the mid-eighteenth century did it begin to appear in respectable English (Lass 1999, 114–16).

Twentieth-century dialect surveys showed that the absence of *r* in the word *here* was typical of eastern New England and the coastal South. Studies in southeastern England at the same time demonstrated that the lack of *r* in *hear* was typical of Kent, Essex, and East Anglia, the three areas from which the most prominent Bostonians came in the seventeenth century (Kurath and McDavid 1961, Map 35; see also Kurath and Lowman 1970, 27). As a later chapter in this book discusses, the pronunciation of *here* was symbolically important in Chicago in its assertion of linguistic independence from New England and southeastern England.

As late as the 1820s, British purists decried the absence of *r* among "the natives of London" in such words as *pearl, girl*, and *card* (*Vulgarities* 1829, 256) even though these pronunciations were rapidly emerging as features of the prestige dialect. In the second half of the seventeenth century, however, the *r*-less pronunciation was emerging as a distinctive feature of American English. New England town records are full of spellings where historical *r* is omitted: *Mos* 'Morse' (1669), *fouth* 'fourth' (1693), *bud* 'bird' (1675). Even more persuasive evidence that *r* was commonly dropped in pronunciation is its appearance following long vowels in spelling: *horsers* 'hawsers' (1655), *geoge* 'George' (1665), *Chals* 'Charles' (1668), *pasneg* 'parsonage' (1666), *Borston* 'Boston' (1694) (Krapp 1960, 2:228–30). These spellings were not common, though, since the great attention to literacy in seventeenth-century New England preserved the historic *r* spellings even if the letter was silent. The words in which *r* is inserted are much more persuasive evidence that the deletion (or vocalization) of *r* was widespread in the region.

The richest seventeenth-century source for information about English in Massachusetts is found in the vast trove of documents preserved from the Salem witch trials of 1692. Salem, a town just north of Boston, caught itself up in a deadly attempt to eliminate witchcraft that seemed to plague the community, and by the time the panic subsided, after just four months, twenty men and women had been executed and many more imprisoned. Nearly obsessive documentation of these proceedings survives, and several scribes transcribing the same testimony produced quite different results, whether in small details or in quite different strategies of summarizing. Some have questioned the worth of these inconsistent reports, but it is certainly the case that they are far more detailed in characterizing speech than any other collection of documents anywhere else in the contemporary English-speaking world. Even if they are sometimes "radically dissimilar" (Grund 2007, 143), they show the same meticulous attention to detail that characterized the earlier records of slander and defamation trials. If people were to die as a consequence of what they did, it was important to record what exactly it was that they said. Of course, different scribes spelled words in different ways, and they thought different expressions had greater or less importance (see Rosenthal et al. 2008; Grund, Kytö, and Rissanen 2004).

For the broad picture of American English attempted here, a specimen of one of the depositions can give sufficient flavor of the kind of speech written down in the proceedings. Here is an extract from the interrogation of one of the accused witches, a woman named Tituba:

TITUBA: the Ind'n Woem'ns Examn March. 1. 1691/2 [March
1,1692]
Why doe you hurt these poor Children? whatt harme have
thay done ont you?
TITUBA: thay doe noe harme to me I noe hurt them att all.
Why have you done itt?
T: I have done nothing; I Can't tell when the Devill works
what doe the Devill tell you that he hurts them?
T: noe he tells me nothing
doe you never see Something appeare in Some shape?
T: noe never See any thing (Boyer and Nissenbaum 1977)

In this passage, the interrogator speaks quite typical seventeenth-century English with one exception: "what do the Devill tell you" rather than "what does the Devill tell you." This use of *do* instead of *does* is not typical of these documents but it was one of the characteristics of the English of East Anglia, the homeland of many of the emigrants to Boston (Kytö 2004, 138).

Tituba's English is far more interesting than that of her questioner. She was a South American, enslaved in Barbados and taught English there by an Englishwoman, Elizabeth Pearsehouse. She arrived in Boston in 1680 as a member of the household of Samuel Parris, a Puritan minister. The ideas she gained of the invisible world of demons came both from the Caribbean and from Anglo-American culture. Her reluctant confession, later recanted, told the court that she had made an agreement with the devil and thus had become a practicing witch (Breslaw 1996).

In this short extract from a longer examination, the distinctive feature for Tituba's English is "I noe hurt them att all." The more usual negative construction, found in other Salem documents, is "I know not the least thinge of witchcraft" or "he do not know any such pitt." "I no hurt them" is just the sort of grammar to be expected of someone from the Caribbean where a creolized form of English was in widespread use. Another scribe who recorded this examination turned Tituba's English in the direction of New England norms: "I do not hurt them" (quoted in Breslaw 1996, 190)—thus transforming the unfamiliar into the usual.

In the second half of the seventeenth century, New England became a backwater among the English colonial outposts in North America. The conquest of Jamaica in 1655 made possible the expansion of very profitable sugar cultivation, which earlier had begun in Barbados. The conquest of New Netherland in 1664 led to a new name for this Dutch colony: New York. It too had great economic potential from trade and from the rich agricultural lands of the Hudson River valley. In 1681, the English monarch granted to William Penn the huge tract of land that would become Pennsylvania; a hallmark of the new colony was religious tolerance extended not only to the Quakers (of which faith Penn was the prominent figure in America) but also to other religious professions. Both for economic and ideological reasons, these new colonies were far more attractive to potential emigrants than was Massachusetts Bay with its short growing season, less fertile lands, and ideological intolerance.

During the seventeenth century, about half a million people left England for the New World and nearly three-quarters of them settled in the Chesapeake and the Caribbean (Horn 1994, 24); these destinations took an increasing share of migrants in the second half of the century. Constantly refreshed by new arrivals, these outposts remained satellites of English culture and very much attuned to linguistic developments taking place there.

Boston struggled. Its population at the end of the seventeenth century was fewer than 5,000. Nonetheless, Benjamin Harris launched the first American newspaper in 1690 amid great hopes that rumors would be scotched and truth reported. He announced:

> It is designed, that the Countrey shall be furnished once a moneth (or if any Glut of Occurrences happen, oftener,) with an Account of such considerable things as have arrived unto our Notice. (*Publick Occurrences, both Foreign and Domestic,* September 25, 1690, 1)

Certainly, there were occurrences of great public interest that flooded upon the community. But Harris's newspaper lasted only one issue, and published reports of considerable things would have to wait until the eighteenth century, when journalism began in earnest (Clark 1991).

Early in the new century, a distinctively American outlook on English began to take hold in New England. In 1704, Sarah Kemble Knight set out from Boston on an overland trip to New York. It took just over a month of steady travel for her to reach New Haven in Connecticut, and she and her guides faced day after day of difficulty as they forded streams, ferried over rivers, and followed roads that were little more than tracks in the forest. Along the way, she encountered people whose interest in language was of interest to her. For example, approaching Kingston, Rhode Island, her sleep was disturbed by two drunkards beyond the thin wall of her sleeping chamber. They were engaged in a heated argument about the meaning of the word *Narragansett*. One declared it was the name of a "prodigious" briar that grew around about; the other that it came from the name of a cold spring. (Neither is correct; Bright 2004.)

From the viewpoint of her refined Boston manners, the people Knight met were mostly clods and bumpkins, and she re-created their rudeness and their improper English. Coming to a house after being lost in a swamp, Knight and her guide entered the principal room.

> My Guide dismounted and very Complaisantly help't me down and shewed the door, signing to me wth his hand to Go in; wch I Gladly did—But had not gone many steps into the Room, ever I was Interogated by a young Lady I understood afterwards was the Eldest daughter

of the family, with these, or words to this purpose, (*viz.*) Law for mee—what in the world brings You here at this time a night? I never see a woman on the Rode so Dreadfull late, in all the days of my versall life. Who are You? Where are You going? I'me scar'd out of my witts—with much now of the same kind. (Knight 1992, 5–6)

The daughter's rude questioning and rustic vernacular showed what was certainly true at the end of the seventeenth century: that English had split into urbane and rustic varieties.

Knight reported another, more complicated story to illustrate the administration of justice in Connecticut.

A negro Slave belonging to a man in yᵉ Town, stole a hogs head from his master, and gave or sold it to an Indian, native of the place. The Indian sold it in the neighbourhood, and so the theft was found out. Thereupon the Heathen was Seized, and carried to the Justices House to be Examined. But his worship (it seems) was gone into the feild, with a Brother in office, to gather in his Pompions [= *pumpkins*]. Whither the malefactor is hurried, and Complaint made, and satisfaction in the name of Justice demanded. Their Worships cann't proceed in form without a Bench: where upon the order one to be Imediately erected, which, for want of fitter materials, they make with pompions—which being finished, down setts their Worships, and the Malefactor call'd, and by the Senior Justice Interrogated after the following manner. You Indian why did You steal from this man? You sho'dn't do so—it's a Grandy wicked thing to steal. Hol't Hol't cryes Justice Junʳ Brother, You speak negro to him. I'le ask him. You sirrah, why did You steal this man's Hoggshead? Hoggshead? (replies the Indian,) me no stomany [< *understand*] No? says his Worship; and pulling off his hatt, Patted his head with his hand, says Tatapa—You, Tatapa—you all one this. Hoggshead all one this. Had! says Netop, now me stomany that. Whereupon the company fell into a great fitt of Laughter, even to Roreing. (Knight 1992, 35–36)

Apart from the makeshift courtroom in the pumpkin patch, the humor of the tale lies in the younger judge defining a *hogshead* 'cask, barrel' by etymology—that is, the man's head is used to explain *hogshead*, a word whose metaphor of *hog* + *head* must have been thoroughly dead at the time of the incident. (*Tatapa* means 'head'; see Goddard 1977, 40.)

From the viewpoint of American English at the end of the seventeenth century, the passage is far more interesting. First, it shows that one judge is prepared to interrogate the witness in "negro." Second, the more perspicacious judge realizes that the examination should be conducted in creole, which he plausibly does in the use of borrowed words like *tatapa* as well as creole grammar: "you all one this." Knight herself knows her way about these language varieties too, and she displays that knowledge by describing the accused as *netop*, a borrowed word for 'friend' that had some subsequent currency among Anglo-Americans talking of themselves as friends of one another.

Now began to be recorded still more voices that were distinctively American. One of these was an African American slave called Onesimus, so named for a biblical slave in a petition written by Paul who sought his freedom. The original Onesimus was called a friend and brother, and that seems to have been the relation of the Boston slave to Cotton Mather in whose household he lived. Though the specimen comes from the following half century, it must have been the kind of voice heard in the second half of the seventeenth century.

> The occasion was the landing of a ship from Barbados in Boston in April 1721. Almost immediately, a small pox epidemic began. Immigrants from Europe who had been exposed to the disease were likely to be immune, but young people and native-born Americans were at great risk. The principal preacher of the day, Cotton Mather, recorded what Onesimus told him.
>
> I have since mett with a Considerable Number of these *Africans*, who all agree in One Story; That in their Countrey *grandy-many* dy of the *Small-Pox*: But now they Learn this Way: People take Juice of *Small-Pox*; and cutty-skin, and putt in a Drop; then by-nd by a little *sicky, sicky:* then very few little things like *Small-Pox;* and no-body dy of it; and no body have *Small-Pox* any more. (Mather 1972, 107; Read 1939, 248)

As shown by this extract, Onesimus spoke the Atlantic creole language used on shipboard and in coastal ports. From Portuguese and Spanish, the expression *grandy-many* means 'very many' (< *grande*); duplication of words for emphasis appears in *Sicky-Sicky*. *Cutty-skin* (< *cut*) and *by-nd by* (< *by-and-by*) 'soon' are both of English origin.

In writing for publication, Mather gave another account of what Onesimus had said:

> ...that People take the Juice of the *Small Pox,* and *Cut the skin,* and put in a drop; then by'nd by a little *Sick,* then few *Small Pox*; and no body dye of it: no body have *Small Pox* any more. (Mather 1721, 9)

In both versions, Mather reported that Onesimus spoke English "brokenly and blunderingly," and the imperfections in his English seemed to him evidence that Onesimus was not attempting to impose a fictitious, and perhaps deadly, remedy. "Reasonable men," Mather wrote, would be more likely to accept inoculation because it was described in a "broken" kind of English.

In the course of the animated debate over the use of inoculation to control smallpox, one anonymous critic hurled a bomb through Mather's window. In the course of its trajectory, the fuse fell out and the accompanying note showed a vernacular style of invective:

> Cotton Mather I was once of your meeting.... You know who made me leave you, you dog. And damn you I will enoculate you with this— with a pox on you. (Brown 1916, 284)

Like the other forms of invective litigated in the previous century, this one uses *dog* as a term of abuse. That the note was carefully preserved is one more example of the impulse toward documentation that had become so common in Boston in the second half of the seventeenth century.

Boston was very much a part of the scientific revolution that took place in the English-speaking world in the last half of the seventeenth century. A fellow of the Royal Society in London, Mather communicated the results of the inoculations he carried out with the help of the premier physician of his day, Zabdiel Boylston. Those who fell ill with the disease numbered just under 6,000 and 844 of them died. Of the 246 inoculated by Mather and Boylston, only six died. Modern epidemiologists have declared this report to be the first use of numbers to evaluate a clinical trial (Best, Neuhauser, and Slavin 2004, 83).

What was American about the English of Boston and its satellites was not that it departed in some important way from the English of southeast England. Some of its features, of course, would have seemed dialectal or archaic in Britain—for instance, *holden* instead of *held* ("Court to be holden at Ipswich") and *agoing* instead of *going* ("I am now agoing"), both of which were in use in East Anglia at the time the Massachusetts colonists left for America (examples from Kytö 2004, 142–44 and Boyer and Nissenbaum 1977).

What was distinctive was the emergence of a speech community in which the literate and the famous interacted with both educated and uneducated, crossing racial and linguistic demarcations. American English at the end of the seventeenth century was a cluster of various ways of speaking, and in this respect it was unlike almost any other community in the world.

4 Charleston, 1700–1750

AMERICAN ENGLISH BEGAN to define itself in new ways at the opening of the eighteenth century, and nowhere was this change more apparent than in South Carolina. Present-day North and South Carolina were still united as a single colony, but their settled places were far apart and very different. Charles Town (as it was then known) from modest beginnings became, by midcentury, one of the wealthiest and most important cities in British North America.[1]

European influence in the region began, of course, much earlier. Five Spanish expeditions traversed the southeast during the sixteenth century, and, from the records created to document them, a detailed picture of the inhabitants and their societies can be discerned. Here as so often elsewhere in the spread of languages, "interpreters" came on board vessels or emerged from the forest to negotiate the exchange of information. In the very first of these expeditions, that led by Hernando de Soto between 1539 and 1543, the interpreter was a French boy who had spent a year in "monolingual

---

1. Throughout the rest of the chapter, I will refer to the city as "Charleston," although people of the period would not have known the city by that name.

isolation" among Native Americans of the Carolina coast and was then pressed into the service of de Soto's Spanish-speaking band (Booker, Hudson, and Rankin 1992, 421). Later, in an expedition of 1566–68, the Spanish encountered an Indian who employed a mixture of Koasati and Spanish and who used it to warn the Spanish of a plot against them (Booker, Hudson, and Rankin 1992, 427). Looking at the linguistic scene three centuries later, one might easily overlook the influence of indigenous languages, particularly given the catastrophic population decline caused by European diseases which destroyed the succession of hereditary chieftains. But these languages—including the pidgins and creoles of Creek and Delaware—survived to have an impact on English.

English settlement began south of Charleston in 1670, and Spanish forces based in Florida immediately threatened the tiny community. Almost before the military campaign had begun, however, a treaty signed in Madrid allocated lands north along the coast from St. Augustine to the English. In fact, though, this political settlement did not have immediate consequences other than to reduce the threat of more military expeditions from the south. South Carolina was very much a frontier and there were many perils. Yellow fever and other tropical diseases had a debilitating effect on European settlers, and the colony did not at first flourish. In 1700, the population of African and European origin numbered about 5,500 in scattered places—Dorchester, for instance, northward from Charleston settled by migrants from Massachusetts in 1696. There were pirates and privateers, French and Spanish enemies, freebooters of all kinds. In response, Charleston became the second walled city in North America (after St. Augustine) with fortifications to repel enemies.

Early in the new century, Gideon Johnston came to South Carolina to oversee the efforts of the Anglican Church in the colony. In 1708, he reported on conditions as he found them in Charleston:

> The People here, generally speaking, are the Vilest race of Men upon the Earth they have neither honour, nor honesty nor Religion enough to entitle them to any tolerable Character, being a perfect Medley or Hotch potch made up of Bank[r]upts, pirates, decayed Libertines, Sectaries and Enthusiasts of all sorts who have transported themselves hither from Bermudas, Jamaica, Barbadoes, Monserat, Antego, Nevio, New England, Pensylvania &c; and are the most factious and Seditious people in the whole World. (Johnston 1946, 22)

In this unflattering profile, Johnston singled out in particular the "dissenters," that is, persons who were not adherents of the Church of England but were Puritans and Presbyterians (among other Christian denominations). Civil rights were limited to Anglicans until after the American Revolution, but South Carolina nonetheless soon had communities of Roman Catholics, Moravians (speaking German), Huguenots (speaking French), and Sephardic Jews (speaking Portuguese and Spanish, though most of this group had spent time in England before migrating; see Hagy 1993, 81; Baranowski 2007). In many of these communities, languages other than English were passed from one generation to the next; not until 1828 were French services entirely abandoned among the protestant Huguenots (Primer 1889, 218). Languages of learning and religious expression were also in use: Hebrew in the synagogue; Arabic among some of the slaves wrested from West Africa for the American plantations; some Latin (and less Greek) among those who had attended school in England.

Precise demographic data are elusive, but the perception of numbers is as revealing as any census count. Johnston and others thought that South Carolina was significantly diverse. Another estimate, this one published in London in 1710, gave an economic profile. Thomas Nairne declared that "All People in this Colony are either Planters, Traders, Artisans, *Indian* Subjects, or Negroe Slaves" (1710, 43). Johnston had not bothered to mention the non-European population, but Nairne presented dramatic figures. Whites were just 12 percent of the population, he wrote: "Negro Slaves" were 22 percent, and "*Indian* Subjects" 66 percent. His subdivision of the white population was also revealing: 70 percent were *planters* (which he defined as persons who oversaw the creation of products for export); 17 percent were artisans, and 13 percent traders. In the course of fifty years these numbers changed: the Native Americans were either exterminated or exiled; the African-descended slaves increased dramatically in numbers but diversified in work since there was a need for skilled and semiskilled labor—coopers, shipwrights, smiths—that could not be supplied by the white tradespeople. Most consequential of all was that English-speaking whites remained a distinct though economically dominant minority in a diverse and polyglot population.

Under these circumstances, who provided the models for the use of English? Though there were some people of education (particularly clergy), there was not yet a cadre of schoolteachers or writers who might offer examples of "proper speaking." Under such circumstances, it was reasonable to look for an influential group whose English might influence those just acquiring the language and those who aspired to influence through speech.

These people were *Barbadians*, though this label served to encompass white immigrants to South Carolina from throughout the Caribbean, especially Bermuda, Jamaica, Antigua, Grenada, and Nevis. They were a hardened bunch, many descended from two or three generations of migrants from Britain to the tropics, knowledgeable in selecting promising lands for settlement, experienced in the brutalities of plantation agriculture, and contemptuous of the soft-handed colonists who had arrived in South Carolina direct from the English port cities. Planting families from Barbados sent representatives to South Carolina and viewed the emerging colony as their outport belonging only technically and logistically to the proprietors in London. Names of places were transferred from Barbados and applied to the streets and parishes of the new settlement; architectural styles developed in the Caribbean to moderate tropical heat were built in Charleston and its satellites (Alleyne and Fraser 1988). New words on the mainland drew upon old contexts: for example, *Barbadian distemper* "yellow fever" and *Barbados sandstone* for an easily quarried building material.

A modern history of South Carolina describes these Barbadians as "tough, experienced, and driven" and praises their hardihood in comparison to the gentlemen adventurers "lollygagging about looking for gold and pearls or planting tobacco in the streets" (Edgar 1998, 49). The Barbadians set their "cultural stamp" on early South Carolina, and, as the eighteenth century unfolded, they formed a political alliance called, among other things, "the Anglican Party" (to ensure that noncommunicants would not be enfranchised) and "the Anti-Proprietary Party" (to assert their independence from the Londoners who "owned" South Carolina) (Edgar 1998, 85). Politically, this alliance enacted a major struggle early in the century. The proprietors in London wanted to attract Scots and Scots-Irish, Jews, French and Swiss Protestants, and others who would create wealth and hence yield dividends. The "Anglican Party" in the colony refused to let them share political power.

Independence had already animated these Barbadians even before they arrived. In 1689, Edward Littleton published in London *The Groans of the Plantations* in which he denounced the interference of England through taxes on sugar and monopoly of shipping. In this essay, Littleton fulminates against such practices:

It may well be imagin'd, (no, it cannot be imagin'd), how the Company and their Agents Lord it over us, having us thus in their power. And if any offer at the Trade beside themselves, they make such Examples of them, that few dare follow them. If they catch us at *Guiney*, they use us downright as Enemies. And at home we are drag'd into the Admiralty Courts, and condemned in a trice. And the word is, that we are found Prize, or contemn'd as Prize, as if we were Forrainers taken in open War. (Littleton 1689, 6–7)

Such expressions are evidence that economic independence was much desired, and political and cultural separation was not entirely beyond imagining.

These economic enterprises were made possible by the slave trade, and the Barbadians were deeply experienced in its practices. Littleton describes the better wisdom of importing a slave from Africa (at £20 a head) than a horse from Britain (at £10). He explains the practice of using cow manure, cane trash, and even human excrement from "both Whites and Blacks" in fertilizing the fields; in carrying baskets of it "upon *Negroes* heads": "Our *Negroes* work at it like Ants or Bees" (Littleton 1689, 18).

Not all Barbadians were brutish planters tyrannizing over those unfortunate enough to be in their power. In 1684, Thomas Tryon published some *Friendly Advice* in support of the conversion of slaves to Christianity. (The practical problem was that Christians might seek emancipation, and it was thus in the planters' interest to keep these evangelizing efforts from being successful.) Tryon presented his argument in the form of a dialogue between a slave and his master, though without doing much to give an air of authenticity to the conversation:

SLAVE: I desire first you would lay that frightful Cudgel a little further off, and then begging Pardon for the Presumption, since this is the Day you observe to *serve God* in, I would crave leave to be a little instructed touching that Service, and wherein it consists.

MASTER: Why? It consists in being *Christians*, as we are—But what should I talk to such a dark ignorant *Heathen*, scarce capable of *common Sense*, much less able to understand things of such an high and mysterious Nature.

SL. I confess we are poor silly dark ignorant Creatures, and for ought I find, so many of the *Bacchararo's* too, as well as we; but that you may not grudge your Time or Pains, I will assure you, that I will attend very seriously to what you say, and possibly may prove somewhat more docile than some of our Complexion; For I was the Son of a *Phitisheer*, that is, a kind of *Priest* in our Country and Way; he was also a *Sophy*, and had studied the Nature of things, and was well skill'd in *Physick* and natural *Magick*.…(Tryon 1684, 150–51)

Tryon inserted a note to explain *Baccharoro's*: "So the *Negro's* in their Language call the *Whites.*" This publication (and the note) provide the first evidence of the word that in its modern spelling is rendered *backra* or *buckra* (Craigie and Hulbert 1938–44; Cassidy and LePage 1980; Allsopp 1996; Collymore 1957).

Buckra is very much an indicator word revealing the Barbadian connection to South Carolina. Today, according to *The Dictionary of American Regional English*, the word is found "chiefly" in coastal South Carolina and Georgia, though it is well known in many regions of the United States (Cassidy and Hall 1985). In the Caribbean, it has been employed in various compounds, though early evidence is lacking for many of them: *backra fire* 'electricity', *backra-johnny* 'poor white', *backra missy* 'daughter of a planter', *backra nigger* 'light-skinned person of mixed black and white ancestry', *backra pickney* 'white child.'

Buckaroo persisted in the Sea Islands of South Carolina. In the 1970s, two investigators examined nicknames of people in the region and noted that the given names were often of English origin and the nicknames of African. The person bearing the nickname *buckaroo* was, they reported, especially skilled in the management of farm animals, and they asserted that the name was derived from *vaquero* 'cow hand' (< Spanish *vaca* 'cow'). More likely, however, is the explanation that it was the special skill rather than the animals that accounted for the nickname (Baird and Twining 1991).

The etymology of *buckra* is well established. It derives from the Efik language of West Africa and describes people with power and knowledge regardless of race. However, it soon became specialized to refer to white people; as one lexicographer explains, "The Efik, being long established middle-men at the slave-trading center at Calabar, E[astern] Nigeria, would prob[ably] have established the item as a loan-word and spread it among slaves of other language groups who also brought it to the New World" (Allsopp 1996). In South Carolina, this spread of *buckra* is evidenced in a report in 1737 of a slave revolt in Antigua. In a letter published in Charleston, a correspondent noted that initial stages of the uprising had been scotched, but on returning home one Major Nugent was told by a slave: "Bockorau go to sleep too soon." Though he would not say more, the informer plucked a hair from his head: "you do no more than so" (*South-Carolina Gazette*, April 16–23, 1737, 2).

In other words, the initial action was many hairs shy of a haircut. The social dimension of this revolt is of interest since an African-born slave was the first leader and the recruits "Top-Tradesmen" among the *Creoles* 'persons born in the island.' Once successful in killing all the whites, the Creoles planned to butcher the *Cormantees*—that is, slaves associated with the West African port of Cromanty and speakers of the Ashanti language—and set up a government on their own. The plot attracted literate slaves, many of them Christians who had sworn on the sacrament to keep the plot secret. The letter published in the *Gazette* made it clear that the evangelizing efforts of the bishop of London had deadly consequences.

Tales of slave uprisings struck fear among the whites of South Carolina, but what is of special linguistic interest in the letter from Antigua is that the reported speech of the informing slave shows evidence of creolized English and employs a variant of *buckra* without any further explanation. And of course nobody needed an explanation since the term was already widely current. The vocabulary of slavery was deeply embedded in the American English of the region, increasingly so as the number of slaves of African-origin in South Carolina grew from about 3,000 in 1700 to nearly 40,000 in 1740. The decade from 1730 to 1740, when this slave population doubled, was the era of the most dramatic increase (Wood 1974, 152). British immigrants and Barbardians alike were immersed in a richly multiracial and polyglot community.

The cultural groups forming that community held firmly to their customs and language. In a natural history of Barbados published in 1750, Griffith Hughes reported the survival of African customs:

> The Negroes in general are very tenaciously addicted to the Rites, Ceremonies, and Superstitions of their own Countries, particularly in their Plays, Dances, Music, Marriages, and Burials. (1750, 15)

Curiosity about these practices was often sympathetically expressed, and Hughes, for one, recognized that the African slaves were as talented as Europeans though brutalized and kept illiterate. An earlier visitor to Barbados, Hans Sloan, was, like Hughes, interested mainly in flora and fauna, but he was sufficiently intrigued by songs to have asked someone to notate them. The lyrics were written down in the African languages, and one song, from Angola, shows the call-and-response pattern that would later figure prominently in American music (Sloan 1707–25, 1:l–li).

Nowhere was this curiosity given more detailed expression than in what Hughes called "ceremonies." Describing Barbados, he explained the practices of the "*Obeah* Negroes, these being a sort of physicians and Conjurers" (1750, 15). Another word of West African origin, *obeah* involves invoking the powers inherent in a small pouch containing shells, plants, and other natural objects. In South Carolina, these practices continued, constantly refreshed by more Africans arriving direct from Africa. Reliable evidence for the language of such ceremonies is elusive, but it is likely that *moco* 'magic, witchcraft' (< Fula *moco* 'medicine man') was in early use. It was noticed in South Carolina and then throughout the South, particularly where cures were attempted by the use of *conjure bags* (Cassidy and Hall 1985–). Eventually *mojo* came into modern use to refer to a dose of cocaine, heroin, or morphine (Lighter 1994–).

Among the African and African-descended slaves of the coastal islands of South Carolina, language survivals endured. In a fifteen-year period beginning in 1932, Lorenzo Dow Turner identified several thousand words in use in the region that had parallels in the languages of West Africa. A few, including *goober* 'peanut,' *gumbo* 'okra,' and *yam* 'sweet potato,' are well known throughout American English, but most of Turner's Africanisms are used only by the Sea Islanders—for instance, *pinto* 'coffin' and *ashantie* 'house' (Turner 1974; Jones-Jackson 1987). Less obvious, but no less African, are loan translations, English phrases based on African models—for instance, *crack one's teeth* 'open one's mouth' in "she didn't crack her teeth when her aunt came to visit" (Cassidy and Hall 1985–). These are regionalisms in modern American English limited to the low country of South Carolina and Georgia and the Sea Islands.

Just how rapidly immigrants learned English (and just what flavor of English it was) has been a matter of scholarly disputation. Contemporary testimony supports the idea that the shift to English, in some form, was rapid. A visitor's account published in London in 1730 asserted that it took only a generation for English to be adopted:

Even the grown Persons brought from *Guinea*, quickly learn *English* enough to be understood in ordinary Matters; but the Children born of *Negro* Parents in the Colonies, are bred up entirely in the *English* Language. (Humphreys 1730, 232)

It is likely that access to and use of English was quite varied: that English was more likely to be heard in towns and villages than in isolated areas; that persons with another common language had less use for English; that mobility, whether or not it was voluntary, made English more important than in more settled circumstances. And even if the change was rapid, the other languages left traces in the use of English.

The longest-preserved words from languages other than English are personal names, though even names might acquire an English form. A French immigrant, Louis Timothée, set himself up as the publisher of *The South-Carolina Gazette* and, to gain custom among the English, altered his name to Lewis Timothy. African-descended persons held to the African custom of naming babies for the day of the week, month, or season of their birth (DeCamp 1967). This tradition was particularly apparent in the names of slaves mentioned in the *South-Carolina Gazette*. A boy born on Friday would receive the name *kofi* in the Twi language of West Africa; in America, the name was generally spelled *Cuffy* and it was attached to place-names—for instance, *Cuffy Creek* in South Carolina. By the time it was first recorded in American English in 1713, it had become a generic name for any Black male, not just in South Carolina but also in the other English-speaking settlements of the Atlantic coast. Before long it had acquired a patronizing or derisive meaning, and not only among whites but also among African-descended persons who looked down on new arrivals as unsophisticated bumpkins. A similar fate overtook *Sambo*, a name for the second boy born in a family. But as Louis Timothée discovered, names could become unremarkably American with just a little adjustment. *Pheba* 'a girl born on a Friday' could easily become *Phoebe* and thus invite people to think of her connection to a Roman goddess rather than, for Africans, to Friday's girl. Similarly, *Cubena* 'a girl born on Tuesday' could, willingly or not, find herself called *Venus* (Holloway and Vasa 1993, 82–83). These names could also be translated into English, and a woman named *Monday* might find her name written as *Mandi*.

The majority of people in South Carolina at the turn of the eighteenth century were Native Americans, and English had acquired (or soon would) the tribal names for them: *Cherokee, Creek, Muskogee* (another name for the Creek), *Tuscarawa, Yamassee, Yuchi*. Direct borrowings of words from their languages were relatively rare: *mananosay* 'soft-shell crab' (1709) is one of the few loans that can be traced to the Carolinas. As in Virginia, English settlers tended to use English elements to name the newly encountered landscape: *arrow-wood, backwoods, black gum* 'a tree,' *flusterer* 'the American coot,' *swaddle bill* 'shoveler duck.' Finding resemblances to existing English words helped the admission of borrowings. *Chunky* was used for a Cherokee game involving throwing a spear at a rolling disk, and its origin lay in *chungke*, an Algonquian word. The use of *chuck* to mean 'toss' helped smooth the way for the borrowing. (American English *chunk* 'hit, throw at' came a century later and is today distributed across the south from South Carolina to Texas [Cassidy and Hall 1985–].)

In the first decade of the century, nearly the sole source of wealth in the colony involved trade with the Native Americans, and economic interdependency led to bilingualism. Export of the hides of white-tailed deer acquired from Native American hunters enriched the traders, but there was an apparently irresistible habit of capturing the hunters. Native Americans engaged in trade might suddenly find themselves captives, taken far away, and enslaved. Naturally enough, this practice led to resentment and retaliation.

Despite conflict, bilingualism impacted American English. A simplified lingua franca had long been in use among Native Americans, and English-speaking traders soon acquired sufficient fluency to engage in trade. Thomas Nairne, whose *Letter* describing South Carolina has already been quoted, was briefly appointed Indian agent in 1707, and he arrested one James Child for assembling a raiding party, capturing 160 Natives friendly to the colonists, and selling them into slavery (Nairne 1988, 13–14). In the ensuing political turmoil, Child was the winner and Nairne put out of his post.

In 1708, Nairne and Thomas Welch set out from Charleston and walked across the South to the Mississippi. In July 1708, Nairne wrote a letter to an English lord in which he outlined an imperial strategy to extend British influence into the lands where French traders had operated from a base at Mobile in present-day Alabama. He was evidently able to communicate with some fluency with the Native Americans he encountered, and in letters he wrote while on the journey he demonstrated detailed knowledge of kinship systems and other beliefs held by those he encountered. Writing in April 1708, he displayed a deep knowledge of the linguistic scene:

> Sir, It something pusled me befor I could thorowly comprehend how the savages came to be this devided into divers Tribes or nations of Diferent Languages, and having constant quarrells one with the other,

yet at the same time pretending kindred, everywhere as far as our trade and Government reach. The Villages for the most part, consist of the same names to their Language be different. Upon the progression of one Tribe out of another, they have still retained the same names but their Language and customs have been much altered. The usual names of their fameiles are the Turkey, Tygare, dear, Bear, Eagle, hauck and bird fameily, Lyslala or demedices, Ogilisa, muctesa, fish etc. Now if a savage of the Tygare or Orilisa fameily become a 1000 miles off, and find any of the same name they own and treat him as their kinsman, even tho the 2 nations have wars together. It is the easyest thing in the world, for an English Traveller to procure kindred among the Indians, It's but taking a mistress of such a name, and he has at once relations in each Village, from Charles Town to the Missisipi, and if in travelling he acquants them with what fameily he is incorporated into, those of that name treat, and wait on him as their kinsman. There are some of our Countrymen of such prudence and forecast, that in case on family should fail them, take care to make themselves akin to severall. (Nairne 1988, 60–61)

These clan names were all potential borrowings into American English, but, if *demedices*, *lysala*, *muctesa*, or *ogilisa* had much currency, their use has escaped the attention of lexicographers. For the chief among the tribal groups, Nairne used a word that had appeared in English in 1555 from Spanish, borrowed by Spanish from the Caribbean: *cacique*. Widely current in English discourse, *cacique* needed no explanation. But Nairne also used the word *mico* (which he spelled *micho*), a term for the same ruler and later used by John Wesley and other visitors to South Carolina and Georgia (32). He also explained two other ranks in Native society: *innehow* 'deputy' and *istechages* 'councilor.'

In towns and on plantations, a drift toward English had begun. In 1710, an Anglican clergyman in the home parish of the most prominent Carolina politicians reported to his sponsors that "The Indian Children of our Neighborhood speak English" (Le Jau 1956, 80). Parallel word lists appeared to assist traders in acquiring the lingua franca of the up-country tribes, but many contacts took place in the context of brutish violence and inhumanity. Some of the more outrageous incidents were reported to the Indian trade commissioners but little was done to ensure justice. Just one report (from 1710) gives the flavor of the contacts:

Jess Crosley, a Trayder, being jealous of a Whore of his, beat and abused an Apalachia Indian Man in a barbarous Manner and also bete Jno. Crocket till he spitt Blood, for onely desiring him to forbear beating the Indian.

Ordered that Jno. Wright, Esq., Agent, do forthwith issue out his Warrant to take the said Crosley and have him brought before the Commissioners to answer to such notorious abuses as he has committed amongst the Indians. (McDowell 1955, 4)

Finally, on Good Friday 1715, the so-called Yamassee War broke out, and Thomas Nairne was one of the first colonists to perish after three days of intense torture. This revolt drove the backcountry colonists in panic to Charleston, and they sent out an alarm to other colonies for assistance. (Only Massachusetts sent material help; Virginia and North Carolina gave only token aid.) Of all the resistance to European settlement along the Atlantic coast, the Yamassee War came closest to success in exterminating the settlers, but a year later raids and battles were nearly over, though episodes continued well into the 1720s (Edgar 1998, 101–2). Nearly all the English "traders" had been killed, and subsequent contacts between the two cultures were for a time delicate and aloof.

Nonetheless, contacts continued, and bilinguals played the role of intermediaries. In 1733, James Oglethorpe passed through Charleston on the way to assert English power in Georgia, and the success of his expedition was promptly reported in the *Gazette*. In Savannah, he was met by two interpreters and a crowd of Creeks claiming power over the lands southward to Florida. This entourage was arrayed, at least to the English mind, in what a European court would have called an order of precedence with eight separate delegations:

From the Tribe of *Coweeta*
Yahou-Lakee, their King or Mico.
Essoboo, their Warrior, the Son of old Breen, lately dead, whom the Spaniard called Emperor of the Creeks, with 8 Men, & 2 Women Attendants....
From the Tribe of *Echetas,*
Chutabeeche, and Robin, 2 War Captains, (the latter was bred amongst the English), with 4 Attendants. (*South-Carolina Gazette*, May 26–June 2, 1733, 3)

Incongruous as the dynamic duo of Chutabeeche and Robin must seem to twenty-first-century observers, it was entirely unremarkable in the first half of the eighteenth century. Oglethorpe's campaign, like other supposedly "European" conflicts, was led by English officers but the fighting was mostly conducted by Natives (some 5,000 soldiers on this expedition). Under such circumstances, bonds of intimacy sprang up, and Englishmen even joined the elaborate war dance that energized the troops, a sign of solidarity thought to be especially welcome to the Natives (Mereness 1916, 221).

The meeting in Savannah at which the alliance was celebrated took place under revealing linguistic circumstances. Two translators, John Musgrove and a Mr. Wiggan, rendered Native eloquence for the English audience. Both in the ideas conveyed and the English employed, it exactly corresponded to the prejudices and preferences of the eighteenth-century listeners. Oueckachumpa, "a very tall old Man," gave both gesture and voice to his thoughts:

He first claim'd all the Land to the southward of the River Savannah, as belonging to the Creek Indians. Next, he said, that tho' they were poor and ignorant, HE, who had given the English Breath, had given them Breath also. That HE, who had made both, had given more wisdom to the White Men. That they were firmly persuaded, that the GREAT POWER, which dwelt in Heaven and all around (and then he spread out his Hands and lengthened the Sound of his Words) and which hath given Breath to all Men, had sent the English thither for the Instruction of them, their Wives and Children. That therefore they gave them up freely, their Right to all the Land which they did not use themselves. (*South-Carolina Gazette*, May 26–June 2, 1733, 3)

Such declamations were entirely satisfying, as the Natives must certainly have learned from prior contacts with the duplicitous colonists. Mary Musgrove, John Musgrove's wife, was not reported to have translated at this grand ceremony, though she was regarded by the English as "the best interpreter in the Trustee's service" and eventually rewarded with a land grant of 600 acres for her work as a translator (Wesley 1988, 12:148).

European languages were commonly spoken in South Carolina, and interpreters were ready to facilitate negotiations between the English and Spanish during the conquest of Georgia and northern Florida. John Wesley's missionary efforts in South Carolina and Georgia led him to encounter a community of Germans knowing no English; he was pleased to lead them in worship, however haltingly, in their language (Wesley 1988, 12:72; McDavid and Lerud 1984). George Whitefield, on a similar mission, found a village of French speakers and assigned one of his assistants to teach the children English. His motive was what now would be called nation building: "I cannot think Children will ever be naturalized to the Colony, till they can talk our Language" (Whitefield 1741, 10). Among the South Carolinians, there was no question that English would be the language of public life. Nor did those being assimilated show much reluctance to adopt it. Evidence from the provincial government shows that some were besting the English at their own games. In 1734, grumbling petitioners complained "that *Negroes* are suffered to buy and sell, and be Hucksters of Corn, Pease, Fowls &c. whereby they watch Night and Day on the several Wharfes, and buy up many Articles necessary for the Support of the Inhabitants, and make them pay an exorbitant Price for the same" (*South-Carolina Gazette*, March 23–30, 1734, 2.1).[2]

Varieties of English were still vividly audible. Persons who escaped from slavery or indenture could be identified by their talk, as the following notices from the newspapers show:

> Run away from Mr. Bryan Reily and Mr. *John CarMichael*, two Irishmen Servants, both talking broad Scotch, one named *Roger O Mony*, a tall pockfretten freckle-faced Fellow, stooping in the Shoulders, his hair cut and wore a linnen cap, a dark brown colour'd Coat and Westcoat, leather breeches, and a new pair of Negro shoes, he has a double thumb with two nails on one hand. The other named *Alexander Sinkler*, a short thick well set, surly looking, long brown hair'd, smooth faced, sharp long nosed fresh coloured fellow, wearing a dark gray coarse kersey new Coat with buttons of the same, a pair of old brown breeches, a pair of gray yarn stockings and a pair of new Negro shoes with two or three lifts, each of them about 24 or 25 Years old. (*South-Carolina Gazette*, March 13–22, 1735, 3.2)

> To be Sold for ready Money. Four choice young Negroe Men Slaves and a Girl, who have each been bred in some useful way, and speak very good (Black-) English. (*South-Carolina Gazette*, March 23–30, 1733/34, 3.3; quoted in Dillard 1972, 34)

---

2. Various subsequent attempts to limit the time or the goods that African-descended people might sell seem not to have been successful because the sellers shared profits with their masters (Easterby 1958, 154–55).

Run away a Fortnight ago from *Barak Norman* at *Dorchester*, a Negro Wench, named *Lucy*, she is a new Negro, and speaks no English.... (*South-Carolina Gazette*, March 12–19, 1737, 3.1)

Run away from *Tho: Hawys* the 9th of this Instant, a Negro Man, named *John, Barbados* born, speaks good English, had on a blue Base Jacket and speckle Shirt, aged about 40. (*South-Carolina Gazette*, May 21–28, 1737, 3.2)

Run away from Robert Williams, the *2d Instant, a* Welch *Servant Man named* Thomas Edwards, *he is about* 24 *Years of Age, of a good Complexion,* 5 *Feet* 9 *Inches high, his Hair almost black, had a small Scar over his right Eye, he speaks but bad* English.... (*South-Carolina Gazette*, February 14, 1743, 2.1)

Run away about the first of *November*, a short thick *Elboa* [i.e., Ibo] Fellow named *Tom*, who formerly belonged to Mr. *Shute*, he had on when he went away a white Negro Cloth Jacket and Breeches, and speaks but very little English. (*South-Carolina Gazette*, February 21, 1743, 3.1)

Run away from *George Ducat*, a Negro Man named *Morrice*, a young Fellow about 25 or 26 Years of Age, A *Calabar* Negro speaks indifferent English, has been gone these 3 Weeks from his Master. (*South-Carolina Gazette*, October 10, 1743, 2.2)

Brought to the Work House ... Also a Negro Man named Sharper, of the Gullah countrey, speaks tolerable good English, 5 feet 4 and a half inches high, 60 or 65 years of age, has a sore on his right leg, and says his master's name is *James Llooden*, in Savanah; the said Negro says his master was killed by the British. (*South-Carolina Gazette and General Advertiser*, August 24–26, 1784, 3)

These advertisements presume a "neutral" form of English against which the varieties can be measured from "no English" to "very little" to "indifferent" to "bad" to "tolerable" to "good." In Charleston there seems to have been a consensus about the properties of these kinds of English and widespread knowledge of their distinctive features. The *Gazette* regularly published items from Scotland, including an amusing anecdote in which readers were required to know the difference between a "burnt Cuttie" and a "sonsy mensful Strapper" (*South-Carolina Gazette*, April 22–29, 1732, 2.2). Even a runaway "Negro man named Joe" could confuse pursuers by his ability "to speak broad Scotch or Northumberland dialect" (*South Carolina & American General Gazette*, January 22–29, 1768, 11).

The people sought through the *Gazette* were property, and South Carolina was wealthy because of their labor. Forest products for shipbuilding, indigo exported to dye fabric, and rice produced enormous wealth after the turn of the eighteenth century, and Charleston became the richest city in British North America. Per capita wealth among unindentured free people was six times that of Philadelphia and seven times that of Boston (Edgar 1998, 161). Citizens were uninhibited by strictures denouncing pleasure, and all of the institutions of London were reproduced on the Carolina shore: libraries, coffeehouses and taverns, a theater, and learned discourse on, for instance, botany. The first public library was founded in Charleston in 1700, but it did not endure owing to the refusal of borrowers to return volumes they had taken out. In 1735, the first opera performed in North America was presented in Charleston, and the following year a purpose-built theater opened with a production of George Farquhar's *Recruiting Officer* (Rogers and Taylor 1994, 15, 26).

Most books were imported from Britain or the northern cities, but the enterprising Timothy family saw an opportunity in publishing John Wesley's *Collection of Psalms and Hymns* (1737) and then two sermons by Alexander Gardner "occasioned by some erroneous notions of certain men who call themselves Methodists" (Garden and Fleet 1741).

In 1737, the *Gazette* reprinted from a Philadelphia newspaper "The Drinker's Dictionary," representing a perennial journalistic excursion into all the synonyms that might be discovered for states of intoxication. Neither the first nor the last such list of what soon would be called *slang*, this inventory contained many familiar expressions in long-established use: *boozy*, for instance, or *in his cups*. Several features make this list interesting for the history of American English, however. One is that a respectable newspaper of increasing regional circulation found it worth printing and regarded "the modern Tavern-Conversation of Tiplers" as a subject for sly celebration (though treated with a tone of moralistic disapproval of "a beastly Vice"). Another is that many of these expressions had a very distinctively American flavor: *he's been at Barbados* (a major source of rum for Charleston); *he's been at an Indian Feast*; *he makes Virginia Fence* (alluding to the zigzag layout of a split rail fence) (*South-Carolina Gazette*, April 30–May 7, 1737, 1–2; Larsen 1937). Racy vernacular language was seldom given much serious attention, but the world of gallants, beaux, and belles was as much an object of curiosity in South Carolina as it was in London.

Education was highly valued, though virtually limited to wealthy young men who were sent abroad for advanced studies. Musical entertainments, literary endeavors, and the visual arts were all encouraged. Literacy among white people in the first half of the eighteenth century was more widespread than it would be again until the twentieth century. Taste for these pleasures extended inland as the sphere of Charleston's influence increased in size.

It is striking that the benefits of education were not limited to the most prosperous. The Society for Propagating the Gospel in Foreign Parts, the London-based missionary society of the Anglican Church, promoted all sorts of efforts to evangelize in South Carolina. According to the *Gazette* in 1743, the Society

> have lately resolved on the following Method of pursuing this good End; *viz.* by purchasing some Country born young Negroes, causing them to be instructed to read the Bible, and in the chief Principles of the Christian Religion, and thenceforth employing them (under the Direction of proper Trustees) as *School-Masters*, for the same Instruction of all such *Negro* or *Indian* Children as may be born in the said Colonies. (*South-Carolina Gazette*, April 11, 1743, 4.2)

This scheme had made such good progress that one teacher was available to begin the work and the article solicited contributions for the construction of a schoolhouse and the maintenance of the teacher.

Such efforts were seldom encouraged and very often forthrightly opposed. In Philadelphia in the spring of 1740, a Mr. Bolton repented of his career as a dancing and concertmaster and resolved to open a school for teaching children to read. It was reported: "Upon his giving notice that he would teach Negroes also, had in 23 days no less than 53 black scholars. For this he was sent for, and arraign'd in court, as a breaker of the Negro law" (*South-Carolina Gazette*, July 12–18, 1740; *Boston News Letter*, August 14–21, 1740). Bolton was acquitted, but the news was duly reported in the *Gazette* in the expectation that readers in Charleston would greet his decision with astonishment and, probably, the surprising demand for education among African-descended youth as disquieting. Among these youth there was a desire for freedom, but, since circumstances made freedom nearly impossible, they yearned for betterment that would arise from knowing English and gaining education.

Even under the harsh and often violent oppression of slavery, some convergence of language variety began to take place. In 1746, a British visitor described life in the southern colonies:

One Thing they ["the better sort"] are very faulty in, with regard to their Children, which is, that when young they suffer them too much to prowl amongst the young Negros, which insensibly causes them to imbibe their Manners and broken Speech. ("Observations" 1746, 330)

Presumably the traits of childhood persisted into adult speech, though the sounds of this English seem not to have been preserved in the written record. Certainly, there were continuing relations of intimacy among Euro-Americans and those of African descent, whether in child-rearing or sexual connections, and these must have produced a leveled kind of English drawing on the special contributions of both sides of the linguistic divide.

Modern scholarship is filled with speculative accounts of the Atlantic creole that is supposed to be the foundation of much later American English, but there is an absence of evidence to support these views—both for and against the notion of a creolized English on the Atlantic seaboard of Africa, the Caribbean, and the southeastern colonies in North America. There are examples that seem both authentic and ancient. In 1922, a rendition of Gullah yields this example: *W'en uh yeddy dat wu'd me h'aa't hebby 'tell 'e ready fuh drap out me t'roat 'pun de du't* 'When I heard that word, my heart was heavy till [= so heavy that] it was ready to drop out of my throat upon the ground' (quoted in Cassidy and Hall 1985–, s.v. *me*). Unfortunately, for the proponents of Gullah as a sign of the creole past, this use of *me* 'my' and *fuh* 'infinitive marker in purpose clauses'—in, for example, "he came over for tell me" (McDavid 1979, 287)—is not attested by the written record before the nineteenth century. Of course Gullah shares traits with Caribbean and West African creoles for which there is earlier evidence than for these examples, but the role of a pan-Atlantic creole language remains a matter of speculation. As the next chapter notes, English was already in widespread use on the west coast of Africa, and the surviving specimens suggest that it was far more intelligible to a range of listeners than the sentence in Gullah just quoted.

Perhaps more than any of the eastern seaboard cities, Charleston was enthralled with the fashions of London. Hugh S. Legaré, the U.S. attorney general and prominent Charlestonian, declared early in the nineteenth century: "Before and just after the Revolution, many, perhaps it would be more accurate to say most, of our youth of opulent families were educated at English schools and universities" (Legaré and Bullen 1846, 7). Henry Laurens (1724–92), the great South Carolinian patriot, was convinced that education in England was a requirement for the young men of the American elite, and his many surviving letters show that he was concerned that these youth have both a classical education and devote themselves assiduously to English. These ideas remained central concerns for him even after the English had imprisoned him in the Tower of London. (Laurens was captured on his return from negotiating the support of the Dutch for the American Revolution. He was eventually released in exchange for Lord Cornwallis, who had surrendered the British forces at Yorktown.)

In a history of the colony written in 1821, John Drayton made much of this Anglophilia: "Before the American war, the citizen of South Carolina was too much prejudiced in favor of British manners, customs and knowledge to imagine that elsewhere than in England anything of advantage could be obtained" (quoted in Primer 1889, 222). English taste and manners thus prevailed among the elite in Charleston, and it seems likely any identifiably "American" habits of speech would have been instantly exterminated.

These conservative values in speech and conduct are everywhere apparent in the letters of Eliza Lucas Pinckney. Her father, an officer stationed in Antigua, moved to Charleston with his family when she was fifteen, and she kept up a lively correspondence. At this time, she had already been to school in England, and her brothers later went there for more education. As a married woman in 1758, she was resident in London, where her husband represented the interests of the colony. As she reported to a friend in England: "Charles Town, the principal one in this province, is a polite, agreeable place. The people live very Gentile and very much in the English taste" (Pinckney 1972, 7). In describing the city to those unfamiliar with it, she regularly emphasized the genteel manners of the people. She corresponded with cousins in Philadelphia and Boston, and, in a remarkably progressive innovation for the time, educated slave children so they might become schoolteachers (Pinckney 1972, 34). Later in life, she sent her sons to be educated in England, and they remained there in their formative years to acquire the education and English of the transnational social class to which they belonged, that of property owners and the higher ranks of military life. When one friend wrote to her after the death of her husband and asked when she would return to England, she declared: "My heart is there tho' all Countrys are now to me alike, nor do I prefer any to another..." (118). While it would be wrong to infer much from the fact that she does not mention varieties of speech, she was given to describing other forms of nuanced social behavior that were summed up in the very eighteenth-century English word *agreeable.*

A more telling fact about the language of Charleston emerges from the mere existence of so many of Pinckney's letters: she was often alone and kept in contact with family and friends by writing to them. Even before she was twenty, she had the sole management of the family plantation, located seventeen miles by land and six by sea from Charleston. The short distance was still a lengthy obstacle to frequent visits, and she wrote to one of her distant cousins of having only six families in the neighborhood social round. Like most gentry in the early eighteenth century, she would have thought of social distinctions in terms of *rank,* that is, the social stratum in which one was born, lived, and died. Social mobility rarely resulted in someone rising or falling from their rank, and one of the fascinations of Samuel Richardson's midcentury novels—Eliza Pinckney read and admired his *Pamela* and *Sir Charles Grandison*—was the theme of love across forbiddingly distant social ranks.

Not until the second half of the century did the idea of social mobility rise to be an imaginable value, and one way that a person might pass as a member of a higher social class was to use the English belonging to the rank above. In both Britain and the North American colonies, a flood of linguistic conduct books was produced and consumed: inventories of "mistakes" and dictionaries of pronunciation, among other works not previously produced and sold. Though she lived through the early decades of this transformation, Eliza Pinckney must have had little interest in it. Her sons were at school in England, the eldest enrolled at Westminster and destined for Oxford. They would have spoken in ways identical to other youth of their own rank, and perhaps some of their cousins and friends in Philadelphia and Boston did the same.

These social practices led to the conservation of older speech forms; when London adopted new ways of speaking, Charleston kept to the old. In South Carolina, the old pronunciation of *gaunt* and *haunt* to rhyme with *pant* and *slant* endured, and only in Charleston did this way of speaking persist among the elite (though it was found elsewhere in the Southeast among lower-class speakers). Similarly, *calm, palm,* and *psalm* all had the vowel of *hat: cam, pam,* and *sam* (Primer 1887, 91; McDavid 1979, 278). The final consonant of the suffix *-ing* was that of *n,* as revealed by Eliza Pinckney's spelling of *quarrelin.* During the nineteenth century, this practice came to be seen as a mistake elsewhere, but in Charleston, as among the English aristocracy in Britain, it persisted among upper-class speakers.

Distinctive Charleston usages made the speech variety well known to outsiders. *Pinder* 'peanut' was an early borrowing from a West African language and incorporated into English in Britain; it continues to be a marker of South Carolina English, though found elsewhere, especially in Georgia and Florida. The coastal plain is known in South Carolina as the *low country*, a usage first attested in English in the early sixteenth century, but now applied only to this region in America. Charlestonians remained aloof from linguistic changes elsewhere in America, and even today the pronunciation of *side* with a pure vowel, so characteristic of other coastal southeastern varieties of English, is not employed in Charleston and Savannah, where the traditional pronunciation of this sound is the diphthong found in other kinds of American English. The elite in Charleston even adopted emergent forms of the prestige standard of eighteenth-century London—particularly the *ah* sound of *glass, dance, path*, a mimicry of the English that only occurred among the most anglophile of newly independent Americans (Primer 1887, 91; McDavid 1979, 278).

Evidence for these distinctive Charlestonian pronunciations comes from a late nineteenth-century description by Sylvester Primer, a scholar thoroughly acquainted with the latest in phonetic techniques and a faculty member at the College of Charleston. When first presented in 1887, Primer's findings were celebrated for their accuracy and particularity. Far from being a cultural hearth for the interior of the colony, Charleston had become increasingly isolated from its hinterland as it declined in economic importance as a port in the late eighteenth century. In the nineteenth, as a desperate and futile act to assert cultural separation from the rest of America, the Civil War commenced at Charleston's battery, from which rebels fired artillery at American soldiers stationed in an island fortification designed to protect the city from attack by foreign forces.

What Primer's description accomplished was to show how the speech of the Charleston oligarchs had become increasingly separated from developments elsewhere in American English. One discussant, a professor at the University of South Carolina, responded in this way:

> I am from South Carolina and Charleston is in South Carolina, but the language of Charleston is not the language of South Carolina. The provincialisms are as strange to us in Columbia as they would be to Philadelphia and almost any where else in the country.... In our South Carolina University at Columbia, we mark a Charleston stu-

dent by his pronunciation, just as we would mark one from Massachusetts or any other part of the country. (Joynes 1887, xix–xx)

The professor made it clear that these students from "the proudest families of Charleston" were seen as ridiculous. In the twentieth century, the pronunciation of *garden* as if spelled *gyardin* was found from Virginia southward to Georgia, but only in uneducated speech. In Charleston, however, some "cultivated" speakers used it as a point of local pride (Kurath and McDavid 1961, 175 and Map 167). In the first half of the eighteenth century, Charleston set itself apart, and the process continued.

In the later eighteenth century, Charleston took pride that it had become the "capital of wealth and ease," but its source of wealth dwindled. No industry developed; even shipbuilding was undertaken elsewhere, and by the early nineteenth century southern crops were mainly exported from northern ports. In a turn of fortunes, "New York's rise hastened Charleston's decline" (Kretzschmar et al. 1993, 386). Charleston was left elegant, genteel, and poor.

Eliza Lucas Pinckney and Henry Laurens were more likely to visit London or the other cities on the Atlantic coast than to journey to the interior of the colony. (The grandees of Charleston commonly spent the summer months in Boston to escape heat, yellow fever, and malaria.) Until 1750, there was some peril in making such a trip into the interior. War between the Cherokee and the Euro-Americans ebbed and flowed, with episodes of considerable stress culminating in sustained warfare in the 1750s. Settlement of the backcountry (as it was known) emerged from a deliberate policy by then colonial governor Robert Johnson. Eleven townships would be established, and they would have two purposes: to put a population between the low-country whites and the Native Americans and to form a barrier to prevent escaped slaves from escaping westward (Johnson 1997, 3). The part of the region that flourished came to be known as the Welsh Tract. Its inhabitants, who soon prospered in the growth and production of indigo, came from Pennsylvania beginning in 1736. By 1747, there were 500 whites and 60 slaves. Word of the prosperity to be found in the region recruited yet more settlers; in 1757, it is estimated that there were 3,300 whites and 300 slaves. Careful study of these early populations reveals that the settlers were not poor. They invested in mills, roads, and other developments needed for their prosperity. Contacts with Charleston (and Georgetown, a port at the mouth of the Pee Dee River, their conduit for bringing goods to market) were initiated from these interior settlers, and by the time of the American Revolution they had established a flourishing market for agricultural products and gained connections with Charleston's financial institutions.

Though slave owners, these new settlers had little else in common with the long-settled communities on the coast, and they are unlikely to have shown any interest in the cultural attractions of Charleston. Part of their motive for leaving Pennsylvania was their fear of liberalizing tendencies in Baptist doctrine, and they found nothing attractive about the genteel culture of the city. The proprietors of the backcountry farms visited Charleston only twice a year: in the fall to sell their harvest and in the spring to obtain supplies for the new growing year. They did not stay long, and they stayed with others like themselves (Johnson 1997, 53). The conviviality of the coffeehouse or the theater held no attractions for them.

In the second half of the eighteenth century, these Separate Baptists of the Welsh Tract were joined by Scots-Irish Presbyterians migrating southeastward from Pennsylvania. Both communities shared strict Calvinist beliefs, and it was not long before they began to agitate for the disestablishment of the Anglican Church in South Carolina and an enlargement of the franchise to include their members in political life. As a consequence of the cultural separation of backcountry from low country, quite different practices emerged, not least ones involving the English language. By the nineteenth century, some of these differences had become institutionalized: *corn house* was the lowland term; *corncrib* the backcountry word (Kurath 1949, figs. 2, 32). What people ate in the uplands was not what they ate in the low country; where people located their cultural ancestors was quite different; and how they used English came to be very different indeed.

Observing a prominent Charlestonian legislator in 1805, Edward Hooker saw his speech as quite distinct from that of the up-country representatives. To Hooker, a visitor from Connecticut, the man's speech was distinctly English in details: "He speaks entirely in the Sheridanian dialect, which is, as far as I have observed, much the most common dialect of well educated Charlestonians" (Hooker 1897, 370). In this observation, Hooker alludes to the first dictionary of English pronunciation, published in London in 1780. Two editions had appeared in North America (from publishers in Philadelphia and Wilmington), but Thomas Sheridan's ideas about the prestigious pronunciation of English seem to have had little influence on American speech—except that of the most anglophile of American cities, Charleston.

Charleston, though a great cultural center in the first half of eighteenth-century America, looked east to the Atlantic rather than west to the mountains. Its English retained an Atlantic flavor that occurred nowhere else along the coast. With the economic decline of the city in exporting American products abroad, the speech of the elite was increasingly recognized as eccentric and hardly worthy of imitation.

5   Philadelphia, 1750–1800

WHEN BENJAMIN FRANKLIN arrived in Philadelphia in 1723, a youth of sixteen, he sought out employment as a printer and, eventually, prospered as both printer and publisher. On his first day in the city, he entered a bakery and asked for *bisket* but the baker did not know the meaning of the word. (*Biskit* in New England was a collective noun like *salt*: "Please give me some bisket.") So Franklin was obliged to buy "great puffy rolls," and he sauntered down Second Street, where he caught a glimpse of his future wife. In this emblematic moment in his *Autobiography*, Franklin starts his upward climb to success and fame.

Bisket, a staple food in Franklin's native Boston, was an unleavened bread made from flower, salt, and water, a food known later in American English as *hardtack*. The contrast between the dry bread of Boston and the yeasty confection of Philadelphia is plain enough, but Franklin had more in mind with this anecdote. Boston and Philadelphia spoke different kinds of English, and they do so to this day. Questioned in the 1960s about names for "bread made with flour," some New Englanders and some southerners responded with *biscuit*. Pennsylvanians never gave that answer.

In 1750, Philadelphia was the third largest city in the British Empire and an outpost of the Enlightenment. Secular and sectarian interests often acted in harmony, though the French and Indian War of the 1760s and the American Revolution a decade later tested the bonds between pacifist Quakers and the more warlike Pennsylvanians who bore the burden of these conflicts. While the wealthiest of the American colonies were those exporting tobacco, Philadelphia was a diversified commercial center exporting finished goods in addition to natural resources like timber, furs, and food. In 1769, Pennsylvania exported £410,757 in products, mainly to southern Europe, Africa, and the West Indies. Only £28,112 of that total went to Britain. New York lagged far behind with total exports valued at £231,906, nearly half of which went to Britain. As these numbers suggest, ships from Pennsylvania went more places and to places where languages other than English were spoken. In 1785, a merchant vessel from Philadelphia reached China.

Finished goods on sale at the Philadelphia waterfront showed just how various the merchandise (and the names for it) could be. In October 1768, John Kaighn, the descendant of prosperous merchants who had emigrated from the Isle of Man a century earlier, offered both European and East Indian goods. Some of these would have been readily recognized on the London market: pins and needles, table knives and forks, thimbles, snuffboxes, coffee mills, brass fenders. Fabrics of all sorts were on offer, and their names show the cosmopolitan character of the English of Philadelphia: *huckaback* (a north of England fabric); *ozenbrigs* (< Osnabrück); *ticklenburgs* (originally from northern Germany); *paduasoy* (< ?*Padua* + *soy* < *soie* from the Italian city where silk was spun and woven); *sectorsoy* (< *silken soy*, a Scottish word for a silk handkerchief square); *culgee, humhum, lungi, romal* (all woven goods deriving from India and the East Indies). Some of these words would have been current in Britain too.

The spices on sale tell a similar story of a thriving international trade in the Indian Ocean: nutmeg, cinnamon, cloves, mace, and pepper (*Pennsylvania Gazette*, October 27, 1768). Another merchant offered "Victuals dressed in the most genteel manner," and included in his bill of fare *ketchup* (a food and a word coming into English from Malay) and *mango pickle* (from the East Indies). The riches of the city are apparent from the goods he advertised: wedding cakes, fresh fruits and vegetables, and "pickled Oysters in Kegs" (*Philadelphia Gazette*, June 21, 1765).

Geographically the center of colonial America, Philadelphia was also the center of intellectual life. Franklin's experiments with electricity were conducted by an American genius in an American city, but his influential findings were published by the Royal Society in London. David Rittenhouse, a clockmaker who built the first telescope in America, observed the transit of Venus across the sun's disk in 1769 and was recognized in Europe as a mathematician of remarkable powers. After the Revolution, Rittenhouse published his account of the transit in the transactions of the American Philosophical Society, an organization modeled on the Royal Society.

Enlightenment ideas were fostered by investment in the intellectual life of the city, beginning, influentially and as a public institution, with the founding of the Library Company of Philadelphia in 1731. In 1749, an essay by Franklin on education led to the establishment of the Pennsylvania Academy, later enlarged into the University of Pennsylvania in 1779. The Union Library and the Southwark Theater were organized in 1759. A medical school prepared its first graduates for practice in 1768, and a school for African American children opened in 1770. Supreme among the achievements of people in Philadelphia was the founding of the United States with a government in which democracy—excluding women and slaves, of course—was given unprecedented scope as a foundation for social life.

The impact of this vibrant cultural capital on American English can be seen firsthand in the life of John Bartram (1699–1777), the great naturalist and explorer. Born in a Quaker family, Bartram was raised by grandparents after his mother died and his father moved elsewhere in the colonies. He started out with few resources and little education. According to his recent biographer, Bartram "was handicapped throughout his career as a naturalist by his poor grammar and inadequate knowledge of Latin" (Thomas 1999, 2:296). This pitiable assessment must have been Bartram's view of himself, and it reflects a dark side of Enlightenment thinking: one must know something of English grammar (or at least avoid solecisms) and a good deal of Latin to be a scientist. Learning of Bartram's fascination with plants, James Logan, a wealthy Philadelphia merchant and agent for the Penn family's interests—lent him books and introduced him by correspondence to naturalists in England. One of these, Peter Collinson, was a member of the Royal Society, and Collinson organized a distinguished set of subscribers to finance Bartram's plant collecting. Once again, the ubiquitous Franklin appeared at a crucial moment; he arranged for Bartram to have access without paying a subscription to the scientific books in the Library Company, and, as postmaster, Franklin granted Bartram franking privileges to enable him to correspond freely with his English sponsors and other intellectuals abroad. Because of his friendship with Carolus Linnaeus, Bartram was elected in 1769 to the Royal Academy of Sciences of Sweden.

While Bartram was not fluent in the languages of Native Americans, he was sympathetic, and he traveled with one of the great translators of the day, Conrad Weiser, to explore the western territory.

Weiser was an important transitional figure in the spread of English in Pennsylvania, and his descendants played emblematic roles in it. Born in Germany in 1696, Weiser had emigrated first to England, in 1709, and then to Pennsylvania in 1710. In his journey to meet with the Mohawks in 1750, he was accompanied by Christian Daniel Claus, then twenty-two years old and later himself a go-between who became fluent in Mohawk. Claus kept his journal in German, but Weiser wrote in English, though not of the most fluent and elegant kind (spelling *bundle* as *pundle* as might be expected from a writer most comfortable in German [Doblin and Starna 1994, 15]). Because he was little concerned with the right spelling of English, Weiser is an important witness to the English of the time.[1] For example, he provides evidence for a new American use of *bush* when he describes an informal caucus outside the council fire as a meeting "in the Bushes," where he was helped by another German-speaking translator, David Zeisberger (Doblin and Starna 1994, 14; Goddard 1988). Bartram was in good company to observe the language interactions.

In his *Observations* published in 1751, Bartram described his tour in the company of Weiser and Shikellamy, the agent of the Iroquois in Pennsylvania. Bartram listened attentively to the exchange of speeches, depending entirely on Weiser (whose native and usual language was German), and Weiser's representation of what the Shawese had to say was in the grand language of eighteenth-century oratory. However, in his report Bartram noted that the Natives expressed approval for the outside visitors by giving "us the *Yohay*, a particular *Indian* expression of approbation, and which is very difficult for a white man to imitate well…" (1751, 22). That *yo-hay* had some currency in the English of Pennsylvanians is suggested by an extract from the journals of William Johnson: "At the end of each sentence one of the chiefs called out—'YO-HAY;'—*do you hear*?" and the response of approbation was general (Stone 1865, l:213). Another visitor to the west, a generation after Bartram, used the same borrowed word to describe the

---

1. Weiser's own report on his travels was written in German (see Weiser 1757).

reaction to his distribution of gifts: "These were received with a full yo-hah or demonstration of joy" (Long 1791, 56).[2]

The 1750s were a time of close contact between English speakers and Native Americans, though not always peaceful contact. Accounts of *pow-wows*—a word coming into American English early in the nineteenth century—were, however, respectful of the diplomacy of both Native Americans and Euro-Americans with rhetorical practices emerging that represented Native oratory in an English way. For instance, *father* was used to refer to allies or to persons in power, first the king and then the president. (This English sense of *father* as used by Native Americans dates from 1751.) Algonquian peoples who allied themselves with the French in the 1760s were dismayed when the French accepted defeat and ceded most of their settlements. When the Iroquois sided with the British during the American Revolution, they too were pushed to the margins when the British withdrew from the emergent United States. Still, this half century was a time in which Native influences continued to appear in English: *nitchie* 'friend' (1791) as a borrowing; *scalping knife* (1759) and *warpath* (1775) as loan translations; *reservation* (1789), a term of special meaning as the Indians were displaced from their lands.

In his journal for January 14, 1766, John Bartram described some of the woody plants of Florida: "The lower rich ground produceth gledistia, pishamins, cephalanthus, ash, cypress and coru femina" (*OED*, s.v. *pishamin*). This casual note encapsulates what was happening to English in America and the place of Americans in the pan-European intellectual life of the second half of the eighteenth century. It is revealed in the words.

Ash and *cypress* are trees found in Europe, and the early explorers of North America identified the American plants with their homegrown counterparts. The *ash* was first reported in 1610 in *A True Declaration of the Estate of Virginia*, the *cypress* in 1637 by Thomas Morton in *New English Canaan*. Both trees were sometimes called *American ash* or *American cypress* in recognition of their membership in a different species. In Bartram's note, there was no need for such distinctions since he (and his eventual readers) would recognize these usages as new in America. These are English words, but they carry American senses and are thus Americanisms.

---

2. In modern Oneida, this exclamation is spelled *ihéh*. Marianne Mithun (Linguistics, University of California, Santa Barbara) believes that it is no longer current, at least in the Cayuga. I am grateful for her assistance with this question.

Pishamin is a distinctively American word, borrowed from an Algonquian source and related to *persimmon*. Once this word had been established, it was applied to a plant producing similar orange fruit and indigenous to Sierra Leone (first noted in 1866). At the end of the twentieth century, the African species under the name *sweet pishamin* was included in an inventory of plants headed "Listing of Potential New Crops for Australia." This English word is an etymological Americanism.

The remaining plants in Bartram's list are drawn from the new scientific nomenclature sweeping the world of biology in the mid-eighteenth century. All three offer insights into English in America. *Cephalanthus* might well have been called *button bush*, the name employed in a book doubtless known to Bartram, Jared Eliot's *A Continuation of the Essay upon Field-Husbandry,* published in New York in 1754 and part of the collection of the Library Company of Pennsylvania. Button bush was, and remains, an Americanism for *Cephalanthus occidentalis. Cornu femina* might as easily been identified as the *gray dogwood* or the *swamp dogwood.* The note also shows something of the limits of Bartram's Latin since it might have been better spelled *Cornus foemina.*

Gleditsia is the most revealing of the names in Bartram's list, and he might well have identified it as *honey locust*, the common name used by John Clayton in the influential *Flora Virginica* (Clayton quoted in Grovinius 1739, s.v. *gleditsia*). Clayton emigrated from England to Virginia and soon began a correspondence with European scientists, particularly Johann Friedrich Grovinius, and sent them specimens of American plants. Grovinius published *Flora Virginica* in Leiden; it was a work of profound scholarship and the first to introduce Linnaeus's new nomenclature for plants.[3] In 1747, Clayton was made a member of the Swedish Royal Society, and Clayton provided a model for Bartram's collecting. Clayton's spelling of *Gleditsia* influenced Bartram's note, but there was also a spelling *Gleditschia* since the species name memorializes the German botanist Johann Gottlieb Gleditsch.

The mixture of "common" and "scientific" names in Bartram's informal note was usual in the intellectual world of eighteenth-century science, and the terms he selected reveal something of the independence (and dependency) of American English even before the nation severed political ties with England. Science was, and is, an international collaboration, and so

---

3. *Flora Virginica* was published in 1739 by Grovinius, drawing heavily on the observations of John Clayton, whose name appears prominently on the title page of the work.

was its language. The languages involved in these examples, however, did not arise from the speaking community but from the community of writing. Latin, still the international language of science, could be relied upon if those most comfortable in vernaculars like English, Dutch, or German needed to seek a common vehicle for communication. In letters to Bartram, Grovinius wrote in both Latin and English.

English settlement along the Delaware River was not the first European incursion into the mid-Atlantic region. As early as 1638, the New Sweden Company had established a colony near modern-day Wilmington, Delaware, and it flourished until 1655, when the Dutch, irritated by Swedish expansionism, absorbed it into New Netherland. Nonetheless, the Swedish community survived, and in 1700 there was published in Philadelphia a Swedish hymnal. In 1742, Benjamin Franklin published a Swedish version of the *Short Catechism* at the direction of the Moravian missionary Nicolaus Zinzendorf. The need for such books is evidence for the continuing use of Swedish in American churches south of the city, and the presence of large numbers of Swedes on British and Dutch vessels coming to North America kept the language alive.

By 1750, though, the Swedish community was in cultural retreat. A visitor from Sweden, Peter Kalm, made detailed records of the way in which English was invading the Swedish language in America. Sometimes these borrowings consisted of English words adapted to Swedish pronunciation and grammar. Kalm provided the following examples:

Det är en kläfver karl. 'That is a *clever* fellow.'
Jag vill gä och öppna gäten. 'I shall go and *open* the gate.'

These loans do not fill any gaps in Swedish, of course, but rather reveal the kind of language mixture usual when bilinguals no longer rigidly separate their languages. Another example shows that Dutch was part of the mixture affecting Swedish:

De begynna skeda ut att tala svenska. 'They are beginning to give up talking Swedish.'

The modern translator of Kalm's travels speculates, plausibly, that *skeda ut* derives from Dutch *uitscheiden* 'to cease or stop' (Kalm 1963, 688).

On May 7, 1750, Kalm composed the following melancholy prediction in his journal:

In the morning we continued our journey from near Maurice River down to Cape May. We had a Swedish guide along who was probably born of Swedish parents, and was married to a Swedish woman but who could not, himself, speak Swedish. There are many such here of both sexes; for since English is the principal language in the land all people gradually get to speak that, and they become ashamed to talk in their own tongue, because they fear they may not in such a case be real English. Consequently many Swedish women are married to Englishmen, and although they can speak Swedish very well it is impossible to make them do so, and when they are spoken to in Swedish they always answer in English. The same condition obtains among the men.... (Kalm 1963, 683)

Kalm concluded this report by saying that Swedish was about to die out as an American vernacular, a prediction almost immediately borne out, at least until the subsequent waves of Scandinavian migration to the upper Midwest in the nineteenth century.

Nonetheless, the Swedes and the English tussled over the names of flora and fauna. According to one report, the Swedes and the Indians called a plant (formerly *Arum virginicum*) the *taw-ho*, while the English called it a *wake-robin*. Another edible plant, *Sagittaria sagittifolia*, was known to Swedes and Indians as *katniss* and to the English as *arrowhead* or *water-archer*, names transferred from the plants of Europe. For yet another edible root, English speakers could borrow the Swedish/Indian *tawkee* or employ *tuckahoe*, the term that had been in American use from the earliest reports and thus fully naturalized as English (Watson 1830, 442–43).

Negotiating over words took place at the mouth of the Delaware River as the founding European colonists, the Dutch and the Swedes, were giving up their languages for English. Nothing of this kind had yet taken place with the largest non-English-speaking European language community in Pennsylvania, the Germans. Waves of immigrants from German-speaking Europe arrived in the colonies, especially in the decades from 1740 to 1760, and most of them entered through Philadelphia. Many remained there, while others migrated north to New York or spread southwestward into the Shenandoah Valley and the uplands of North Carolina. In 1760, there were more than 50,000 Germans in Pennsylvania and western Maryland, and in these areas they were equal in numbers to the English-speaking white population (Fogelman 1996, 8). Even more significant was the fact that the natural increase in population was more rapid in the German community than in the English.[4]

Printing in German in Philadelphia began in 1728, and between that date and 1830 more than 3,000 titles were published, most of them newspapers and magazines, works of devotion, calendars, and almanacs (Bötte 1989). In 1732, Franklin published the *Philadelphische Zeitung*, a newspaper that lasted for only two ill-printed issues. At Germantown, Christopher Saur began a long career as printer and publisher in 1738 when he recognized that Franklin (who had published his first German title in 1730) was prospering from the market for such works. In 1742, Franklin published Martin Luther's *Kurzer Catechismus*, and in 1743 Saur responded with Luther's translation into German of the Old and New Testaments. (Not until 1782 was the Bible first published in America in English.) Noting Franklin's success with the *Philadelphia Gazette*, Saur published *Der hoch-deutsch pensylvanische Geschicht-Schreiber* (1739–46) and its successor the *Pensylvanische Berichte* (1746–62). The paper continued under the direction of Christopher Saur's grandson, Christopher III. Other newspapers directed to a German-speaking audience were founded, and those that did well were published in towns in the hinterland: *Die Germantowner Zeitung* (published in 1776–77) and *Neue unpartheyische Läncaster Zeitung* (from 1787 to 1797).

German-language journalism was an important part of civic life, and the Parliament in London took note of it by proposing to double the tax imposed upon printed papers written or published in languages other than English.[5] While soon repealed under the pressure of American opposition (and the more consequential opposition of William Pitt in the Parliament), the Stamp Act was the first legislative attempt to suppress any language other than English in what would become the United States.

---

4. While Germans were the largest of the non-English white immigrant groups, they were only a part of the great wave of settlement across the Atlantic that culminated in 1760. The previous two decades produced the highest proportion of immigrants to resident population in the history of America since 1700—more than the proportion in later periods regarded as immigrant eras, such as the decades from 1840 to 1860 or 1880 to 1919 (Fogelman 1996, 156–57). With the huge influx of immigrants, the time was ripe for change in English.

5. The Stamp Act stated: "For every skin or piece of vellum or parchment, or sheet or piece of paper, on which any instrument, proceeding, or other matter or thing aforesaid, shall be ingrossed, written, or printed, within the said colonies and plantations, in any other than the English language, a stamp duty of double the amount of the respective duties being charged thereon" (ahp.gatech.edu/stamp_act_bp_1765.html, viewed July 26, 2005). At the time of the controversy, Franklin was suspected of having influenced the introduction of this provision, an assertion denied by his modern editors. Certainly, Franklin had more to gain than any American printer by its adoption.

Such disparate treatment of their language did little to increase the allegiance of Germans to the British government, and the Stamp Act had the unintended but important consequence of urging Germans to seek citizenship (and thus become voters) before the new tax was imposed. The Stamp Act also did little to diminish the flow of publications in German as it increased the interest of Germans in civic life. The first news of the signing of the Declaration of Independence appeared in the *Pennsylvanischer Staatsbote* on July 5, 1776, and on July 9 the same paper published the first translation of the document (Verhoeven 2005, 77).

Though numerous and prosperous, the Germans did not at first participate, proportionate to their numbers, in the intellectual, social, and political movements that made Philadelphia a center of influence for America. Some of the aloofness from these developments can be explained by the fervent activity of Germans in Christian endeavors. Saur himself was closely connected to the Ephrata Cloister, and his son, Christopher Saur II, became a bishop in the German-Baptist Brethren (known as the *Dunkards*). Missionary work among the Indians in the western part of the state led to many conversions and promotion of the German language among these converts (Heckewelder 1820). In April 1748, the young George Washington made his initial trip beyond the Alleghenies and encountered Indians for the first time. He was vexed that "they would never speak English but when spoken to they speak all Dutch"—that is, German (Washington 1931–44, 1:11).

German voters in the colony favored their language and the status quo, supporting the Quaker candidates who embraced both pacifism and abhorrence of high taxes. Religious tolerance allowed them to refine various denominations of Protestantism, and wealth from farming supported a relatively affluent life. Secular intellectual pursuits conducted in English held little interest for most Germans, and the only Germans active in the Library Company in its first decades were recent immigrants rather than long-established Pennsylvanians. In 1771 Franklin took pride that the Library Company "made the common tradesmen and farmers as intelligent as most gentlemen from other countries" (quoted in Nash 2002, 33). The kind of "intelligence" fostered by Philadelphia's scientific societies and schools did not seem valuable to many Germans, particularly in the rural hinterland where German-language institutions were strongest.

When there were few Germans in the Pennsylvania Assembly, their "threat" to the English-speaking community could be utilized for political advantage. While resident abroad, Franklin exploited this issue, and he denounced Germans in a very public place—*The Gentleman's Magazine* in London:

> A nation well regulated is like a polypus; cut it in two, and each deficient part shall speedily grow out of the part remaining. Thus if you have room and subsistence enough, as you may by dividing, make ten polypusses out of one, you may of one make ten nations, equally populous and powerful.
>
> And since detachments of *English* from *Britain* sent to *America*, will have their places at home so soon supplied, and increase so largely here [i.e., in Britain]; why should the *palatine Boors* be suffered to swarm into our settlements, and by herding together establish their language and Manners, to the exclusion of ours. (Franklin 1755, 485)

Franklin's strong views did him little good politically when news of this article reached Philadelphia and the Germans came to know of it.[6] In the 1750s, Franklin saw the problem of the English and Germans competing for sovereignty and struggling to see which of them would become "populous and powerful." Certainly he did not envision a time when English speakers would learn German, and in both public and private he denounced the German community for ignorance (even when the literacy rate was likely to have been higher among the Germans than among the English). Franklin was even willing to rouse English fears in imagining that the intermarriage of Germans and English-descended Americans would result in mixed-race children "of what we call a swarthy Complexion" (Verhoeven 2005, 81).

In 1750, Christopher Saur I opposed opening an English-language school, fearful that it would harm the institutions of German culture.[7] Saur became even more suspicious of such schools when in 1753 the proprietors of the colony in London established "charity schools" for German children, and he recognized, correctly, that such schools were intended as tools of assimilation. Yet Saur was willing to promote cultural balance

---

6. The article was reprinted in Boston in 1755, but the controversy over it only erupted in 1764 when the *Pennsylvania Journal* (September 27, supplement) excoriated Franklin over the phrase "Palatine Boors" (Verhoeven 2005, 99).

7. At the same time, Saur was encouraging his friend Christopher Dock to compose a treatise on education to make known how kindness toward children might replace the violence typical of common schools at the time. Dock's teaching took place in German communities, but he was known to the larger world of Pennsylvania and able to use English when it was required (see Studer 1967).

between the two communities, and he published a textbook to assist Germans in learning English (*Nützliche* 1751). Such a work brought into Saur's list of books a topic already made popular in 1748 in *Grammatica Anglicana Concentrata* (Arnold 1748), which contained an appendix "whereby an Englishman may easily attain to the knowledge of the German language" (96). The book contained a variety of dialogues showing English and German in parallel columns. For example:

VIII. *To take a Lod[g]ing*
Mistress, have you any good Room to let?
Yes, sir. Will you have it forwards or backwards?
That's all one.
Let me see one.
Will you give your self the Trouble to walk up.
There's a very good Room, and a Closet, both very lightsome.
Is the Feather-bed good?
As good as any in Town. (Arnold 1748, 72–73)

While awkward in spots—for instance, *forwards* and *backwards* instead of *in front* or *in back*—the specimen dialogue shows the fragmentary sentences of authentic conversation, and the book itself foresees a bilingual community in which landladies and tenants can communicate in both languages.

After his father's death in 1658, Christopher Saur II took a less dogmatic view of the language situation, and he even printed (in English) the agreement that led to the founding of an English-language school in Germantown (Germantown Academy 1760). Christopher Saur II was an enterprising man, building a paper mill and a type foundry, and he became one of the wealthiest men in the colonies. His devotion to the world as he knew it inevitably led to his supporting the monarchy during the Revolution, and in 1778, when the British withdrew from Philadelphia, state officials confiscated his property and sold it.

While many Germans lived in prosperous towns outside Philadelphia, there were some who involved themselves in Enlightenment science and cross-linguistic inquiry. One of these was Conrad Weiser's grandson, Henry Muhlenberg, who, as a schoolboy in Trappe, Pennsylvania, became bilingual in German and English. Henry accompanied his two older brothers to Halle—his father's university—where he spent a year engaged in theological studies and acquired Latin, Greek, and Hebrew. Returning to Pennsylvania, he was named assistant to his father, the most prominent Lutheran pastor in the colony and an eloquent preacher in English, German, and Dutch. After the Revolution, in which he and his brothers were warm adherents of the American cause, Henry settled in Lancaster, Pennsylvania, where he spent the rest of his life.

Henry Muhlenberg, like his older contemporary Bartram, became a self-taught and tireless botanist, and he too entered into frequent correspondence with European scientists, but he was unfortunate in his collaborators. Johann David Schöpf, for instance, published in Germany *Materia Medica Americana* in 1787, substantially derived from Muhlenberg's original research but without so much as a mention of him.[8] As his recent biographer notes, "[F]ew botanists have written so much but published so little" (Boewe 2000). Muhlenberg's manuscripts are still largely unpublished, and the American Philosophical Society preserves his monograph describing the plants roundabout Lancaster with, in addition to botanical description, their "local names in German, English, and Indian languages" (Muhlenberg 1784–1813, item 12).

The sheer size and cultural integrity of the Germans in Pennsylvania meant that multilingualism (like Muhlenberg's) was rare, especially outside Philadelphia, and consequently the influence of German on English was limited. In 1775, one of the German newspapers began to publish some notices in English—*Henrich Millers pennsylvanischer Staatsbote* (1775–79)—and late in the century others followed suit. Assimilationist efforts only began in earnest in the nineteenth century in *The People's Instructor = Volksunterrichter* (1810–13), a weekly journal with double-column format published in Easton, Pennsylvania, by Christian Jacob Hütter. The only well-known word in modern English to come from German in Pennsylvania during this era is *sauerkraut* (Leacock 1776, 30). Other German words associated with German settlement in Pennsylvania are recorded much later: *Belsnickel* 'Santa Claus' (1823), *schnitz* 'dried apples' (1848), *moshey* 'candy of boiled sugar syrup' (1849), *lager* 'beer' (1855), *knepp* 'dumpling' (1869), *fasnacht* 'dough nut' (1869), *outen* 'to extinguish' (1878). Many of these terms are still in use in Pennsylvania. Most other words to enter English from German in America were the result of

---

8. In 1801, Schöpf repaid his enormous intellectual debt in part by naming a species of turtle presented to him by Muhlenberg *Testudo muhlenbergii*. In the late twentieth century *Muhlenberg's turtle* was classified as a threatened species and its habitat thus the focus of strenuous conservation efforts. After his death, Muhlenberg was recognized as the botanist personally responsible for about 150 species of plants (Lee 1999).

waves of nineteenth-century immigration and settlement in the heartland of the country.

Satisfied with their tolerant culture and agricultural prosperity, the Germans in Philadelphia were not necessarily eager to embrace change. In
1785, *The Pennsylvania Gazette* published (in English) an appeal to Germans that had appeared earlier in an unnamed German newspaper. Its
purpose was to foster the development of German-language schools in villages like Reading, Lebanon, Lancaster, or Manheim, where the students
would not be tempted by "those vices which always prevail in large towns."
The author represented himself as "a friend to equal liberty and learning in
Pennsylvania," and he foresaw the ascension of a class of learned Germans
to positions of authority in government. He wrote:

> I anticipate a revolution in our stage, big with human happiness, when
> the farmer and the scholar shall be blended together, and when the
> same men who have been competitors for fame in our Colleges, shall
> be competitors for honor in the Councils of the State. (*Pennsylvania
> Gazette*, August 31, 1785, 3)

This optimistic prospect must have seemed entirely reasonable to many,
particularly those in the English-speaking community influenced by
Thomas Jefferson's ideal of government by yeoman-scholars.

In this letter, the author attempted to counter arguments against a
German-language school. First of all, an educated populace would not be
duped by "lawyers of other societies" nor given bad medical treatment by
"quacks of their own nation." Another argument, described and rejected,
asserted that it would be better for Germans to enroll in existing English
schools. But in that case, the Germans would be at an educational disad-
vantage; a solid grounding in their own language would lead them to seek
the knowledge found in English books. Educated German youth would
meet those descended from the English or the Irish on equal footing. Still
another argument to be countered was that book-learning would turn
youth from prosperous labor as farmers to the indolence of the learned
but unemployed. (This argument was also current in Britain in the late
eighteenth century; the Parliament in London heard arguments of exactly
this kind in deciding not to make primary education universal.) Here the
author embraced the Enlightenment idea that applied knowledge could
make for agricultural prosperity through the best modern notions of hus-
bandry. Finally, he pointed out that many legislators in Connecticut and

Massachusetts were graduates of Yale and Harvard and their efforts had produced excellent constitutions and "freedom and dignity" in their government.

Appealing to national pride—"the Germans in Europe are wise and Learned"—the writer hoped that Pennsylvania Germans would seek charters from the legislature to establish these German-language schools. There was also a need, though he did not mention it, for American-educated ministers in the Lutheran and Reformed congregations since these churches could no longer anticipate the arrival of Germans from Europe to serve them. Ministers of the prominent German churches in Philadelphia saw this need and urged action. In 1783, the German department of the University of Pennsylvania was established, led by two Philadelphia ministers, to instruct monolingual German youth, but the pressures on these students to learn English were so intense that it did not continue to attract the children of prosperous families. In 1787, it was closed.

Almost certainly the letter published in *The Pennsylvania Gazette* was composed by Peter Muhlenberg, Henry's older brother, lately a major-general in the American forces in the Revolution, and, eventually, a United States senator. He was one of the advocates for establishing a German college in Lancaster. Peter Muhlenberg contributed £50 toward the establishment of such an institution, and he persuaded Benjamin Franklin to be another of the subscribers. Having put aside his earlier reservations about the likelihood of German assimilation, Franklin contributed £200 and thus was given honor in the name of the institution: Franklin College. In the petition to the legislature, the proponents established the purpose:

> The design of the this institution is to promote an accurate knowledge of the German and English languages, also of the learned languages, of mathematics, morals, and natural philosophy, divinity, and all such other branches of literature as will tend to make good men and useful citizens. (Quoted in Dubbs 1903, 19)

Readers might reasonably imagine that Franklin College was designed to enroll German-speaking young people and to provide them with a balanced bilingual education.

The program for the dedication on June 5, 1787, was printed in both German and English on facing pages. A sermon in each of the two languages was preached, prayers were offered in both, and an ode was recited, a verse composed and recited in German and translated and recited in

English. A line from it gives the flavor of the composition: "Fliehe, fliehe Unwissenheit" / "Begone! Begone! Ignorance." So great was the national and international interest in the founding of the college that a translation of the program into French appeared in the *Mercure de France* (Sutterfield 1945, 11).

Certain features of the great ceremony displayed the fact that the college was not designed to put the two languages on equal footing. On the day before the ceremony, Benjamin Rush addressed his fellow trustees. (Rush was a Philadelphia eminence, a signatory of the Declaration of Independence, and a remarkable and innovative physician.) He outlined a series of benefits that might ensue through education in the college, particularly "the partition wall which has long seperated [*sic*] the English & German inhabitants of the state." He allowed that German might eventually have some official status in Pennsylvania, but Germans could not expect it to play a role "in our federal councils." Yet "by means of this College the German language will be preserved from extinction & corruption by being taught in a grammatical manner" (Sutterfield 1945, 16–17). Rush's companion at dinner, William Rawle, a Quaker and member of the American Philosophical Society, smoothed over the contentious issues in Rush's address by conversing with the gathered worthies in German.

Events the next day did not bode so well for German. The English sermon was preached by Joseph Hutchins, the Episcopal minister in Lancaster. Like other members of his denomination, he was suspected of royalism and of having an interest in making his church the "established" (or state-sponsored) faith of Pennsylvania. He alleged that Franklin College would be a vehicle for absorbing Germans (and their language) into English-speaking society, and he said as much in bald terms: "As the limited capacity of man can very seldom attain excellence in more than one language, the study of English will consequently demand the principal attention of your children" (Hutchins 1806, 15). To speak in this way to an audience of capable bilinguals was an affront to those who understood him and expressed the view that advocates of the college for Germans most feared. Wisely for his own position in Lancaster, Hutchins deferred publication of his sermon for twenty years.

Henry Muhlenberg was named the first president, and Franklin College continued as an outpost of higher learning for Germans into the nineteenth century. But the forces of assimilation were inexorable. In his old age, Henry Muhlenberg published a German-English bilingual dictionary in Lancaster. In the preface, he and his collaborator explained their hopes for the use of German:

> An Acquaintance with the German language, independent of its importance to the reader, in enabling him to peruse the most valuable works in the original, is also of high interest to every man of business in this country where the language has been so much diffused. (Muhlenberg and Schipper 1812, iii)

Unfortunately, there is nothing very "American" about the work since it lacks entries for such current American English words as *catalpa*, *skunk*, *pone*, or *wolverine*. American words that are included are defined from a European perspective: for example, *moose* "der americanische Hirsch" ("the American deer").

Franklin College became an increasingly English institution, renamed in the nineteenth century as Franklin and Marshall College. From the perspective of English, the influence of Pennsylvania Germans on the language appeared only once German diminished as a language of commercial and intellectual life. Pennsylvania German endures to this day in the life of the Amish and other pietist communities, but they are a people deliberately set apart as they maintain their cultural and religious purity by separating themselves from most innovations of modern life.

The end of the second half of the eighteenth century put Germans on the threshold of change. Benjamin Rush, once again, was a reliable witness to the events of his day:

> The intercourse of the Germans with each other, is kept up chiefly in their own language; but most of their men who visit the capital, and trading or country towns of the state, speak the English language. A certain number of the laws are now printed in German, for the benefit of those of them, who cannot read English. A large number of German news-papers are likewise circulated through the State, through which knowledge and intelligence have been conveyed, much to the advantage of the government. There is scarcely an instance of a German, of either sex, in Pennsylvania, that cannon *read*; but many of the wives and daughters of the German farmers cannot *write*. The present state of society among them renders this accomplishment of little consequence to their improvement or happiness. (Rush and Rupp 1875, 54–55)

At the end of the eighteenth century—Rush wrote in 1789—Germans were likely to attend church services in their language, trade with people within their community, marry within the group, and use German in the home.

The early nineteenth century witnessed the rapid disappearance of the German language in these communities. Proposals to provide for a bilingual legislature in Pennsylvania failed at the end of the century. (They would succeed in the new government formed a decade later in Louisiana Territory.) The elites, particularly those in cities and towns, gave up their language; those in rural and pietist communities preserved it down to this day. Like the Swedes fifty years earlier, Germans turned to English without much apparent sense of regret.

The largest of the immigrant groups in the period 1750–1800 traced their ancestry to Africa, and nearly all of them were brought to America by force rather than choice. The complex transactions of the slave trade required that there be *linguisters* at both ends of the journey. In 1750, a medical doctor from Philadelphia, William Chancellor, signed on as physician to a slave ship and traveled to the west coast of Africa, where he encountered what he called "trading men[,] that is those that talk English" (Wax 1968, 478). He was curious about these intermediaries and speculated that they took a third of the purchase price of the slaves they provided. He observed:

> *Sunday, July* 8 [1750]. As soon as you arrive at Annamaboo, you will have negroes come off to you to desire you to take their Sons on board, to learn them English, which they generally do, & keep them in the cabbin to wait on you neither is there any thing, the negroes so much esteem as a negro who talks English, and by thr. Country men they are very much esteem'd. (Wax 1968, 476)

English was sufficiently well-established in West Africa that Antera Duke kept a diary in it from 1785 to 1788. Duke's English, though showing traces of creole features, is remarkable for its fluency and range (Forde 1956).

In the American colonies, slavery existed in every colony, everywhere characterized by high levels of restriction. In Philadelphia in the 1760s there were 1,500 slaves—four of them owned by Franklin: Peter, Jemima, King, and Othello. Quakers recognized that slavery was inimical to their religious profession and so abolished slave-holding among their members, and from 1770 onward Franklin himself became an increasingly ardent advocate of Abolition. During and after the Revolution, freed slaves (and those escaping slavery) found haven in Philadelphia. An act of the legislature in 1780 declared free any slave brought into Pennsylvania and remaining there for six months. In 1785, Olaudah Equiano arrived at what he called "this favourite old town" since it had been for him in his earliest days of his slavery a dreamed-of destination. He was delighted to see in Philadelphia that the Quakers had erected a free school for African-descended children of all denominations (*Slave Narratives* 2000, 231).

The growth in the African-descended population culminated in a wave of migration in the 1790s when the slave revolt in Haiti caused many slaves (and their owners) to flee the Caribbean. In the 1790 census, 10,000 African Americans were enumerated for Pennsylvania.

The impact of African Americans on the variety of English forming in Philadelphia is difficult to identify (just as it is difficult to discern the work of African American artisans and laborers in the growth of the magnificent city). Scraps of evidence suggest that the group was more likely to have been at sea and employed in shipping, more likely to have traveled widely, and more likely to be multilingual. In 1762, a notice of a runaway named Joseph Boudron reveals all three of these factors. He had been born in the Caribbean and lived in Charleston and New York. According to the advertisement, he "speaks good English, French, Spanish, and Portuguese" (*Philadelphia Gazette*, August 26, 1762). In addition, he was a good cook and just twenty-three years old.

What is missing from the record is an accurate sense of the vernacular, and one of the few words of African origin to turn up first in English in Philadelphia reached the language by a roundabout route. In 1769, a Georgia planter writing from Savannah communicated to the American Philosophical Society a method of extracting sesame oil from seeds. Instead of using *sesame,* a word long established in English, he described the *bene seed* and enclosed a small keg of the oil to demonstrate its excellence. *Bene* (also spelled *benne*) was a West African word, and it is likely that the seeds and the method of cultivating them came from Africa too (Morel 1771, 239–40).

Before the Revolution, African-descended persons, both slave and free, met in what became Washington Square for singing, dancing, and socializing—"'each in their own tongue,' after the customs of their several nations in Africa" (Watson 1830, 483). Though tantalizingly vague, this report suggests that African languages survived for some time on American soil refreshed by sailors and new immigrants from abroad. It is reasonable to assume that all these multilingual Americans displayed a great variety of inflections and accents, but racism among the literate reduced their speaking to a series of stereotypes in the written record which, though to some extent revealing, do little to illuminate the details of this variety.

Among the earliest of these representations appeared in John Leacock's 1776 play with the arresting title: *The Fall of British Tyranny*. The subtitle proclaims that it had been "lately planned at the Royal Theatrum Pandemonium at St. James," but it was very unlikely to have been performed by anyone anywhere. There is small plot and less action, but the vignettes show the British behaving badly and meddling with American liberty. In one of the scenes the British villain, Lord Kidnapper, attempts to rouse slaves to revolt:

Well, my brave blacks, are you come to list?
CUDJO. Eas, massa Lord, you preasee.
KIDNAPPER. How many are there of you?
CUDJO. Twenty-two, massa.
KIDNAPPER. Very well, did you all run away from your masters?
CUDJO. Eas, massa Lord, eb'ry one, me too.
KIDNAPPER. That's clever; they have no right to make you slaves, I
    wish all the Negroes wou'd do the same, I'll make 'em free—what
    part did you come from?
CUDJO. Disse brack man, disse one, disse one, disse one, disse one,
    come from Hamton, disse one, disse one, disse one, come from
    Nawfok, me come from Nawfok too.
KIDNAPPER. Very well, what was your master's name?
CUDJO. Me massa name Cunney Tomsee.
KIDNAPPER. Well then I'll make you a major—and what's your
    name?
CUDJO. Me massa cawra me Cudjo.
KIDNAPPER. Cudjo?—very good—was you ever christened, Cudjo?
CUDJO. No, massa, me no chrissen.
KIDNAPPER. Well then I'll christen you—you shall be called major
    Cudjo Thompson, and if you behave well, I'll make you a greater
    man than your master.... (Leacock 1776, 46–47)

The name *Cudjo* derived from the West African practice of naming infants for the day of the week on which they were born: Cudjo was born on a Monday. Just a few features composed this stereotype of African-influenced speech: *me* for *I*; reduction of consonant clusters in *master* and *christen*; substitution of *d* for *th* in *this*; *b* for *v* in *every*; a vowel or *r* for the *l* sound in *please* and *colonel*, an *r* for the *l* in *black*.

That such stereotypes flourished in Philadelphia reflects an idea about speech but not necessarily speech itself. To give another example, in 1782, a report appeared in *The Pennsylvania Gazette* from an officer in General Nathaniel Greene's army of American forces then fighting in the South. According to the report, a Captain Randolph attempted to break a blockade in the Ashley River, and he did so by drifting a small boat down on the tide in the dark of night, with his troops concealed by heaps of straw. The report continued:

> When he got within sixty yards, he was challenged by the sentinel; he answered in the negro dialect, that some poor negroes were going to town to sell some live stock: "Massa, we got some fat goose, will you buy?" "Yes, yes," replied the sailor, "heave to and let us look at them." As soon as the boat struck the sid[e] of the vessel, the men jumped up, mounted the deck, knocked the sentinel's brains out and shut down the hatches, by which he secured 20 prisoners, three officers included, and captured a very fine sloop of ten or twelve guns. He was obliged to burn the vessel, but he brought off the prisoners. (May 15, 1782, 3)

Here the trick seems to have been successful by the use of the word *Massa* 'Master' alone.

In both these examples, the speech represented comes from the South, not from Philadelphia. No such accounts suggest that the emergent class of African-descended tradespersons and intellectuals spoke a distinctive Philadelphia form of English. There were certainly occasions when such stereotypes might have been invoked—for instance, when Pennsylvania slaves embraced the promise of freedom and fought against the rebels to achieve it, or when it was alleged that African Americans shirked their duties during the terrible plague of yellow fever in 1793.

Stereotypes of this sort were part of the lore about the emergent country. "The inhabitants of almost every state in America are distinguished by some particularities, either of speech or behaviour, peculiar to themselves," asserted an essay published in *The Federal Gazette and Philadelphia Evening Post*. The piece singled out New Englanders as the most peculiar of American voices and gave as an instance this enthusiastic outburst: "*Odds swamp it, as sure as snakes, it must be tarnation clever fun*" (September 9, 1792, 2). One should not conclude that all Yankees talked this way; John Adams certainly did not. Nor should one infer that African Americans like Absalom Jones habitually used *Massa* or *ebery*. Exactly this point was urged by the author of this essay: "To judge of a whole people by a few individuals argues want of experience, an unacquaintance with men and manners, and a mind clouded with prejudice and absorbed in ignorance."

Of the language communities in eighteenth-century Philadelphia, the most distinctive spoke a variety of English derived from Scotland and Ireland. Part of the joke in the essay just quoted concerned the attraction of membership in the Sons of St. Patrick to those of every origin seeking an occasion and fellowship for getting drunk while having "tarnation clever fun." Without counting such would-be Irishmen, the 1790 census found the Scots-Irish part of the white population of Pennsylvania to be 23.1 percent, not too far behind that designated as "English." The great majority of these migrants were Protestants from the northern part of Ireland, many of whom claimed descent from the Scots "planted" there in the seventeenth century by the English government in an attempt to outweigh the Catholic population of Ireland. Famine, rack-renting, and trade depressions all fueled the migration to America, so much so that James Logan wrote to John Penn in 1729: "there are some grounds for the common apprehension of the people that if some speedy Method be not taken, they will soon make themselves Proprietors of the Province" (quoted in Dunaway 1944, 37). In the 1740s, the Scots-Irish arrived at the rate of nearly 12,000 a year, and in 1771–73, many more sailed from Belfast, Dublin, Cork, Waterford, and other Irish ports to North American towns and cities, most of them to destinations along the Delaware River. More than 100,000 arrived in the years just before the American Revolution (Dunaway 1944, 39–40). For most, their destination was westward to the frontier beyond Lancaster, many following the route laid out by Germans to the uplands of Virginia and North Carolina.

Most Scots-Irish immigrants arrived penniless and were indentured for extended periods to pay off their passage. Many of them ran away, and those holding their contracts advertised for their capture and return. In the years from 1729 to 1760, 1,185 notices of runaways appeared in *The Pennsylvania Gazette*. Of the number identified by national origin, 476 were from Ireland (417 men, thirty-three women, and twenty-six children)

(Meaders 1993, 507). Constituting nearly two-thirds of the runaways, "Irish" people were far more numerous than any other identifiably white group. (Second in rank was "England" with 179.)

Only a handful of these immigrants were speakers of Gaelic, and those who were also used English. One John Connell was described as one of this group: "speaks in the Irish dialect, and can converse in the Irish tongue" (*Pennsylvania Gazette*, July 8, 1795). Patrick Birds from Dublin could be known by his dialect, and a recent convict migrant, Robert Lyon, "speaks much in the 'Scotch dialect'" (*Pennsylvania Gazette*, August 4, 1784, July 9, 1784). Mary Lawless could be recognized by her language too: her English "is a little mixed with the brogue" (*Pennsylvania Gazette*, February 25, 1784). In many of these advertisements, the phrase "speaks bad English" was sufficiently descriptive, and this "bad English" took many forms. One might know an escaped slave named Cato because he was a native New Englander and his language was "somewhat on the Dutch dialect" (*Pennsylvania Gazette*, October 11, 1780). Another, named Bacchus, was born in Guinea and could be known by his accent (*Pennsylvania Gazette*, May 1, 1782). A Welsh convict-migrant spoke another kind of "bad English" (*Pennsylvania Gazette*, June 30, 1768). Philip Marks, a Jew, could be identified by yet another form of "bad English" (*Pennsylvania Gazette*, March 29, 1775).

Dialect differences within the colonies were also described. For example, two African-descended slaves, a man and a woman, "can speak but very bad English, so as they cannot be well understood, but from what can be gathered from their dialect, it is apprehended they left some part of Maryland or Virginia" (*Pennsylvania Gazette,* July 28, 1779). Not all distinctive kinds of English were bad, of course. A runaway named Cuffy, originally from Montserrat, "speaks good English and French" (*Pennsylvania Gazette*, May 17, 1747).

These notices provide invaluable insight into the varieties of English and the status of multilingualism in Philadelphia in the second half of the eighteenth century. Runaways might change clothing or disguise their features, but they could not easily change their language.

Little information is available about the fate of these runaways and how many of them were returned. Enterprising escapees wanted to get away far and fast, and masters of ships were especially urged to be on the lookout. An alternative to taking a ship was to go west, through the dense communities of German speakers where English newspapers were little read and beyond those communities to the west.

The Quakers remained distinctive in spoken English by their adherence to "plain language." This consisted mainly of using *thee* instead of *ye* or *you*, so *thee* was used for the Deity and all sorts and conditions of persons. (*Ye* and *you* were earlier used among equals, *thee* and *thou* for the high and the low.) This usage roused the contempt of Benjamin Perkins, who, in 1806, called it a "perversion." He complained particularly about the generalization of *thee*:

How dost *thee* do?
Wilt *thee* go into the country? (Perkins 1806, 4)

Like many purists, Perkins joined the campaign as the battle was nearly over, and the Quaker *thee* did not last long in the nineteenth century.

New England travelers early in the nineteenth century described, sometimes with horror ("I actually seemed to be among foreigners in a foreign country" [Smith 1958, 199]), the passage through the German-speaking parts of Pennsylvania. As they moved westward, they came back into English-speaking country but among the Scots-Irish: "It was with the greatest difficulty that I could understand any thing that was said" (Smith 1958, 200). In 1810, Margaret Dwight wrote home to describe her arrival at the frontier:

We have almost got out of the land of Dutchmen, but the waggoners are worse—— The people here talk curiously, they all reckon instead of expect— Youns is a word I have heard used several times, but what it means I don't know, they use it so strangely. (Dwight 1991, 37)

Youns, equivalent to *you all* as the second-person plural pronoun, is still widespread in central and western Pennsylvania, and it comes to America from the north of Ireland (Macafee 1996, 400).

Many more influences from the Scots-Irish appeared in Pennsylvania and spread westward into the Ohio River valley. While textual evidence for some of them dates only to the nineteenth century, they were certainly in widespread use in the late eighteenth. *Poke* 'a bag, sack' represents such a word. Obsolete in England, *poke* remained (and remains) in use in Scotland and Northern Ireland. In modern American English, its use is centered in western Pennsylvania, southeastern Ohio, West Virginia, and eastern Kentucky. The use of *poke* in the interior South shows a spread characteristic of American dialects in which the Scots-Irish word followed the path pioneered by German settlers as they turned south from western Pennsylvania into the great valley of Virginia. A word with a similar history is *redd* 'tidy' (as in "Please redd up your room before you go to school"). Written evidence seems not to appear in America until the nineteenth century, but its origins in Scotland and Northern Ireland are well-documented. In present-day American English, its main area of use is in western Pennsylvania with additional use in southeastern Ohio and West Virginia. Many other expressions arrived with Scots-Irish people in Pennsylvania and extended westward: *till* 'to' (in "quarter till three") and *all* with interrogative pronouns (in "What all did she want?").

Characterizing earlier American English, visitors often commented on the uniformity or purity of the language, usually considering it in comparison to the many localized forms of speech found in Britain. By the end of the eighteenth century, homegrown observers were beginning to characterize its diversity and difference. In Philadelphia, in 1792, an essay reprinted from a Georgia newspaper caught the flavor of this new way of thinking about English in America:

> The inhabitants of almost every state in America are distinguished by some particularities, either of speech or behaviour, peculiar to themselves. The most apparent national distinctions appear to exist between the natives of the New-England states and the Inhabitants of all the others, from their frequently stigmatizing each other with the satirical appellations of Cracker, Yankee, Lovers of Pork and Molasses, bad Pronouncers of their own tongue, and many other such like elegant epithets. (*Federal Gazette and Philadelphia Evening Post,* September 6, 1792, 2)

While the author of these reflections was not specific about just who the "bad pronouncers" were, he acknowledged that New England towns were the source of good English from "the number and diversity of excellent literary institutions established in every part." The belief that the English of Massachusetts and Connecticut was a model for other Americans flourished in the nineteenth century and continued to be a vigorous, and influential, idea in the twentieth.

While Philadelphia might have been predicted to be the hearth and origin of English for western America, it was not to be so. In 1793, an outbreak of yellow fever had a devastating effect; in a city of 45,000, more than 5,000 died, and in the epidemic "the city's social fabric collapsed"

(Nash 2002, 127). Both the state and federal governments fled, and, in 1800, the permanent settlement of the federal government in Washington diminished Philadelphia as a destination for those seeking power and privilege.

Yet the economic vigor of the city was soon restored, and manufacturing created an inexhaustible demand for labor. By 1810, the population had increased to 91,000. No longer were the Irish immigrants seen as improvident drunkards but rather as essential workers in both commerce and intellectual life. These new citizens, suspicious of anglophile tendencies among the longer-established Philadelphians, became ardent followers of Thomas Jefferson, whose politics shifted emphasis from the seaboard cities to the western frontiers.

Symbolic of this change is John Murdoch's 1795 play *The Triumphs of Love*. Patrick, the Irish suitor, prevails over "English Dick" in winning the hand of Jenny and finds a patron to set him up as a grocer: "Shir, I hope you will not be affronted at my taking you by the hand. I fale more in my heart than I can spake wid my tongue" (78). While he has not yet lost his brogue, he has become thoroughly American.

6   New Orleans, 1800–1850

FEW DESCRIPTIONS OF travel present so dismal a scene as that describing Christmas morning 1827 when Frances Trollope and three of her children left the "bright blue waves" of the Caribbean and encountered the muddy water staining the sea at Balize, Louisiana. "I have never beheld a scene so utterly desolate as this entrance of the Mississippi," she wrote in *Domestic Manners of the Americans* (1832, 1). It took two days to beat upriver to New Orleans, and the visitors saw uprooted trees. She continued:

> Sometimes several of these, entangled together, collect among their boughs a quantity of floating rubbish, that gives the mass the appearance of a moving island, bearing a forest, with its roots mocking the heavens; while the dishonoured branches lash the tide in idle vengeance; this, as it approaches the vessel, and glides swiftly past, looks like the fragment of a world in ruins. (2)

An economic exile from England, Trollope encountered the New World with much skepticism and prejudice. The landscape, she reported, displayed a "total want of beauty" (3). But she found New Orleans deeply engaging, a society in which the languages spoken were mostly French and Spanish. She landed in the most Caribbean of North American cities, and she marveled at the nuances of caste, color, and language she saw and heard around her.

There were no American towns in the lands of the Louisiana Purchase— at least if "American" was measured by Boston, New York, Philadelphia, or Charleston. All the visitors reported just how exotic the area was. Trollope observed "the grace and beauty of the elegant Quadroons; the occasional groups of wild and savage-looking Indians" (5). Another English visitor, Harriet Martineau, arriving in 1835 thought the same thing, and she was at first astonished at "a multitude of every shade of complexion" at worship in St. Louis Cathedral with "no separation." But it was a far less cordial scene than it first appeared: "The division between the American and French factions is visible even in the drawing-room. The French complain that the Americans will not speak French; will not meet their neighbors even half way in accommodation of speech" (Martineau 2000, 115). Visitors from the northeast of the United States heard themselves called *foreigners*. Thomas Nichols, describing a visit in 1837, reported: "Strange groups everywhere, and everywhere a foreign language met the ear…" (1844, 1:189).

Trollope, Martineau, and Nichols saw a society in New Orleans that appeared to have reached an equilibrium among diverse groups. And so it had, at least in comparison to the situation when the Louisiana Purchase was consummated in 1803. As might be expected in a nation founded as a democracy, the federal government gave first priority to conducting a census of the new territory, and the results, published in 1811, displayed some unexpected numbers. Louisiana—the only part of the Purchase with a significant Euro-American population—was urban. Nearly a third of the population (17,000 people) lived in Orleans parish. Only five American cities were larger in 1800: New York (with 60,515), Philadelphia (41,220), Baltimore (26,514), Boston (24,937), and Charleston (18,864). Many people lived nearby and found the Mississippi a convenient way to make brief or extended visits, so the comings-and-goings were frequent. By contrast, New York City was only 10 percent of the population of its state in 1800, making it a far less dominant metropolis for its hinterland than New Orleans was for its.

A second surprising demographic fact about New Orleans was that it was dominated by men and boys, at least among the white population: 56 percent were male. This demographic fact put women in an unusually competitive position in selecting sexual and marriage partners. (African-descended women, children, and men were not counted separately in the census.) Visitors observed, and often disapproved of, what seemed to be a perpetual round of dalliance and courtship. Women were well positioned to lead salons in which music and the arts were discussed and enjoyed.

A third fact, though not startling to those acquainted with Charleston, was that nearly half of the population of Louisiana as a whole was of African origin, and in Orleans parish it was 63 percent (*Message* 1811). While without property and cruelly treated, Americans of African descent exerted a cultural presence noticed by every visitor; it was particularly common for visitors to observe the enthusiasm of women of African origin at mass in the cathedral. Everywhere visitors went in the crowded city, they encountered African American slaves, but privileged whites of the day were quite used to finding servants of all conditions unremarked and invisible. What was exotically visible was the population of what the census called "freemen and women and children of color": 2,312 of them. Some of them commanded property, or at least fine clothes, and it seemed almost obligatory for visitors to describe horse races and cotillions at which elegantly dressed women of color made a prominent appearance. As Nichols wrote, "[T]he maddest abolitionist could not wish for an exhibition of greater equality or a more perfect amalgamation, than is to be found in New Orleans..." (1844, 1:188).

A fourth fact is central to understanding the transformation of English that took place in the region. Louisiana was the most compactly multilingual place in the country: Amerindian and African languages, Caribbean creoles, German, Spanish, French, and English were all routinely spoken by persons permanently resident in New Orleans—and the brisk trading along the levee brought still more languages. (*Levee* was introduced as an English word in the eighteenth century to describe the embankments protecting New Orleans from flooding.)

While loyalties (and animosities) based on language were certainly strong, multilingualism was a fact of everyday life. At first, English was not a consequential part of the mix, and the events of 1806 revealed this fact in a startling way. Governor William Claiborne addressed the militia urging them to prepare for the onslaught of rebels coming down the river under the command of Aaron Burr. In speaking English, and English only, he congratulated the troops on their willingness to march to the field of battle, and an hour later a special issue of the *Gazette* was published expressing his heartfelt thanks for their volunteer spirit. Soon word spread in French of what the governor had said. In less than an hour after that, the citizens "swarmed around the government" to clarify the fact that they had certainly not volunteered to fight a large army on behalf of a distant government in Washington (*Faithful Picture* 1809, 10).

Foresighted persons could see that English would eventually come to be important in the government of the territory, but that did not mean that large numbers of the long-time residents rushed to learn it. Almost immediately, there was some anxiety that language rights might be overlooked, and there must have been some awareness that the rights of language minorities were ignored or abused in other states and territories. Consequently, in 1804, a petition to Congress was circulated declaring the patriotism of the signatories (and the "modesty and wisdom" of their address): "They pray that when it [Louisiana] first be taken as a State into the Union, that they (*"whose language is English"*) may be indulged in having the Legislative and Judicial proceeding conducted in their 'mother tongue.'" Additional signers might call at the store of Benjamin Morgan, Esq. to inspect it (*Louisiana Gazette*, October 10, 1804, 3). These petitioners feared that they would be obliged to learn French, and they very much did not want to do so.

In these first days of U.S. sovereignty, two lawyers advertised their ability to represent clients, "let the language of the party be what it may," and declared themselves ready to give assistance in French, English, and Spanish (*Louisiana Gazette*, November 30, 1804, 3). The *Gazette* itself, in that same month, reported that new fonts of type had arrived from Philadelphia, and the proprietors declared themselves ready to print cards, handbills, shipping papers, and all kinds of blanks in both French and English. In an adjacent column, Henry Labruere offered for sale a slave named Peter; he thought it prudent to advertise in both of these languages (November 11, 1804, 3).

New Orleans grew rapidly, and commerce flourished. Fortune hunters from around the world (and upstream) flocked there in search of wealth. Describing the place in 1817, Samuel R. Brown rhapsodized about commerce:

The market is plentifully furnished with the necessities and luxuries of every clime. It is upon the levee fronting the city that the universe is to be seen in miniature. It is crowded with vessels from every part of the world; and with boats from a thousand different places in the "upper country." Here in half an hour you can see, and speak to

Frenchmen, Spaniards, Danes, Swedes, Germans, Englishmen, Portuguese, Hollanders, Mexicans, Kentuckians, Tennesseans, Ohionians, Pennsylvanians, New-Yorkers, New-Englanders and a motley groupe [*sic*] of Indians, Quadroons, Africans, &c. (148)

Brown saw this linguistic abundance as something genuinely remarkable, a social fact not equaled elsewhere in his broad survey of the United States and the territories dependent upon it.

New Orleans became a destination for visitors both foreign and domestic.

America's great architect of the period, Benjamin Latrobe, came to New Orleans in 1818 to design a lighthouse at Balize and other public buildings. In his journal he described the remarkable fluidity of the culture of the city:

What is the state of society in New Orleans? is one of many questions which I am required to answer by a friend who seems not to be aware that this question is equivalent to that of Hamlet to Polonius, He might as well ask, What is the shape of a cloud? (1951, 32)

In answering the question, Latrobe provided three categories: the French, the American, and the mixed. But the cloud was even more amorphous than Latrobe described. Persons prominent in the community one day might be dead the next. Yellow fever and cholera erupted every summer, and the epidemics were severe. Many of the prosperous fled to more temperate regions in the north and east, but the diseases were no respecter of persons. Henry Latrobe, Benjamin's son, came to New Orleans to design and build a water system, and in 1817 he died from yellow fever. Exactly a year later, Benjamin died from it, too.

Historians of American English have not commonly recognized that New Orleans became a city much resembling London in the mid-fourteenth century. Seasonal diseases resulted in many deaths, and deaths distributed through the population, so the educated, the prosperous, and the elite (like Latrobe and his son) shared equally in the catastrophe. Like the medieval plagues, men (especially young men) were more likely to be victims, thus creating a gender imbalance (Hatcher 1977, 59). This fact of mortality gave women more effective control of their own destinies and of wealth. They could even impose their linguistic tastes on their suitors. Despite the threat of contagion, London, like New Orleans, had lured outsiders, and the demand for expensive pleasures increased, both for material goods and for pleasures of the senses. Death in town produced prosperity in the hinterlands. In medieval England, cloth-making for export flourished in the villages far from the contagion of the city. In Louisiana, the cotton and sugar plantations grew prosperous at a distance from pestilential New Orleans.

The parallels between London from 1348 (when the plague began) and New Orleans from 1803 (when American sovereignty was imposed) should be persuasive for language historians. The conservative forces that inhibit language change were challenged: an established elite with a preferred way of speaking was displaced; literacy practices that constitute a drag on oral styles were in jeopardy; a threat of mortality discouraged silence and obedience and encouraged articulation and exuberance. "Courtly love," the code of courtship so influential in medieval literature, expressed itself with special fervor in the works of Chaucer, all of which were written, read, and performed when the plague had tipped the balance of the population in favor of women. In New Orleans, in the first decades of the nineteenth century, love poetry (especially in French) became the fashion.

The linguistic effects of the fourteenth-century plague were rapid and enduring, particularly in striking a balance between Germanic and Latin-Romance elements in the English vocabulary that persists today. English was more open than ever to loanwords, and the increase in communication and contact between distant places and London brought dialect leveling, as can be seen in the surviving correspondence from the period. Distinctions between languages and dialects simply collapsed.

New Orleans in the early nineteenth century differed from medieval London in several important ways, of course. In London the population failed for two centuries to rebound to its size before the plague. In New Orleans, the yellow fever and cholera seem hardly to have discouraged migrants. Between 1810 and 1860, the population of Louisiana increased by ninefold; in the state of New York, population increased only fourfold. Far more than any place under the sovereignty of the United States, New Orleans was a focus of immigration and a center of influence linking the Caribbean with the Mississippi valley.

In understanding the role of New Orleans at the time of the Purchase, it is important to recognize that the mouth of the Mississippi had been multilingual long before the Americans arrived. In fact, the region had been multilingual before any Europeans appeared in the Western Hemisphere.

The word *bayou* 'a creek or small river, esp. one characterized by a sluggish current' is useful in drawing attention to an important part of the pre-Columbian linguistic setting. In the *Dictionary of American Regional English* (from which this gloss is quoted), the etymology is "LaFr from Choctaw *bayuk* creek, river," and the current distribution of this sense is shown to be limited to Louisiana, Mississippi, Arkansas, and (two reports) eastern Texas. The etymology is far more complex (and interesting), as Emanuel Dreschsel explains in his fine monograph devoted to Mobilian Jargon. This pidgin language was in widespread use in the lower part of the Mississippi watershed from Georgia to Texas and northward into Illinois and eastern Missouri. Like the other pidgins of the eastern woodlands— particularly Delaware Jargon of the territory of the fur trade—Mobilian incorporated words from a variety of sources, particularly the Muskogean from which its basic word order also derives. The region in which it was spoken was very diverse linguistically, exceeded in richness on this continent only by the complex of languages spoken in California and the Pacific Northwest (Dreschsel 1997, 10). *Bayou*, Dreschsel believes, entered French from Mobilian and thence was borrowed into English. Its history is thus a nexus of many Amerindian languages rather than just one. The "wild and savage-looking Indians" encountered by Frances Trollope on the streets of New Orleans in 1828 were certainly speakers of Mobilian, but they were doubtless multilingual in other languages native to the region as well.

Since only a few speakers of Mobilian survived until the end of the twentieth century, it is difficult to estimate the balance among the contributor languages to Mobilian, and the fact that the survivors were mostly speakers of Choctaw as a first language gives a bias in favor of words like *bayou* that were incorporated in Mobilian from that language. Most of the words whose etymologies can be traced came from one of the Muskogean languages, but there are elements from Algonquian and European languages as well, not to mention "words of mixed, uncertain, or unidentified sources" (Dreschsel 1997, 75). The only word of undisputed Algonquian origin in Mobilian is *sonak* or *šonak* 'money,' a concept unknown in pre-Columbian culture and, at the end of Mobilian as a language, "a kind of lexical identification marker for Mobilian Jargon" (Dreschsel 1997, 89). However confident Dreschsel is in this etymology—he gives several cognates in Algonquian languages—he cannot reject the proposal that the word is connected with Romani *sunakai* 'gold' since there were "Gypsies" in early Louisiana (known there as *Bohémiens*) and some of them may have made use of Mobilian (88 n. 13).

In the mid-eighteenth century, English observers were just discerning the nature of society in Louisiana. In 1766, Harry Gordon was dispatched by General Thomas Gage to discover if the newly ceded western territory obtained from the French could be profitably defended against illicit traders. Traveling down the Ohio from what is modern Pittsburgh, Gordon found most fortified places ruinous or of dubious value. He discovered that the British made a "foolish figure," and General Gage reported to London the discouraging prospects for British trade:

> Advices from the Illinois mention an illicit Trade, whereby French Goods are Smuggled up the Ohio and to the Lakes, and the Peltry of those Countreys carried down the Mississippi to New Orleans; where Skins and Furs bear a Price of ten Pence Pr. Pound higher, than at any British Market. (Mereness 1916, 477)

Britain might have had political sway but it lacked economic power to compete with the French traders. Approaching New Orleans, Gordon found a colony of "Poor Acadians" (Mereness 1916, 482) from Canada, and in the city an uneasy competition between the French and the politically ascendant Spanish. There were, though, signs of economic activity, particularly in the production of pitch and tar, which yielded "a very good Trade with La Vera Cruz" in Mexico (460).[1]

By the time of the Louisiana Purchase, the situation of the European languages had become even more complex than what Gordon had found in 1766. French migrants, especially military and governmental personnel, used the varieties of French then current in their new homeland (and they were by no means uniform), but there were at least some forms of French recognizable to European visitors, and most Francophones acknowledged the "superiority" of European French even if they used one of the North American varieties. A second group of French speakers were the descendants of the *Acadians*, a term in print since 1707 for the residents of Acadia in eastern Canada. These settlers were expelled by the British in 1755 and migrated south to the more congenial hospitality of French Louisiana.

---

1. Gordon's journal also provides the first English attestation of *bayou* (Mereness 1916, 484).

Visitors regularly noted them as a distinct group, although the modern name *Cajun* did not emerge in print until the end of the nineteenth century. The French of this community was regarded as "archaic" (by those sympathetic to the Cajuns) or "debased" (by those not). The successful revolt by slaves in Haiti brought a third distinct group, those of both European and African descent who spoke the variety of French now known as *Kreyol*. These refugees arrived in two waves, the first in 1780 and the second, and larger, group in 1809 when the Spanish, in a response to the wars of Napoleon, expelled the former Haitians who had settled in Cuba (Labbé 1998). These speakers, in a French-based language much influenced by African languages, constituted a third community within the French of New Orleans.[2] Though not attested in print until the third quarter of the nineteenth century, the words *hoodoo* and *voodoo* 'a system of religious beliefs' come from an African source through *Kreyol*, and *hoodoo* remains distinctive of Louisiana and the regions influenced by it.

Thus language variety among French speakers was rich and diverse. Yet another visitor from the 1830s, Thomas Hamilton, was particularly scornful of the French of slaves. They "jabber a sort of *patois* unlike any thing I ever heard in France, though my intercourse with the French peasantry has been tolerable extensive" (1833, 311). In this sneer Hamilton was almost certainly right since *Kreyol* must have been current among the Haitian refugees at the time of his observations of New Orleans. Similarly, John James Audubon was contemptuous of the language of riverboat men (as well as the men themselves), who were often *métis*: "This is a breed of animals that neither speak French, English nor Spanish correctly, but have a jargon composed of the impure parts of these three" (John James Audubon quoted in Crété 1978, 127).[3]

A third language group recognized by the travelers in the early years of American sovereignty was Spanish speakers, though the Spanish rule over the territory had been both brief and nominal. Nonetheless, Spanish had been an early presence and remained there as part of the trade patterns in the western Caribbean and overland to Texas. At the end of the eighteenth century, a French traveler, James Pitot, noted both the presence of the

---

2. A very perceptive view of "slave French" was provided by Claude-Charles Robin, who noted in particular the drastic reduction in the number of pronouns and the use of a single form for all tenses and modes of verbs (1807, 186–87).

3. The quotation comes originally from *The Journal of John James Audubon: Made during His Trip to New Orleans in* 1820–1821.

"Acadian refugees" (the French they spoke was typical of Brittany, he claimed) and of migrants from the Canary Islands whose language was Spanish (Pitot 1979, 66). This community retained its distinctive variety of Spanish, though now markedly influenced by English and Louisiana French (Lipski 1990; Holloway 1997). No expressions from these groups have entered English with the exception of the names, *isleño* and *brulé*. Both words are, like *hoodoo*, only found in print in English at the end of the nineteenth century, but both have local currency in Louisiana according to the evidence presented in the *Dictionary of American Regional English* (Cassidy and Hall 1985–).

Still another European language group important at the time of the Purchase was the German speakers settled on "the German coast" of the Mississippi, and they had largely assimilated culturally and linguistically to the French. This small core of German culture attracted more immigrants, most of them arriving from the port city of Bremen. One well-remembered group was later called *redemptioners*. They had been robbed of their passage money, but the German government provided them with transportation to be repaid by the sale of their labor on their arrival in Louisiana. Many died on the journey, and the survivors were sold as white slaves and dispersed throughout the region. Some were able to remain in New Orleans and on the nearby German coast. *Redemptioner*, the term used to describe them, became an American usage in 1771, according to the *Dictionary of Americanisms* (Bartlett 1859), to designate migrants who agreed to redeem their passage money through their labor.

In addition to these groups using languages other than English, there were also persons arriving in the area who spoke distinctive varieties of English, the Irish prominent among them. Before the Purchase, skilled migrants and persons experienced in commerce saw opportunities for wealth in a large, comfortably Roman Catholic city. Afterward, significant numbers of impoverished and unskilled Irish arrived. They came in family groups and settled in close-knit communities where their distinctive English was regularly remarked by visitors and transmitted across generations, and where they were particularly prone to the yellow fever (Labbé 1998, 539).

Language diversity within English was most dramatically seen in the swarms of people who arrived from elsewhere in the United States, and first among these were "westerners" from Kentucky who had attempted to seize the Ohio and Mississippi trade route in order to free themselves from the vexations of overland travel and the rapacious practices of exporters in the eastern cities.[4]

The intensity of feeling about these internal migrants was captured in the travel narrative of William Darby, and his views were published in the English-language press of New Orleans soon after they appeared in print in New York and Philadelphia. The anglophone American who published the *Louisiana Advertiser* wrote in 1820 of the "gallantry and firmness" of the "Creoles of our country" in the late war, and he heartily endorsed Darby's views of the lately arrived migrants to New Orleans:

> The cordiality with which the Louisianans hailed their introduction into the United States government has received a check from the misconduct of too many Americans. The moment the change was effected, an host of needy adventurers, allured by the softness of the climate, the hopes of gain, and inflated by extravagant expectations, spread themselves along the Mississippi. Many men of candid minds, classical education, and useful professional endowments, have removed and settled in Louisiana; but some without education or moral principle, prejudiced against the people as a nation whom they came to abuse and reside amongst. Too ignorant to acquire the language of the country, or to appreciate the qualities of the people, this class of men have engendered most of the hatred existing between the two nations that inhabit Louisiana. The evil of national animosity will gradually subside, as a more numerous and orderly race of people become the improvers of the public lands. (*Louisiana Advertiser*, April 29, 1820, 2.4–5; quoting Darby)

It is difficult to tell if readers of the *Advertiser* shared the ameliorist optimism of the Yankee visitor or if they were too offended by the "needy adventurers" to see a hopeful prospect for future civility.

A German visitor, Karl Anton Pöstl, certainly did not hold these optimistic views. Pöstl published under the pseudonym of "Charles Sealsfield," and his books on the South and West were soon translated into English.

---

4. It was exactly this lure of a new way of bringing the riches of the interior to a world market that had motivated Gordon's survey of the route in 1766. Then opposition from the Spanish and French had made it impossible for British interests to make use of the waterways; now, with the Purchase, those obstacles were removed.

Having described the advantages of the Purchase for the established inhabitants of Louisiana, Pöstl reported in 1827 on the nature of the new arrivals who afflicted them:

> But the moment the cession was made, crowds of needy Yankees, and what is worse, Kentuckians, spread all over the country, attracted by the hope of gain; the latter treating the inhabitants as little better than a purchased property. Full of prejudice towards the descendants of a nation, of which they knew little more than the proverb, "French dog," they, without knowing or condescending to learn their language, behaved towards these people as if the lands, as well as the inhabitants, could be seized without ceremony. This was certainly not the way of thinking, or the conduct of all the northern new comers, there being amongst them many a useful mechanic, merchant planter, or lawyer; but the greater number came with a degree of presumption, which was in an inverse ratio of their unbounded and absolute ignorance. The creoles, with a proper sense of their own independence, naturally retreated from the intercourse of these intruders. (1828, 169–70)

Turning from this scathing indictment, Pöstl then criticized the Creoles for their addiction to pleasures and their failure to resist the onslaught of Yankees, but his sympathy was clearly with the long-time residents despite their indulgence in "frivolous amusements" and "the luxurious enjoyment of the other sex" (171).[5]

With this rich array of languages and language varieties, New Orleans was a hotbed of linguistic change. The long-resident elite, the Creoles, disdained learning English, and the others in the city had little chance of making their usage general since the French of the Acadians and of the slaves lacked the high-status accents of Paris. The Germans and Irish were poor and few; the Spanish even fewer and marginalized once they had ceded political power first to the French and then to the Americans. No single variety of English was singled out as the model because there were few cultural institutions by which it might be disseminated—schools and

---

5. Before fleeing Europe, Pöstl had been a monk. His use of *creole* in this passage is typical of the usage of the day in Louisiana; it meant simply 'native' and did not carry implications of racial mixture, as was widely presumed by outsiders. A circumstantial and well-documented history of this complex term is found in Tregle (1999, 337–43).

the theater, for instance—and as late as 1845 a visitor lamented that there was no public library, the former one having vanished at a sheriff's sale because of indifference to reading (Norman 1845, 79–80). Protestant churches were established, but, because of the climate (and the yellow fever), the ministers did not remain long, and thus they often did not have the influence on English expected of them elsewhere on the frontier.

Tumultuous linguistic times resulted in great attention to the languages of the community, although much of it consisted of jocular or censorious criticism of the way people talked. Such comments should not be taken too seriously as evidence of the varieties that were merging and emerging, and stereotypes of English speech were much in evidence in these specimens. It is worthwhile, even so, to scrutinize the way in which varieties of English were held up for comment.

Before the removal of the Cherokees westward, viable and important Native American communities were to be found in Tennessee and along the Mississippi. In particular, the traffic along the Natchez Trace made Natchez, a satellite of New Orleans, a locus of linguistic intermingling. In 1830, Natchez was home to most free Blacks in the new state of Mississippi. Born in this town in 1810 or 1811 was Warner McCary, eventually known as Okah Tubbee. Later inquiry has revealed that he was probably the child of a slave woman named Franky and a white cabinetmaker resident in Natchez. At his father's death in 1813, McCary was obliged by the terms of the will to be held as a slave, along with his future children (Littlefield 1988, xiii). To escape from this dismal future, Warner created for himself a new identity, claiming to be the son of Moshulatubbee, a chief of the Choctaws.

Under the name Okah Tubbee, McCary became first a musician in a militia band, then a solo performer as an instrumentalist, storyteller, and singer, and finally an "Indian" physician promising cures using a secret knowledge of herbs and simples. His "Indian" identity was not invented before 1847, and the details of his life were then created with the help of his wife Laah Ceil, a woman of literary talent and of undisputed Native American parenthood. Together they produced *A Sketch of the Life of Okah Tubbee*; it was sold in support of McCary's career as a performer and physician and underwent several updatings.

In the *Life*, McCary described how as a youngster in Natchez he was the object of special curiosity among visiting Native Americans, and, one day at their approach, they became "wild with delight" and imagined he was their child. Suddenly, he found himself speaking in a tongue that "was neither English, Spanish, or French," and they later told him that he had asked in Choctaw for his father. While the miraculous ability to speak Choctaw is the point of this tale, it is significant that the boy could recognize the three European languages most frequently encountered in the 1820s when this revelation took place. Elaborating further, McCary produced the following specimen of "imperfect English":

[T]he Indians loudly asked where and to whom does this child belong? some one answered to a colored woman. The clouds seemed to grow darker on their way [*wry*], yet to me, sweet face, the same one said, to a slave woman, and he is a slave. The Indian held his hands high above his head and said, but white man lie, he no good, him no slave, no niger, no, bad white man steal him, his skin is red; this was repeated in imperfect English by them all—me, I love him—the crowd were some smoking, laughing, some mocking, angry and cursing—the Indians conversed in a low tone together, here some of the crowd interfered, and separated me from my new, but dear friends—while all the time, bad white man lie, he steal him, I no niger, him Indian boy, now and then reached my ears. I was then torn from them—My feelings toward them I cannot attempt to explain. (Allen 1848, 26)[6]

Here is a vivid representation of American Indian Pidgin English, though hardly accurate in details. A speaker of this contact language would not have said both "he no niger" and "his skin is red," and the "me, I love him" sentence is also grammatically implausible in this variety. The best that can be said of specimens like this one is that authors (and their readers) in the nineteenth century thought that this was how Native Americans ought to speak English.

Okah Tubbee's importance in the speech community of the upper Mississippi increased with his conversion to the Church of the Latter-Day Saints. He embraced the doctrine of plural marriage and acquired several wives; he declared himself a prophet. His African ancestry, however, brought him into conflict with other Mormon prophets, and he was soon excommunicated. Some believe that Okah Tubbee was the person who

---

6. Littlefield republished the 1852 Toronto version of the *Life*. Because of some textual differences that seem to me important, I quote the first edition here as likely to represent more accurately McCary's dictation to the Rev. Mr. L. L. Allen.

led to his own exclusion (and all like him) from participation in the Church until 1978 when another revelation lifted the ban. When the Mormons reached Utah, some efforts were made to regulate English, including the creation of the Deseret alphabet to ensure that vowels and consonants would have the same values among Mormon English speakers. There was no sympathy for Okah Tubbee's peculiar English.

Other varieties of English in New Orleans were stock sources of criticism and ridicule. Almost no British visitor in this era described American society without a sneer at the English used here, and in New Orleans in 1836–37, James Logan found that the language used was "inelegant." He particularly objected to *clever* 'pretty' and *handsomely* 'cleverly': "what a *clever* bonnet this is" and "how *handsomely* I did that" (1838, 197). Domestic critics also found inelegant expressions or even ones excessively elegant. So, for instance, in 1844, *The Daily Picayune* ridiculed euphemisms and other attempts at verbal gentility: *indissolubly united in the holy bonds of matrimony* 'married'; *diurnal journals* 'daily papers'; *repose in the arms of Morpheus* 'go to bed' (July 11, 2.2).

The American vernacular in several forms attracted amused attention and, in a subsequent issue of the *Picayune*, the editor saw fit to reprint an anecdote from a New York paper:

Jonathan walks in, takes a seat, and looks at Sukey. Sukey rakes up the fire, blows out the candle, and don't look at Jonathan. Jonathan hitches and wiggles about in his chair, and Sukey sits perfectly still. At length Jonathan musters courage and speaketh:
"Sewkey?"
"Well, Jonathan."
"I love you like pizen and sweetmeats."
"Dew tell!"
It's a fact and no mistake—wi—will-now—will you have me, Sewkey?"
Jonathan Higgins, what am your politics?"
"I'm for Polk, straight."
"Wall, sir, you can walk right strait hum, cors I won't have nobody than aint for Clay—that's flat."
"Three cheers for the 'mill boy of the slashes,'" sung out Jonathan.
"That's your sort," says Sukey. "When shall we be married, Jonathan?"
"Soon's Clay's elected."
"Ahem! a-a-hem!"
"What's the matter, Sukey?"

"S'posin' he aint elected?"

Jonathan didn't go away till next morning, but whether he answered the last question, this deponent knoweth not. (November 16, 2.3)

This story depends greatly on the Yankee created by Thomas Chandler Halliburton in his tales of Sam Slick, but the New England "short *o*" in *home* was authentic, and the spelling of *pizen* reflected both the New England pronunciation and the emergent stereotype of the Kentuckian. It was a usage attributed to Andrew Jackson, the hero of the Battle of New Orleans (Cassidy and Hall 1985, s.v. *poison*).

Irish voices, heard in increasing numbers in the city, were also worthy of observation by the paper. Having printed a well-worn Irish anecdote, the editor of the *Picayune* presented what he called firsthand observation:

Yesterday, out of curiosity, we listened to one of their *conversaziones* in Camp street, and it certainly proved highly amusing to us. The parties were congregated on and about an empty dray in the shade; they numbered about half a dozen, and the word attack and rejoinder were bandied about from one to another indiscriminately.

"Ah, boys," said one, "did ye hear that Tom broke the pledge? and be all that's bad, he did; and they're goin' to expel him from the society."

"O, be gor," said another, "Tom nivir put his hand in any thing that he didn't brake. He broke himself, and he'd brake Biddle's bank the richest day ivir it was."

"Yis, Mick," said Tom, in reply to the last speaker—"and iv me mim'ry sarves me right I broke your head wanst. D'ye remimber that?"

"Ah, thin, did yer, Tom?" said another who seemed rejoiced that he gave Mick a Roland for his Oliver—"did yer ever thry the hardness of Mick's head wid yer shillelah?"

"Troth, then, I did," said Tom—"I gave him a tip wanst between the lug and the horn where the Connaught man sthruk his ass, and faith I left him as aisy es iv he was magnetized—I put him in an iligant magnetic sleep!" (September 8, 1844, 2.2)

Some of these "Irishisms" may have been conventional, but certain details suggest some care in observation—for instance, the inversion in *iver it was*, the raising of the vowel in *niver, iver, mimry,* and *thin,* and the palatized consonants in *thry* and *sthruk.*

Of the specimens of dialect representation, perhaps the most revealing is the earliest, a fictitious report of a meeting held by the "Bosson Bobilition Society" and composed especially for the *Louisiana Advertiser* in 1820 (April 29, 1.5). This virulently racist piece of humor presented the Boston Abolition Society as if it conducted its meeting and transcribed its minutes in African American English. The subject of the deliberation was the question before the Congress that would result in the "Missouri Compromise" on the extension of slavery. This meeting purported to be an occasion to celebrate the efforts of Massachusetts senator Rufus King to reject the "compromise" and to provide for the immediate abolition of slavery (with compensation to "owners" and "colonization" for those wishing to migrate to Africa).

Some of the linguistic features of this document represent eye-dialect or merely humorous misspellings, for instance: *compremise, cuntry, devided, interduce, offen, rite* (for *right*), *sellebrate* (for *celebrate*). A few are certainly fictitious. It was widely known in the era that some Britons added (or deleted) initial *h*, but this was never a feature of American English and so *hanniversary* 'anniversary' is likely to have been manufactured. Other words are not consistently represented; for instance, *society* and *seciety* are both used, and *pass* and *past* (for *passed*) appear in the same sentence as do *meetin* and *following.*

Many features are precisely observed, however. The substitution of *b* for *v* appears in such words as *eber* 'ever,' *gib* 'give,' *lib* 'live,' and *Slabery* 'slavery.' *D* and *t* appear for the interdental fricatives: *dat* 'that,' *de* 'the,' *dis* 'this,' *furder* 'further,' *mout* 'mouth,' *Soudern* 'southern,' *tanks* 'thanks,' and *widout* 'without.' Consonant cluster simplification is put vividly on display: initially (*tanding* 'standing,' *tate* 'state'), finally (*cole* 'cold,' *funs* 'funds,' *hole* 'hold,' *lef* 'left'), and both initially and finally in *tan* 'stand.' Other initial sounds may be modified or deleted: *Bobilition* 'abolition' and *firmative* 'affirmative,' for instance. Final consonants expressing past tense also vanish in such verbs as *continued, declared, informed,* and *removed,* and the final syllable of the past-tense *presented* is also omitted. Final consonant cluster reduction in singular nouns also yields a predictable plural, *toases* 'toasts.'

By far the most interesting features are grammatical, and these show up toward the end of the list of toasts, reflecting, in this fiction, the progressive loss of linguistic inhibition that goes with inebriation as the meeting moves to its conclusion. (I omit the names of the "tunes" called for to punctuate them.)

4. Our fair Sisters of de soudern tates—May he white man no be so fond of crossing he breed.
5. De Day we sellebrate—may he come as offen as he can.
6. De happy millenium what de African preacher talk about—when de plow-shear be turn into sword, den no more plow corn all day.
7. De Army and Naby—what he do witout colored drummer lass war?
8. De land we lib in—He good land and plenty on hin [? for *him*].
9. Ole king George what dead—Massa General Washington beat him and giv him ten.
10. De far color seck—Hope he no expose heself in too much in de sun, fear he git him tan.

The relative-clause marker *what* is of great interest here and the monophthongal nucleus of *far* 'fair.' Most distinctive is the use of *he* for various personal pronouns including *his*, *it*, and *she*, as well as *heself* for *himself*. These are aspects of the pan-Caribbean creole English common in New Orleans, and it is unfortunate that the debate about the presence of African American creoles on the mainland has not given attention to Louisiana, which is, regrettably, seen as part of the "marginal South" in recent investigation of the matter (Kautzsch 2002, 156).

Presuming that the excellent index to early New Orleans newspapers is reliable, there seem to be no "humorous" treatments of French- or Spanish-influenced English. In part this may be the result of the self-imposed isolation of these two language groups from the invasion of vulgarians and Yankees. Still, in the first year of the Purchase, the Anglophones asserted their sovereignty, and a judge declared to a newly empanelled Grand Jury that "all its pleadings shall be in French *and* English" (my emphasis; *Louisiana Gazette*, November 9, 1804, 3.2). English could be a stick with which to beat the French, but there were carrots, too. Among the shrewd actions of the United States at the time of the Purchase was to appoint sons of the five leading French families to cadetships at West Point (Foley 1989, 141).

It did not take long before only the most militant French separatists clung to monolingualism, and observers saw that English would eventually prevail. Gottfried Duden published letters in Germany that described conditions in the "western states of North America," and his promotion of emigration was part of a campaign that changed America. The grandchildren of the Germans who came before and just after the Purchase no longer spoke "their mother tongue," and older people did not read or write German. He recognized a certain bigotry against Germans from xenophobes: "Fluency in the English language is a sure protection against the annoying arrogance of such Americans" (Duden 1980, 94). Duden, a Rhinelander, held the dialects and customs of the early arrivals from Germany in low esteem—they did not maintain the distinction between *du* and *sie*, for instance—and he thought they behaved better when speaking English than when they spoke German (94–95). Newcomers would be well advised to attach themselves to Americans who knew only English. The vital communities of French speakers he observed in Louisiana and upstream had been abandoned by France, he thought, and they had "retired into stricter isolation" (95) that had no promising future.

The decade of the 1820s seems to have been the time when the isolation of these groups began to end, and *L'Abeille*, then a newspaper publishing mainly in French, contained three ads that reveal the cultural transformation: an advertisement (in French) for English-language instruction; another (in Spanish) offering the same; and a third (in French) inviting applicants interested in operating a store the opportunity to apply for a job. The proprietor offered a salary of "2,000 piastres" and a 6 percent interest in the operation to a person able to speak all three languages: French, English, and Spanish (November 17, 1827, 1.4). The following week *L'Abeille* capitulated to changing tastes by renaming itself *The Bee* (November 24, 1827, 3.4).

The most important fact that made New Orleans the foundation of English for the Louisiana Purchase was the introduction of the steamboat into the Mississippi waterway. In 1811, the *New Orleans* was built in Pittsburgh and became the first steam-powered ship to travel downriver to New Orleans. Keelboats, barges, bateaux, and other vessels continued as strong competitors, and they were able to handle huge cargos going downstream. But on the return voyage they had to be poled and manhandled around snags, bars, and currents. The French-speaking boatmen—the most reliable were thought to come from St. Louis—made French the language of the river, but, with the introduction of many steamers, the boatmen could no longer compete, even for the bulkiest products of agriculture and industry. In 1820, when steam power had become established, goods could be brought by steamer from New Orleans to Louisville for $2 in two weeks; the keelboats and barges could not promise delivery in less than three months and the cost was $5 a hundredweight. Even more significantly, the water route made the overland passage from Pittsburgh no longer competitive. In 1829, the cost of delivery from Pittsburgh to Cincinnati by land was between $5 and $8 a hundredweight. The goods could be delivered the much longer distance from New Orleans by steam for only $1 (Baldwin 1941, 193).

A "Yankee," Joseph H. Ingraham, who visited in the early 1830s, described the vessels moored along the levee near Bienville Street in New Orleans: "Spanish and French coasting vessels,—traders to Mexico, Texas, Florida, &c" (1835, 1:104). He imagined some of them as pirates. Next to them were massed an immense number of steamboats bound for many destinations. And finally he described the river traffic:

> The next station, though it presents a more humble appearance than the others, is not the least interesting. Here are congregated the primitive navies of Indiana, Ohio, and the adjoining states manned (I have not understood whether they are *officered* or not) by "Real Kentucks"—"Buck eyes"—"Hooshers"—and "Snorters." There were about two hundred of these craft without masts, consisting of flat-boats, which resemble, only being much shorter, the "Down East" gundalow, (gondola) so common on the Rivers of Maine,.... These are filled with the produce of all kinds, brought from the "Upper country," (as the northwestern states are termed here) by the very farmers themselves who have raised it;—also, horses, cattle, hogs, poultry, mules, and every other thing raiseable and saleable are piled into these huge flats, which an old farmer and half a dozen Golia[t]hs of sons can begin and complete in less than a week, from the felling of the first tree to the driving of the last pin. (1835, 1:105–6)

Since the export of produce and livestock was only downstream, it was possible for these flatboats to continue in use long after steam was established, and the farmer could dismantle the craft, sell the lumber, and return home swiftly by steamer.

By 1844, the newly constructed Ocean House resort hotel of Newport, Rhode Island, tried to attract business by advertising in *The Daily Picayune* (July 2, 1.3), and at the same time advertisements appeared for ships bound for such places as Philadelphia, New York (with stops in Key West and Charleston), and Liverpool. Steamboats were embarking passengers for all upriver destinations as far as Louisville and Cincinnati. The packet *J. M. White* offered, it was claimed, "accommodations unsurpassed by any boat on the Western Waters"; it was "elegant, new, and fast-running" and bound for St. Louis (*Daily Picayune*, July 10, 1844, 3.4–6).

Convenient and inexpensive transportation brought people from far and near. In 1848, Walt Whitman arrived from Brooklyn for a three-month stint as a writer for the New Orleans *Crescent*. He was mainly engaged in routine editorial tasks, and it is his 1887 recollection of those days that provides insight into the condition of New Orleans as a cultural center. He remembered the bustle of troops returning from the conquest of Mexico and the gay appearance of Zachary Taylor and his officers at a theatrical entertainment, the leisurely breakfasts (and excellent coffee), and the usual parade of people on the levees noted by every visitor since Frances Trollope. What is most striking, however, is Whitman's regret that he did not learn more from this mix of people—he names particularly the French and Spanish in "New Orleans in 1848": "I have an idea that there is much and of importance about the Latin race contributions to American nationality in the South and Southwest that will never be put with sympathetic understanding and tact on record" (1964, 606–7). He recognized there was something unusual in what he observed, something not typical of the Atlantic-coast cities he knew.

The census of 1850 showed just how unusual Orleans parish was among American cities. Only 43 percent of the people there were born in Louisiana; 14 percent were born elsewhere in the United States: 43 percent came from foreign countries. The gender imbalance among the white population was pronounced: 52,878 residents were male; 38,563 were women. The number of persons of African descent in the parish had diminished in comparison to the white population: 9,961 were free; 18,068 were slaves. New Orleans continued to dominate Louisiana and the lower Mississippi: 43 percent of those counted in the census lived in Orleans parish. Culturally, New Orleans influenced its hinterland far more than any other American city, and foreign-born Louisianans were likely to live in the city and influence their compatriots living elsewhere in the region. There were really three foreign-born groups of consequence: Irish (24,266), German (17,507), and French (11,552). Eighty percent of those of European origin in Louisiana came from these three.

Some sense of just how unusual this situation was can be seen by a comparison with New York. That state had by far the biggest population in the country in 1850 (with just over three million), and 78 percent were born in the state and provided the cultural matrix to which immigrants adapted. New York's huge population of persons born abroad (651,801) constituted only 21 percent of the total for the state, and, lower Manhattan excepted, New York was a "normal" American state for the era. Louisiana, in contrast, was a destination of foreigners from abroad and at home. Some came from the Northeast (especially New York, Pennsylvania, and Massachusetts), and many more from the South (Georgia, South Carolina, Tennessee, and Virginia). It was impossible to maintain that a single cultural "identity" could encompass Louisiana, and visitors in this era could hardly restrain their astonishment at the variety of voices heard in New Orleans.

There are few modern traces of the influence of New Orleans as a "hearth" for its hinterland, and only a handful of its distinctive expressions reach much above the Arkansas border (Carver 1987, 137–43; Coles 1997). Yet the city was the entry point for many migrants, and the leveling of dialect differences that took place there was influential for what happened to English in the upriver settlement communities, particularly St. Louis, where the actual transfer of title to the Louisiana Territory took place. Like London in the fourteenth century, New Orleans was a place where language change was rapid, and uniformity emerged from multilingual and multidialectal diversity. As with other places where English came late—for instance in Cornwall and the Highlands of Scotland at the end of the eighteenth century—a variety emerged that was "purer" than that of communities nearby: Mississippi, for instance, or Texas. It has sometimes been argued that the "standardization" of the heartland was imposed by bigoted (and powerful!) Yankee schoolteachers who arrogantly forced the dialect of the "Inland Northern" region on the hapless children of the Prairies. The main advocate of this view now recognizes that it was the Germans (and others) who, having decided to abandon their languages, determined to follow Gottfried Duden's advice and model their language and conduct on that of the "refined" Americans they encountered (Fraser 1996, 95; Bailey 2006). New Orleans was the place where the great cleansing of American English took place.

It was the Civil War and its aftermath that reduced New Orleans from a port of entry into an impoverished backwater. From 1850 to 1860, Louisiana grew by 36 percent; from 1860 to 1870, the population increase was only 2.5 percent. Steamer traffic that made its influence felt upriver was supplanted by railroad transport of goods and people. The north-south axis of the American heartland shifted to the east-west routes—like the Erie Canal and the national road—that in 1800 did not even exist.

Agricultural products for export declined in value, as sugar and cotton could be produced more cheaply outside the United States. Starved for capital by the Reconstruction governments in Washington, Louisiana did not take part in the transformation to an industrial economy that made for great fortunes elsewhere in the heartland. Yet in the first half-century after the Purchase, Louisiana was a destination, an entry point, and a cultural center for the entire Mississippi, Ohio, and Missouri basin.

7 New York, 1850–1900

IN 1850, METROPOLITAN New York was the most populous area in the United States. The census reported 515,547 people in Manhattan and 138,882 in Brooklyn. In 1900, the five boroughs of the city had 3,437,202 people. Growth had been explosive, and the city was rich in cultural and linguistic variety.

This diversity had already begun to develop before 1850. Refugees from the famine in Ireland arrived in droves; revolutionaries from the European uprisings in 1848 brought in flotillas of Germans and French (among other nationalities). Yet it was not immediately apparent how these newcomers would affect English. A historian writing for publication in 1853 repeated what had been received wisdom articulated by foreign visitors for a century: America was blessed in the uniformity of its English—particularly in comparison to the British Isles. As Tocqueville alleged, American democracy was "unconstrained" by one powerful group claiming hegemony over the others: "These circumstances have given to New-York a purer English dialect than can be found in most places where the English language is spoken" (Curry 1853, 309).

In place of the increasingly implausible idea that New Yorkers spoke "a purer English dialect," a new theory of language variety emerged, captured by historian Mary Louise Booth in 1867. New York was comprised of a "strange mosaic of different nations" and English had gained "floating material from every nation under the sun wherewith to form and mold a new people." Booth asserted:

> Fit language, indeed, is the English for such a nation; as yet a mass of crude material, gathered from the lexicons of every dialect that sprung from the confusion of tongues, to be molded by time and use, and the master hand of genius, into a symmetrical form, perfect because all-comprehensive, and fitting to become a universal language—the only tongue that should be spoken by the people of a New World. (Booth 1867, 661–62)

Mary Louise Booth had a different idea from that of her predecessors. What God had put asunder, New Yorkers could join together into a perfected if not a pure language. Though the expression *melting pot* did not become common until the twentieth century—with Israel Zangwill's play *The Melting Pot*—here was that very idea in mid-nineteenth-century America.

In 1782, a French visitor earlier than Tocqueville, J. Hector St. John de Crèvecoeur, reported that in America "all nations are melted into a new race of men" (*OED*, s.v. *melting*). The image of smelting disparate metals into a nation did not take hold immediately, but it became increasingly popular in the second half of the nineteenth century.

The first distinctively New York voices were not an amalgam of foreign influences but rather the local speech of native urban ruffians, the *b'hoys* who dominated street life in lower Manhattan, particularly in the Five Points district already infamous for debauchery and crime. The gents were dandies, members of fire companies and baseball teams, and in literary representation they echoed the ring-tailed roarers of the western frontier. One contemporary journalist described them as virtuosity carried to excess:

> Thus, their courage is quarrelsomeness; their frankness is vulgarity; their magnanimity subsides to thriftlessness; their fun expands to rowdyism; their feeling of friendship and brotherhood seeks danger-

ous activity in mobs and gangs who conspire against the public piece.
(Foster 1849, 44)

Those lacking firsthand knowledge of the b'hoys could learn all about them
from newspapers—the extract just quoted appeared in the *New York Tribune*—and from their representation on stage and in novels (Buntline 1849).

Here is a specimen of a dandy stepping into the street after courting
Julia, a young woman he plans to seduce:

> If I aint gallus, ter night, then I'm a pup! Wonder wot 'a thunder the
> gov'nor wants ter skin that mister Orson for; he's a nice ole rooster
> enough, an' as for that ere Jule, if she isn't a perfect bird-ee, then I
> wouldn't say so! I wouldn't mind havin' her for my *heifer*, *I* wouldn' t;
> 'cause she's one o' them g'hals as 'd set a feller off nice, when he's drivin'
> his team out on the Avenue. (Buntline 1850, 181)

Gallus means 'attractive, splendid,' then a relatively new slang coinage derived from the phrase *fit for the gallows.* As with the subsequent development of *gangster fiction* (and even later *gangsta rap*), these characters were,
at times, low-life heroes. Ned Buntline, the author of the novel from which
this passage was drawn, was among the social radicals who saw characters
like those in their fiction as representing young men for whom there was
no work and young women for which there was no respectable
employment.

Having shown how the b'hoys talked, Buntline represented how women
in the Bowery used English:

> "Ah, Misses Burton," returned Mrs. Granger, piteously, "we orten to be
> so crooel on the poor creeters! Remember, they was pressed very hard
> by misfortin'!"
> "Wot then?" demanded Mrs. Burton, indignantly; "is that any reason
> they should bring disgrace upon their broughten-up, by goin' on the
> town? I'm sure if every poor girl acted so, 'cos she was a little misfor-
> tinated, the city wouldn't be big enough to hold 'em!" (Buntline
> 1850, 194)

In fact, New York was hardly big enough "to hold 'em" when the pay for
piecework in the clothing industry dipped below starvation wages.

Voices like these were used in a series of plays representing *b'hoys* and *g'hals* through the characters of Mose and Lize beginning with Benjamin Baker's play *A Glance at New York*. Wildly successful, this play—with F. S. Chanfrau and Mary Taylor as the principal characters—led to an emerging saga culminating with the migration of Mose and Lize to California, accompanied by their children Lil Mose and Lil Lize. Their voices were fashioned of the same material as Buntline's fiction.

> MOSE: Lize, ain't you a gallows gal?
> LIZE: I ain't nothing else, Mose. (Quoted in Bartlett 1859,
>   s.v. *nothing else*)

This construction with *else* was described by a contemporary observer as "the strongest American (slang) way of putting an affirmation." A clergyman, in this account, asked a Bowery boy, "Wilt thou have this woman?" He replied, "I won't have any one else" (Bristed 1852, 120).

Observers, both domestic and foreign, were astonished by the number and variety of voices to be heard in New York streets. Pedestrians bustling up and down Broadway and the other major streets made a constant hubbub. Given how crowded and densely packed were the apartments and tenements, it is not surprising that many spent their days on the street (if they did not in fact live there). For Walt Whitman, in *Leaves of Grass*, there was a resonance of sound:

> The blab of the pave.... the tires of carts and sluff of bootsoles and
> talk of the promenaders,
> The heavy omnibus, the driver with his interrogating thumb, the
> clank of the shod horses on the granite floor,
> The carnival of sleighs, the clinking and shouted jokes, and pelts of
> snowballs;
> ...
> What living and buried speech is always vibrating here.
> (Whitman 1982, 83–84)

Whitman's enthusiasm for this language was unbounded: "Great is the English speech.... / It is the mother of the brood that must rule the earth" (1982, 144).

The "blab of the pave" held special power for Whitman, and he believed that popular speech was the great source of innovation and poetry. He wrote:

Language, be it remember'd, is not an abstract construction of the learn'd, or of dictionary-makers, but is something arising out of the work, needs, ties, joys, affections, tastes, of long generations of humanity, and has its bases broad and low, close to the ground. Its final decisions are made by the masses, people nearest the concrete, having most to do with actual land and sea. (Whitman 1982, 1166)

Of course there was no shortage of purists in New York, but even among them there was a kind of grudging admiration of the vigor of the vernacular.

Fascination with low-life New York even produced dictionaries, ostensibly as guides to the unwary but actually part of a long-standing tradition of romanticizing criminal behavior. The energetic Buntline produced, as part of one of his tales of the b'hoys and g'hals, a glossary of more than a hundred terms, many of which arose from the blab near the concrete into respectable American English: *bus* (shortened from *omnibus*), *jug* 'prison,' *tramp* 'to walk,' *whiff* 'a puff of smoke' (Coleman 2004, 2:245). Another journalist, who became the first chief of the New York metropolitan police, published a more ambitious lexicon, one deeply indebted to the long tradition of criminal argot and cant in English. That officer, George Washington Matsell, saw in the vitality of slang a source of innovation. Like Whitman, he marveled that these expressions rose into the usage of New York's *upperten*—a shortened form of *uppertendom*—for the richest ten thousand citizens:

> ...so that while they [the expressions] are in common use among the footpads that infest the land, the *élite* of the Fifth Avenue pay homage to their worth, by frequently using them to express thoughts that could not otherwise, find a fitting representative. (Matsell 1859, v)

Though even more derivative than Buntline's list, Matsell provided the earliest evidence so far discovered for such words as *carom* 'to rebound' in billiards, *cash* 'to exchange' gambling chips for money, *piker* 'a gambler who places only small bets,' *wash* 'a fictitious sale of stock shares.' Matsell also documented early borrowings into English from German or Yiddish: *ryebuck* 'good, excellent,' *spieler* 'gambler,' *Yiddisher* 'a Jew.' Matsell took romanticizing crime to unprecedented levels of luridness in founding and publishing the *National Police Gazette*.

Comments on New York speech did not at first reflect the polyglot and polydialectal city. The uppertendom were a numerous and powerful group, but they did not represent a very broad picture of Manhattan, which, in the 1850 census numbered just over half a million. When William Cullen Bryant first came to New York about 1820 (from his native Massachusetts), he made a list of distinctive expressions that were not reported fifty years later as characteristic of New York English: diphthongs in *forty* and *born,* a full final syllable in *taken* and *mistaken,* a syllabic final consonant in *barrel,* a short vowel in *jist* 'just' and *sich* 'such', and various past tenses and past participles that were not familiar to him (like *have went, I seen, I guv* [for *gave*]) (Bryant 1941, 157). None of these formed a prominent place in what would be recognized as New York English at the end of the century.

One of the first observers to write on varieties of American English was Charles Astor Bristed, the grandson of John Jacob Aster, the first American multimillionaire. Bristed was educated at Yale and Cambridge and wrote in a volume published in London to present the wisdom of graduates of the University. (He had won prizes while a scholar at Trinity College.) Bristed gave many details of New England speech and provided useful views of southern American English. But his native New York did not provide him with much to report: "we find very few expressions *peculiar* to New Yorkers" (Bristed 1855, 68), though he noted Dutch borrowings like *stoop, loafer* 'an idler', and *boss* (which he said was "confined entirely to the labouring classes" [69]). Despite the large numbers of Irish immigrants in the city, he said, there were no Hibernicisms in use.

Bristed took a visiting Englishman to the races and wrote this report of the crowd:

All up the rough broad steps, that were used indifferently to sit or stand upon; all around the oyster and liquor stands, that filled the recess under the steps; all over the ground between the stand and the track, was a throng of low, shabby, dirty men, different in their ages, sizes and professions; for some were farmers, some country tavern-keepers, some city ditto, some horse-dealers, some gamblers, some loafers in general, but alike in their slang and "rowdy" speech. There is something peculiarly disagreeable in an American crowd, from the fact that no class has any distinctive dress. (Bristed 1852, 227)

Bristed's basis of comparison seems to have been an English race-track crowd, where "distinctive dress" served to set off the *hoi polloi* (an expression Bristed himself favored) from the toffs. What is more remarkable is that this promiscuous crowd was alike in "rowdy speech." As his perspective reveals, Bristed was no enthusiast for democracy, but the American crowd displayed it in both uniformity and variety.

The ideology of language played itself out violently in the Astor Place riot of 1849, when the adherents of the American actor Edward Forrest did battle with the fans of the English actor William Charles Macready. The militia fired on the crowd and in the end some thirty people were killed. More than 170 militia were badly hurt by pavers thrown by the angry mob. The causes of the riot were complex, but Forrest and Macready framed their rivalry on national grounds: Was American or British English the superior vehicle for performing Shakespeare? Macready played to the lower classes in the Bowery Theatre (and later in larger venues in the United States and abroad) and declared that if Shakespeare were alive, he would sound American. Forrest played to the upper classes in the glorious Astor Opera House, requiring elegant dress, and used the elegant British diction of the day. A detailed account of the rivalry and riot offered, among other causes, the question of language: "…the feelings against England and Englishmen, handed down to us from the Revolution and kept fresh by the insults and abuse of British writers on American manners" (Ranney 1849, 15). Like the sullen crowd observed by Bristed, the adherents of Forrest resented the presumption that English speech was superior to American.

The years of the Civil War, 1861–65, saw the transformation of New York. In 1860, the metropolitan region grew to 1.1 million, and there were vast population shifts as people moved in from the hinterlands, went off to war and to the west, and arrived from abroad. The focus of attention was still on Five Points in lower Manhattan:

> Every state in the Union, and every nation almost in the world, have representatives in this foul and dangerous locality. Its tenant and cellar population exceed half a million. One block contains 382 families. Persons composing these families were, 812 Irish, 218 Germans, 186 Italians, 189 Poles, 12 French, 9 English, 7 Portuguese, 2 Welsh, 39 Negroes, 10 Americans. (Smith 1868, 206)

With the belief that statistics would lead to answers, nineteenth-century observers enumerated to their hearts' content. These particular numbers showed that English was a majority language in this block, though only fifty of these persons were speakers of American English. The likelihood, however, is that those who did not speak it would soon do so, bringing with them traces of their linguistic origins.

Another guide to New York presented a more vivid picture of the languages of the Bowery at about the same time:

> Germans are so numerous there, one might fancy himself in Frankfort [*sic*] or Hamburg. Irish so abound that Cork and Dublin appear to have come over in the vast ships lying at not distant piers. Italians prattle, in Ariosto's language, of the beauties of bananas and the importance of pennies. Frenchmen jabber; Spaniards look grave; Chinamen stand sad and silent; colored men stare vacantly, or laugh unctuously, in that singular hub-bub of humanity. (Browne 1868, 130)

Every one of the groups mentioned in this report acquired a derogatory nickname in the maelstrom of New York languages: *greaser* 'Spanish person' (1849), *mick* 'Irish person' (1850), *sauer-kraut* 'a German' (1858), *dago* 'foreigner' (1858), *froggy* 'French person' (1872), and *chink* 'Chinese person' (1901). The hubbub of humanity was not a peaceful place.

For what the New York crowd lacked in affection, it made up in expression. A native of the Lower East Side, Thomas D. Rice knew African Americans, and he later traveled along the Ohio River, where he mastered African American stereotypes and turned them into song. Returning to New York in the 1830s, Rice created the character Jim Crow, whom he impersonated in several popular shows, and the song "Jump Jim Crow" was widely known. Rice was acknowledged as the "father" of the American minstrel show in which he, and others, sang and danced in *blackface* (1869). (Following the Civil War, Rice's character gave the name to *Jim Crow Laws,* regulations enforcing racial segregation in the nation.)

Minstrel shows gave wide currency to ideas of how African Americans talked, and there was an endless array of songs and stories expressing them. Here is a specimen from a series of newspaper articles published in *The New York Pickayune*:

> De fust ting I did arter gittin fru de Custom House…was to find my way to a eatin house. As soon as I sat down a waiter come to me wid all de grace ob a grasshopper stepin ober a newly plowd field—den my trubble wid de tongue begin. De waiter understood jus nuff Eng-

lish to put him asleep, so sez I, "Hab you any soups?" "We, we!" sez
he; "ze soup am ze potash." "No! no!" sez I, "not potash soup, some
odder kind." (Hannibal 1857, 362)

The minstrel shows and the comic turns changed the public face of language variety in New York. In the example just quoted, a Jewish writer put
American Black English on display, and there was no scarcity of boundary
crossings. In 1851, Christy's Minstrels performed Stephen Foster's "Old
Folks at Home" on the New York stage and established the minstrel line
with Mr. Bones at one end and Mr. Tambo at the other. The interlocutor,
sitting in the middle, was the straight man asking Bones and Tambo questions which they answered in humorous ways. In 1859, Emmett's Minstrels
introduced in New York the song "I Wish I Was in Dixie," which shortly
became the unofficial anthem of the Confederate States of America. This
tradition culminated in 1935 with *Porgy and Bess*, an opera by George Gershwin, Ira Gershwin, and DuBose Heyward. In the New York premiere, the
entire cast consisted of African American performers. With that, the tradition of *blackface* comedy began to disappear.

An observer of lower Manhattan in 1869 declared: "The *b'hoy* is fast
disappearing from among us, and the day is not far off, we apprehend,
when the Bowery will know him no more" (*New York Home Journal*, June
17, 1868 quoted in Schele de Vere 1872, 583). But if the distinctive voices of
the *b'hoys* and *g'hals* were no longer heard, there were plenty of others.
Dion Boucicault, the Irish actor and playwright, became popular on the
New York stage, particularly with *The Octoroon* (1859), an antislavery
melodrama set in Louisiana, and *The Shaughraun* (1872), another melodrama set in Ireland. Both plays had dialect-speaking characters and were
popular both in New York and abroad.

In 1869, a novel of college life presented as a principal character "a handsome fellow with a strong New York accent" (Washburn 1869, 5). Just what
this accent consisted of is left mysterious, but the handsome fellow was
certainly a member of the uppertendom, and his character seems to belie
Bristed's claim that there was no such thing as a New York accent.

Enthusiasm for varieties of New York English led to the publication of
recitation books enabling amateurs to enact various types in declamations
and performances. Typical examples were *Burdett's Negro Dialect Readings*
(Burdett 1884) and *Brudder Gardner's Stump Speeches and Comic Lectures*
(Carey 1884). The latter bore an elaborate subtitle: *containing some of the
Best Hits of the Leading Negro Delineators of the Present Day. Comprising*

the Most Amusing and Side-Splitting Contribution of Oratorical Effusions Which has Ever been Produced to the Public. Still another expanded the repertoire to *Yankee, Italian, and Hebrew Dialect* (Cooper 1891.)

Fascinated by language variety, New Yorkers realized that they could leverage language improvement for the general betterment and, sometimes, for a worthy cause. In 1865, *Godey's Lady's Book*, a New York magazine with a national circulation, reflected on "Titles of Office, Rank, Respect." The author argued that introducing new words might give women their due by the use of forms that would demonstrate equality with men: *doctoress, professoress, teacheress.* The drift of the argument is apparent in the advocacy for *Americaness*:

> We hope this new title will be approved. It is definite and dignified, and seems to give the idea of nationality to our countrywomen which no other form of expressions can so well convey. ("Titles" 1865, 276)

Apart from novelties, the author wanted to make existing usages symmetrical so *woman midwife* would be the opposite of *man midwife. Wifeless* would be understood as the contrary of *husbandless.* These forms were widely recognized if not widely admired (or used). Maximilian Schele de Vere, a Swedish philologist who was professor of English at the University of Virginia, regarded them as "offspring of the agitation of so-called Women's Rights" (1872, 655), and he added to the list *bankeress, brokeress, sculptoress, masoness* 'member of a Female Lodge,' *chairwoman,* and *chairwomen.* (None of these was either new or coined in America.)

If these particular expressions did not capture the national imagination, there was certainly a change in the way women were represented in writing. In the large, computer-searchable sample of written works from the period captured in the Corpus of Historical American English (COHA), the pronoun *she* increased in frequency from 3,737 per million words in 1850 to 5,250 per million in 1900. In the same period, the word *girl* increased from 218 to 492 per million. *Boy* increased at a far slower rate: 261 to 353. *Woman* went from 343 to 537, while *female* dropped from 47 to 23. In 1900 by far the most frequent compound with *woman* was *woman suffrage.* (These data come from Davies 2010.)

Improving English gained momentum with the 1856 volume *Over* 1000 *Mistakes Corrected.* The author's intention was to reduce "cases of grammatical embarrassment" (3) and to provide instruction for those who would attempt "newspaper literature." Many fine points were examined and argued: for instance, whether it was better to say *the Misses Gould* or *the Miss Goulds*. Mistakes specific to New York included *voiolent* for *violent*, *afeared* for *afraid,* and *debbuty* for *deputy* (*Over* 1856, 179). Similar books continued to appear over the next half century, culminating in 1905, with W. H. P. Phyfe's *Ten Thousand Words often Mispronounced*.

Correctness became increasingly important. William Cullen Bryant, having become America's most celebrated poet, took to editing the *New York Evening Post* and issued a style sheet listing forbidden usages. He objected to *authoress* and, whether or not we can attribute its decline to his influence, it is a fact that the word dropped (according to COHA) from 1.15 per million words in 1850 to just 0.84 in 1870. His objection to *poetess* had a similar baleful effect. *Sucesh* 'secessionist,' though common in 1860, rapidly vanished with the end of the Civil War.

More fundamentally, Bryant objected to usages that other purists found objectionable. *Standpoint* seemed to Bryant and others an unwanted borrowing from German, and they urged the use of *point of view* instead. In this case they failed: *standpoint* increased from 0.36 in 1850 to 12.44 per million in 1900 in the COHA data. Bryant also forbade the use of "is being done (and all passives of this form)" (1920, 386). That verb phrase was first noticed in England in the late eighteenth century and was much criticized by purists on both sides of the Atlantic. The kind of thing they objected to was "every effort is being made to lower miners' wages" and "at Hilton Head a railroad is being built" (both examples from the 1870s). In this effort, Bryant's campaign (and those of the like-minded) was even less influential, with the structure increasing from 1.5 to 2.3 per million words in 1850 to 11.9 to 17.8 per million in 1900 for the various forms of the *be* verb (according to COHA data). Nowadays, of course, no one pays any never mind to such structures (Bryant 1920, 386–87).

While the uppertendom and their allies bickered over the niceties of English usage, New York City became a richly multilingual society. An out-of-town guidebook published the information for visitors who might have the temerity to visit Gotham (a name applied to New York in the 1850s and used by, among others, Charles Astor Bristed). The book reported that there were daily papers in French, German, Italian, Spanish, and Czech, and this was just the beginning:

And if we take into account the weekly and monthly publications, we find New York a veritable Babel of tongues, with papers in Russian, Swedish and Norwegian, Danish, Portuguese, Greek, Arabic,

Chinese, Hebrew, and almost every language in the world. (Schepp
1894, 455)

The texture of the city's linguistic life was transformed by the many tight-
knit linguistic enclaves in lower Manhattan, and, in the prosperity following the Civil War, the uppertendom moved north along the avenues
paralleling Central Park (which had been designated in 1857). This migration left the southern part of the island to immigrants where languages
other than English flourished.

Between 1892 and 1928, millions of Europeans entered New York though
the immigration facility on Ellis Island in New York harbor. Many of them
passed through the city to western destinations like Buffalo, Cleveland,
Detroit, Chicago, and Milwaukee, but some remained in New York. The
most numerous were speakers of Italian, German, and Russian, and the
district between the Bowery and the East River came to be known as
Kleindeutschland 'Little Germany.' The immigrants did just what their
predecessors had done: they renamed the landscape in their own language.
Thus Essex Street in Kleindeutschland was renamed *Esikstrit* based on the
Yiddish word for *vinegar* (Kliger and Peltz 2002, 99). In the 1880s, Irving
Place, just to the north, became known as the *rialto* because of the concentration of English-language theaters there. (In the twentieth century, the
theater district followed the uppertendom farther north to the streets adjacent to Times Square.) Second Avenue became the *Yiddish Rialto* because of the concentration of Yiddish theaters and concert halls along it.

One point of intersection between English and these other languages
was food. Delmonico's, the most famous New York restaurant of the era,
published its menu in French, but the diners spoke many languages and
shared a fondness for French food. Borrowed words for "foreign" food
flooded into English: *kugel* (1846), *wiener schnitzel* (1854), *au jus* (1866),
béarnaise sauce (1877), *chop suey* (1888), *sauerbraten* (1889), *oregano* (1889),
gnocchi (1891), *paella* (1892), *kreplach* (1892). Hungry people crossed language barriers.

People noticed such innovations. New Yorkers seemed increasingly to
talk in odd ways, and out-of-towners were curious. Here's a report from
Connecticut:

"Me name's Dutchy, I shines, sells papers, and works de growler for de
gang." "What's the growler?" I asked. "Don't you know?" he replied,
looking at me in undisguised contempt. "De growler? Why dats de

pail dey gets de beer in when the gang's in luck. I gets only de froth. We wus out to-night and took in de te-a-ter (theatre), and I wus barred out of de house and wus snoozin when you comed along." (Campbell 1895, 253)

It became usual to treat such expressions as folk terms and to speculate about their origin. *Growler*, for example, was traced to *growling* or *grumbling* among children who resisted the homely chore of fetching buckets of beer (Ralph 1897, 90).

Scattered loan words and casual innovation were not, however, sufficient to explain the major changes that were transforming New York English at the end of the nineteenth century.

The most influential language shaping the transformation did not even have an English name until 1875: *Yiddish*. Despite publications and theater productions, Yiddish did not have a powerful impact on English until nearly the last decade of the century. In the 1870s, there were just two words borrowed from Yiddish; in the 1880s, six. In the 1890s, however, there were thirty-nine, and the twentieth century brought in a flood of them, current especially in New York but increasingly known elsewhere. (Just precisely which borrowings came into English in New York is difficult to know; at the same time, Israel Zangwill was introducing Yiddish words in his tales of ghetto life in London, and his books were promptly republished in New York.)

Yiddish words covered wide spheres of life, not just food or customs. New York Jews were increasingly bilingual in English, and they brought with them broad areas of conversational expressions: for example, *oy vey* 'alas' (1892) and *nu* 'so?' (1892). Corresponding words from French like *alors* or from German like *ach* did not crossover into English in the same way. Social stereotypes kept their Yiddish names too: *chutzpah* 'audacity' (1892), *meshuga* 'crazy' (1885), *schlemiel* 'bungler' (1892), and *schnorrer* 'freeloader' (1892). Social roles like *bubbe* 'grandmother' (1895) and *rebbe* 'rabbi' (1881) also began turning up in otherwise English contexts. The twentieth century, of course, was the great heyday for Yiddish borrowings, and expressions became more widely known through broadcasting, film, and theater.

Naturalism, a movement in the arts, became popular at the end of the nineteenth century, and William Dean Howells, the American novelist, became one of its chief exponents. Having read a short story by Abraham Cahan, Howells invited Cahan to his New York apartment and became his patron. With Howells's encouragement, Cahan published a novella in 1896, *Yekl: A Tale of the New York Ghetto*.

Yekl presented New York English in a new light. When the eponymous Yekl is represented as speaking or thinking in Yiddish, Cahan used fluent English, but when Yekl speaks English, it is "broken" and foreign. This narrative strategy reflects the catastrophe of Yekl's assimilation to English-speaking culture; his English is as defective as his character (Wirth-Nesher 2006, 1–31). Yet we see him not as linguistically defective but as having a full range of intellectual and moral choices in his native tongue. Consider this passage:

> "You mush vant you twenty-fife dollars," he presently nerved himself up to say in English, breaking an awkward pause.
> "I should cough!" Mamie rejoined.
> "In a coupel o' veeksh, Mamie, as sure as my name is Jake."
> "In a couple o' veeks! No, sirree! I mus' have my money at oncet. I don't know vere you will get it, dough...." (Cahan 1970, 50)

Cahan was sensitive to linguistic nuance, distinguishing the less English *coupel o' veeksh* in Yekl/Jake's speech from the more English *couple o' veeks* in Maimie's. He illustrated pronunciation variants that would become important markers of New York speech in the twentieth century: *dough* 'though,' *foinitsha* 'furniture,' *t'ink* 'think,' *goil* 'girl,' *bluffin'* 'bluffing,' and many others (Cahan 1970, 50–51). But his more important accomplishment was illustrating different degrees of fluency in English and showing that Yekl is a bilingual with one well-formed language and another broken one. Thus Yekl is not a one-dimensional character with his language illustrating a stereotype, but a fully-formed user of his two languages, one of them imperfect.[1]

Other naturalist writers also depicted New York speech, though in less sophisticated ways than Cahan. Cahan represented multilingualism, though writing solely in English, and a variety of dialects in the English of the city. O. Henry's characters are often New Yorkers, but their speech is not as nuanced and localized as Cahan's.

In *Maggie: A Girl of the Streets* (1896), Stephen Crane depicted the Irish American side of ghetto life, and his characters are more plausibly New Yorkers. William Dean Howells was ingenious in his praise, attributing to Crane a tragic cast and to Cahan a comic streak. But it was the vernacular that interested him most.

---

1. The features listed here became important variables in Labov's study of the Lower East Side in 1963 (Labov 1966).

Maggie's brother Pete, a brawler, is given to angry outbursts, as in the following:

"An' den when dat Sadie MacMallister next door to us was sent the di devil by dat feller what worked in di soap factory, didn't I tell our Mag if she—"
"Ah, dat's anudder story," interrupted the brother. (Crane 1991, 40)

Here there are only two features that became prominent in New York English: *dat* 'that' (and similar words) and the vocalization of word-final *r* (indicated by the spelling *feller* and pronounced *fellah*). The range of Cahan's and the variety of New York features were not attempted in Crane, though Irish Americans certainly made use of them.

Howells celebrated Cahan's fluency in "natural" English when representing his New York characters: "I had almost forgotten to speak of his [Cahan's] English. In its simplicity and its purity, as the English of a man born to write Russian, it is simply marvelous" (Howells 1896, 18).

One event that changed the nature of New York English was the opening of the Brooklyn Bridge in 1883. The crowded slums of the Lower East Side now had an outlet to the east allowing people to flood across the East River while still keeping their jobs in the factories of lower Manhattan. Long-established passenger ferries made crossing the river easy, but the new bridge swelled the volume of traffic and migration. The "Brooklyn accent"—with its shibboleth *Toity-toid 'n' toid* 'Thirty-third [Street] and Third [Avenue]'—consolidated features of New York speech and gave an enduring quality to the dialect well into the twentieth century. Dominance by the uppertendom of Midtown and upper Manhattan effectively blocked expansion of New York English, in its most marked forms, northward.

Founding of the American Dialect Society (ADS) in 1889 provided a forum for talking about New York English, and we are thus in possession of scholarly and reliable accounts of the dialect. The most important of these was "The English of the Lower Classes in New York City and Vicinity" by E. H. Babbitt of Columbia (also the secretary of ADS). What a good thing it would have been had Babbitt's short paper been seen as a model for further contributions to the field. First, he noticed that New York English was class-stratified (as indicated by his title). Babbitt observed, "The upper class live a life of their own" (1896, 459), educated in private schools, traveling widely in America and abroad, and living in social institutions exclusive to their own. "Their language," he concluded, "is therefore independent of the environment to a large extent, though there are individuals who have all the local peculiarities, and very few escape some of them" (1896, 459). Since the first audio recordings of speech became available at the end of the decade, we can hear the voice of Theodore Roosevelt, very much a member of the uppertendom and about to become president in the new century. Roosevelt's speech had few of the "local peculiarities" apart from the vocalization of *r* before consonants and in word-final position: for instance, *water, pleasure*. In this respect he shared a marker of East Coast speakers of the day.

Assimilation to New York English was rapid, Babbitt observed: "I think that no child under ten retains any trace of any other pronunciation after two years in the New York school and street life" (1896, 459). Consequently, he thought, New York English was the property of youth and spoken in gangs and social networks formed by them. This wise observation placed the locus of New York English among young people, with adults as marginal participants in the vernacular culture. (The Irish, he thought, might be an exception, preserving Irish American features a little longer than the other groups.) He was not beguiled by the importance of ethnicity and national origin, as were the Chicago sociologists discussed in the next chapter, and he saw the primacy of street-corner society over the ties of German or Italian descent in forming New York speech.

Babbitt targeted a phonological variable that remains highly salient today: "The treatment of the various vowels when followed by *r* is undoubtedly the most important matter in local variations of pronunciation in the United States, if not elsewhere where English is spoken" (Babbitt 1896, 462). The *r*-lessness of New York speech had long been noted, but Babbitt, who had spent time doing "phonetic investigation" in Philadelphia, noted (correctly) that it was not in use there. The vocalization of *r* after vowels was nearly everywhere in the city (though not elsewhere in the state of New York), as was the insertion of *r* after words ending in vowels like *idear* or *vanillar*. The result of this process for New Yorkers was that *father* and *farther* were homophones, and *four* rhymed with *law*. Babbitt also remarked that there were word-by-word variants, so *girl* might be pronounced by one person as *gel* and by another as *goil* (which was parodied in the "Bowery dialect" in the newspapers). In such observations, he captured something of social stratification (*gel* is more upper-class than *goil*) but also of individual variation (where more careful speech has one form and less careful another).

Babbitt was even more explicit about stylistic variation in a single speaker. Every New Yorker could employ both *this* for *dis* and *dat* for *that*. Some explanation might be found in the frequency of the word in question: *ritmetic* was more common than *arithmetic,* but nearly everyone said *method* and *parenthesis*. Babbitt did not believe that the predictive factors for these pronunciations were random or unstructured, but that some explanation might be found to account for them.

Another distinction in New York speech was that the words pronounced in Boston (and southeast England) as *dance, ask,* and *path* had the vowel of *hat* rather than being said *dahnce, ahsk,* or *pahk*. Other vowels followed suit, giving *hend* for *hand, keb* for *cab,* and *hef pest* for *half past*. (All of these vowels were subject to varying degrees of nasalization.) These two vowels entered into individual, stylistic, and social patterns within the large community of New Yorkers.

Babbitt's vision of language variety was revolutionary given the current state of inquiry in the American Dialect Society and elsewhere. Unfortunately, he found few imitators in the investigations that followed, and he did not return to the study of New York in his subsequent scholarship.

New York, Babbitt wrote, "is and always has been something distinct" from the rest of America (1896, 457), and except for the "commutation district" there was very little evidence of New York English in the upstate counties or the towns only a short distance from the city in New Jersey and New York. This judgment was confirmed by his colleague, B. S. Monroe, speaking at the same meeting on his study of dialect in the southern tier of New York counties. Thus, at the opening of the new century, New York grew more and more to dominate the cultural, commercial, and political life of the nation, yet its distinctive English was widely despised and even scorned. How different this was from the European model, where the court and the capital were seen as the locus of model speech and norms could be promoted based on it. Some New Yorkers, particularly members of the uppertendom, attempted to model their speaking norms on those of southeast England, extending the Anglophilia already well-established on the American stage to the emergent movie industry and to the rarified discourse of learned topics. New York was the head of the country but without a voice; the search for the articulate American would have to be pursued to the west.

Despite the prestige English of New Yorkers such as Theodore Roosevelt, there was still something profoundly troubling about the lack of a norm for good English. Roosevelt certainly did not speak like a Bowery Boy or a *Yiddish mensch*, but even so there seemed to be no cultivated dialect of the uppertendom that would distinguish its speakers from the less fortunate. What could be to blame?

Two of the great novelists of the end of the century discovered the cause: Women.

Speaking at the commencement at Bryn Mawr (near Philadelphia), Henry James excoriated the graduates for their poor use of English. In Britain, he found American women were widely derided for their speech, and he singled out for special criticism "the poor children of the rich" (James 1906–7, 18). Howells, for all his celebration of Cahan's dialogue, was equally scornful of women, particularly mentioning those educated at the private colleges for women (including Bryn Mawr). Nonetheless, Howells thought better days were coming, particularly if women's clubs would bring their forces to bear on speech improvement. He remarked:

> What woman was in her superiority to all men, the American woman was in her superiority to all other women. She had beauty, she had mind, she had manner, she had money, the most in the world and without doubt she had the sweetest voice in the world, as she often had evinced in operatic song, but she had not always thought how to use it in her daily speech. For this reason alone she sometimes spoke through her nose, she twanged, she whiffled, she snuffled, she whined, she whinnied the brilliant things which she was always incontestably saying. (Howells 1906, 930)

New York remained a contentious swarm of varieties of English, not one of them gaining consensus as a standard or even taking on the role of a local norm. Those seeking excellent English were obliged to look elsewhere, but the agents of improvement were at hand. Mothers could discipline daughters; teachers could send ill-speaking girls home for punishment and improvement; the rightly powerful women's clubs could devise rewards and punishments to improve speech. There was no shortage of models of good English—though there were persnickety debates about the details—and opinion leaders like James and Howells were confident that something could be done.

8   Chicago, 1900–1950

IN *SISTER CARRIE* (1900), Theodore Dreiser imagined a young woman, Caroline Meeber, taking the train from some westward point of departure toward Chicago. She is bent on seeking her fortune, and the grinding toil afflicting her sister, already settled in Chicago, is not to her taste. She soon discovers a more attractive life being supported in leisure by men, and she eventually prospers as a renowned actress in New York.

While morally relaxed, Carrie is linguistically fastidious. In her brief stint of factory work, she is distressed to find that the talk of the other workers is "graced by the current slang." They are not particular about their language: "there was something hard and low about it all" (Dreiser 1961, 39). The other young women engage in playful banter, make new friends, and speak the language of the city. Carrie is above such connections and such language. She has given up the secure linguistic home of "Crescent City" for Chicago; she is "two generations removed from the immigrant" (2) and ready for something new and different. Dreiser was not reluctant to moralize, though the content of his morality was unlike that of contemporary novelists. At the outset of the tale, the narrator declares that there are only two alternatives for a young woman migrating from a country town to Chicago: "Either she falls into saving hands and becomes better, or she rapidly assumes the cosmopolitan standard of virtue and becomes worse" (1). For Carrie, the "saving hands" were those making Chicago English respectable.

Chicago became a linguistic center for English in America in the first half of the twentieth century, partly by attracting migrants from the South and from abroad, and partly by its powerful influence on the norms for good English in the heartland. A journalist before he was a novelist, Dreiser interviewed Philip Danforth Armour in 1896 and wondered at the size of his meatpacking business. Most marvelous of all was Armour's communications hub:

> Though he sits all day at a desk which has direct cable connection with London, Liverpool, Calcutta, and other great centers of trade, with which he is in constant connection,—though he has at his hand long-distance telephone connection with New York, New Orleans, and San Francisco, and direct wires from his room to almost all parts of the world, conveying messages in short sentences upon subjects which involve the moving of vast amounts of stock and cereals, and the exchange of millions in money, he is not, seemingly, an over-worked man. (Dreiser 1985, 126)

What was new here was not the telegraph and cable, but the telephone connections that brought Armour into voice-to-voice contact with people across the nation and the world.

In the first half of the twentieth century, Chicago became a home to campaigns for linguistic betterment, and all the energy devoted in New York to assimilating immigrant languages to English was now turned to uplifting the kind of English used in the heartland of America. By 1900, Chicago had become the "second city," trailing only New York in the U.S. census. The World's Columbian Exposition in 1893 had turned the frontier town into a center of innovation and created a love affair with science. The single permanent building for the Exposition—all the rest were plaster and wood—became the Museum of Science and Industry. Daniel Burnham, the architect for these buildings, was a Chicagoan who designed the Flatiron Building in New York and Union Station in Washington. He created the tallest building in the world in Chicago, 310 feet high, and his imagination led to new buildings by Louis Sullivan and Frank Lloyd Wright. One of the earliest citations of the word *skyscraper* in the

OED is from a Chicago newspaper, *The Daily Inter-Ocean*: "1888 30 Dec. 10/5 The 'sky-scrapers' of Chicago outrival anything of their kind in the world."

The west was a land of optimism. In 1890, John D. Rockefeller provided the money for the University of Chicago to combine the liberal-arts tradition with scientific research. Rockefeller might have put his university in western Pennsylvania (where his first fortune had been made) or in New York, but, perhaps owing to the vast profits of Standard Oil of Indiana in nearby Whiting, he chose instead to invest in up-and-coming Chicago. It was there, he thought, that merit might be nurtured rather than inherited wealth, and, imitating the Prussian universities where science had flourished, he made it a particular point to install physics as one of the major disciplinary emphases. For these dreams to be realized, good English was a necessity, and among his goals for philanthropy Rockefeller listed "progress in literature and language" (Rockefeller 1913, 158). Progress in English meant making the language better.

More practical and more locally effective was the Armour Institute, founded by the immensely wealthy Philip Armour and now known as the Illinois Institute of Technology. If Rockefeller's university was theoretical in focus, Armour's was practical. Founded in 1892, the institute was devoted to engineering; most important of all, it enrolled students regardless of ethnicity, religion, or race. Thus it provided a vehicle for upward mobility for the hardworking, and it blended people from many and quite separated communities into a middle class whose professional language was English (Grossman, Keating, and Reiff 2004, 407–8).

For many people, linguistic improvement did not oblige them to look eastward for models. In a Chicago novel published in 1903, *True Love: A Comedy of the Affections*, Emily, the principal character, has traveled widely with her wealthy grandfather and thus knows the English of the eastern cities as well as that spoken in Britain. Though seemingly destined to marry into a rich and snobbish family, she changes her mind. And language is part of how she realizes what she wants:

> The door-bell rang. She heard someone asking for her in a quiet, good-natured voice with rich middle-west r's loudly rolled. (Wyatt 1903, 195)

In terms of English, Emily had returned happily home (Woolley 2000). Unfortunately, Emily dwelt in a land of linguistic anxiety.

In 1900, the *Chicago Daily Tribune* declared in a headline: "Bad English 'Chicagoese.'" The story reported that the district school superintendents had collectively declared that "teachers do not understand the language and cannot use or teach it correctly" (April 4, 1900, 10). The list included all sorts of shibboleths from the use of *ain't* to sentence-final prepositions. Blaming teachers for what was regarded as the poor English of pupils was a theme that continued with increasing force during the twentieth century.

One anguished resident, Sarah Willard Hiestand, wrote in 1906 to an eastern magazine:

Where shall we find the teachers, who "may do much" to restore to our children their lost inheritance? Not in Chicago's schools. Here [there are] dozens of schools in which not one teacher is capable of setting an example of pure and beautiful speech.... Some of us are sending our sons and daughters East to college, hoping thus to repair in some measure the damage done by sheer force of numbers in this huge, prosperous Philistia. (73)

Her letter shows little sign of optimism that the standard of English in Chicago could be elevated.

This view of Chicagoese was not limited to a few purists. So great a linguistic eminence as Leonard Bloomfield wrote for publication in 1935: "The rapid cultural advance, during the last fifty years, of the CW [Central-Western] area involves universal schooling by semi-educated teachers, and wide reading..." (107 n. 15). In his treatment of Chicago English, Bloomfield identified "elegant middle-class" forms like *chaise-lounge* (for *chaise-longue*) and the noun *envelope* with [ɛ] rather than [ɑ] as its initial vowel. The culprits in the decline of English in Chicago were teachers: "Schoolteachers," Bloomfield asserted, "who are otherwise innocent of any attempt at B[ritish] pronunciation, will try to make their pupils use [ɑ] [my translation of Bloomfield's phonetic character into IPA] in a few words like *laugh*. Social climbers betray themselves by hyper-urbanisms, such as [ɑ] in *bass* or *lass*, or even *and, man, shadow*" (106). While these were "isolated phenomena," they were nonetheless the subject of Bloomfield's puristic scorn.

Chicagoans at large were sometimes ambivalent about the question of good English. In 1910, the University of Chicago imported a German philologist, Professor Lorenz Morbach, to teach the history of the language, and he promptly declared that slang was a great vice that needed correction. The *Tribune* might accept domestic criticism but it was offended by a foreign authority's putting down the vernacular of the city. In its report of Professor Morbach's appointment, the paper "translated" his remarks into the vernacular:

> Slang is goin' to put the everlastin' kibosh on your mother lingo. It's gotta be stowed together with a lot of other loose jaw rattle, or it will be as hard for posterity to get hep to our English as it would be to translate a grammaphone record with a hieroglyphic dictionary. (October 6, 1910, 2)

Of course nobody really talked like that, but the passage displays a covert civic pride in the rootin'-tootin' English of the "west."

Into this cultural maelstrom about English stepped an entrepreneur from Michigan, one who embraced the up-and-at-'em spirit of Philip Armour: Sherwin Cody. He joined the meatpacker of great wealth in believing that anyone could overcome any obstacle with application and hard work. Cody marketed self-help volumes to the linguistically anxious (e.g., Cody 1903), and he shrewdly played to fears created by scorn heaped on Chicagoese. In 1903, one of his advertisements in the *Chicago Daily Tribune* had the arresting headline "Good English Pays." The advertisement continued:

> Do you know that Marshall Field & Co. pay their employees $1 for every error in English one of them finds in any of the printed matter issued by the house? Nowadays nothing harms a man's prestige with the educated like careless English. (November 17, 2)

The solution, Cody wrote, lay in the purchase of a series: four books, each containing seven home-study lessons. These could be obtained for $3, and for just $2 more the purchaser would receive *System*, a magazine revealing all that was necessary to master "business methods." In fact, for a limited time, both books and magazine could be purchased at the astonishing price of $3 by entering your name and address in the blank space provided for the purpose in the advertisement. Only fifteen minutes of study each day was required for achieving mastery.

Before the United States entered World War I, there was relatively little comment on the use of languages other than English in Chicago or the possible ill effects of foreign-accented English, even though foreign languages abounded. In 1900, two-thirds of the population of the city regularly used languages other than English, and, in many neighborhoods, English was seldom heard. A professor at the University of Chicago, Carl Darling Buck, expressed pride that Chicago had larger communities of the following languages than anywhere else in the United States: Polish (125,000), Swedish (100,000), Czech (90,000), Norwegian (50,000), Dutch (35,000), and Danish (20,000) (Buck 1903). The largest of these communities was German with half a million speakers. These, and much smaller enclaves, supported newspapers, theaters, schools, and religious services conducted in the language of the community.

At Hull House, Jane Addams developed "settlement" programs designed to teach immigrants American ways, but at first learning English was only incidental to immigrants participating in civic life. Public schools offered evening classes to substantial numbers where English might be learned, and one observer noted with astonishment that young Lithuanian women became fluently bilingual in nearly no time: "To the American she speaks English without a flaw. Just where she manages to learn her English is a miracle to me" ("Lithuanian Girls of Chicago" 1908, F1). At first, English speakers seem not to have been disturbed by the tightly knit communities within the city where the languages of Europe flourished. Most of the worry about English was centered on the supposed faults of those who spoke it natively.

This observation should not mask the competition and, often, hostility expressed by (or against) the ethnic groups in Chicago. Some terms of abuse were used within groups to distinguish among various degrees of scorn. For example, *saltwater Irish* were recent immigrants; *shanty Irish* were less refined than *lace-curtain Irish*. Some of these terms spilled over into wider usage—especially *shanty Irish*—but the distinctions were as much within the Irish community as outside it. Most of these terms, however, were used by outsiders to disparage or offend. Urban Chicagoans sneered at their rural neighbors, calling them *hicks*, *hillbillies*, and *stump-jumpers* (Pederson 1971b, 188). As with other parts of America at the time, Catholics, Jews, and African-descended Americans were particular targets. One term, though, was specific to Chicago: *Lugan* (or *Lugon*) for persons and things Lithuanian. *Lugan* (and the variant *loogy*) was used only by persons with social or business contacts in the neighborhood of "Little Lithuania" in the neighborhood known as Back of the Yards, but not by Lithuanians themselves. *Lugon* seems to be used nowadays only by elderly people, but it was very much alive in the 1940s. A study of Chicago terms of abuse found that *Lugan* was not familiar to WASPs 'white Anglo-Saxon Protestants' interviewed: "it is virtually unknown in their well-insulated subculture" (Pederson 1964, 48 n. 42). But it was common among the Lithuanians' near neighbors.

Lithuanians in 1900 were estimated to number 10,000 in Chicago, and their comparatively modest number came to national and international prominence with the publication of Upton Sinclair's novel *The Jungle* (1906). Sinclair drew attention to the brutal and unsanitary working conditions of the slaughterhouses, and his story was based on intensive study of the Lithuanian community. The novel begins with a party celebrating a wedding. On the way, the bride is able to berate the driver of her carriage in Polish (when she discovers he does not speak Lithuanian), and when she arrives we learn that, in the many generations of guests, the old people speak only Lithuanian, but times are changing.

> Of these older people many wear clothing reminiscent in some degree of home—an embroidered waistcoat or stomacher, or a gaily colored handkerchief, or a coat with large cuffs and fancy buttons. All these things are carefully avoided by the young, most of whom have learned to speak English and to affect the latest style of clothing. (Sinclair 2003, 13)

While their English may be imperfect, these young people are well on the road to Americanization.

As noted earlier, it was not the bad English of migrants but that of the native born that aroused anger. Campaigns to improve the language gained increasing force. The Chicago Woman's Club was a leader in urging action. One member wrote of her distress at the English of children of the "best" families:

> Yet I know of a certain group of children in the most fashionable part of Chicago where the so-called *old* families of Chicago live. These children, fifty or sixty in number, never have had their speech affected by foreign-born children. They play in a private playground. They attend the best private schools in Chicago, where the teachers speak a most cultivated English. Most of the children have English or French governesses with excellent voices. Yet these children when they are

together almost without exception try to talk as badly as they can. (Robbins 1918, 167)

Such criticisms reveal a deep anxiety about English and the perils of poor speaking. If the contagion could affect children quarantined from the vernacular of the city, what could be done to cure them?

When this woman italicized *old* in "*old* families" or Bloomfield criticized schooling of the previous fifty years, they both acknowledged that Chicago was not a very old place. Having been destroyed by fire in 1871, the city was rebuilt in a frenzy of construction on a street plan that anticipated it would become a great metropolis. And so it did with remarkable speed, drawing immigrants from abroad but also migrants from elsewhere in the United States. The English of the region was already a matter for comedy late in the nineteenth century in works like Edward Eggleston's *Hoosier Schoolmaster* (1871) and *Peck's Bad Boy and his Pa* (Peck 1883). These fictions gave national publicity to the vernacular of the heartland, but both books dealt mainly with rural life.

Now came the voices of Chicago. Some of them were jesters—the wise fools found in many cultures—who could speak truth to power in ways that would have aroused anger and retribution if expressed in the normal voices of English. One of these voices was expressed in newspaper columns by Finley Peter Dunne, who created the vivid "Mr. Dooley," a South Side saloon keeper. Mr. Dooley took umbrage at an English don "that's about ready to declare war on us because he says we're corruptin' th' dilect they call the English language in England with our slang." Following a long American tradition, he asserted that all language begins in slang and it is a sign of vitality: "Faith, whin us free born Americans get through with th' English language we'll make it look as though it had been run over be a musical comedy" (Dunne 1913, 39). Dunne's columns met with national favor as he expressed the new idea that, following the Spanish-American War—a five-month campaign—America had become a global and imperial power. Dooley expatiated on what this might mean for the language and for Americanizing the world through exporting slang.

Another Chicago journalist, George Ade, also exploited the local vernacular for entertainment. In *Fables in Slang* (1899) and *In Babel: Stories of Chicago* (1903), he gathered these journalistic essays into popular volumes. In his preface to the latter, Ade wrote that he hoped the stories, which "are supposed to deal, more or less truthfully, with every-day life in Chicago," "may serve as an antidote for the slang that has been administered to the public in such frequent doses of late" (1903, iii). The truth about Chicago was that people spoke in different voices, and, like his model, Mark Twain, Ade wanted to give these voices life, and he did so in an unashamed use of colloquial English.

A successor to Dunne and Ade was Ring Lardner, who made a similar reputation for himself in the Chicago newspapers. Lardner's most famous creation was the "busher," a novice baseball player with the Chicago White Sox, who wrote letters describing his pride in his athletic talent in the face of his failures as a pitcher. The collection of "letters," *You Know Me Al* (1916), gave Lardner scope for phonetic spellings—for instance, *De Lukes* for *deluxe*—in addition to the vernacular usage—for example, *ain't*—already exploited by Dunne and Ade.

As early as 1894, the young Hamlin Garland decried the attachment in East Coast cities to the literature and language of England. What was new in the west did not fit the tradition; most writers barely noticed the emergence of something new in Chicago:

[The writer] does not see the wealth of material which lies at his hand, in the mixture of races going on with inconceivable celerity everywhere in America, but with especial picturesqueness in the West. If he sees it, he has not the courage to write of it. (Garland 1894, 12)

In a prose poem published in 1917, "Song of the Soul of Chicago," Sherwood Anderson expressed Garland's idea with greater vigor: "We want to give this democracy thing they talk so big about a whirl. We want to see if we are any good out here we Americans from all over hell. That's what we want?" (Friebert and Young 1995, 42). Anderson was a powerful influence on the fiction writers who emerged after World War I, and his assertion here, as well as in the example of his own writing, inspired others to make their own exploration of "this democracy thing."

Not long after, writers began to explore the vernacular in new ways, and their successors used Chicago, and the voices of its people, to explore a gritty reality of ethnic and racial conflict. James T. Farrell in the *Studs Lonigan* trilogy (1932–35) presented the city from the perspective of the Irish American community on the South Side but a side of life never shown by Mr. Dooley. He described in vivid detail the four-day race riot in the summer of 1919 to readers suddenly aware of the inequities of American life as a consequence of the economic depression following the end of World War I. For instance:

Studs made a face at Bill, as if to say: Go soak yer head!
"Bill's a loogin who always tries to wisecrack," Studs said.
"Studs is a little fruity!" Bill said, and they laughed.
"Such awful slang you boys use!" Helen Borax said. (Farrell 1993, 41)

These were new voices in the written record of American English.

Richard Wright's *Native Son* (1940) showed stark differences between a young African American man—one nearly inarticulate—in a catastrophe brought on by the vast social distance between his life on the streets and the citadel of privilege created by wealthy whites. In *The Man with the Golden Arm* (1949), Nelson Algren dramatized the denizens of Division Street; the title character is a gambler destroyed by his morphine addiction:

They retch, they sweat, they itch—then the big drive hits'n here they come out of it cryin' like a baby'r laughin' like a loon. (Algren 1949, 58)

Poetry, especially that by Carl Sandberg, added depth to the image of Chicago as a tough, violent, and tough-talking city. All of these created, in dialogue, the English of a gritty and unforgiving place.

Early in the century, the English of the city flowed outward in print and through the communication channels seen with such awe by Dreiser in Philip Armour's office in the last decade of the nineteenth century. The *Chicago Defender*, founded in 1905, became influential in the South, partly because it was distributed there by Pullman porters, and it had a huge circulation outside Chicago. Langston Hughes, known as one of the leading figures of the Harlem Renaissance in New York, came to be known nationally to African Americans through the *Defender* and other African American newspapers syndicating his writing. The *Defender* also promoted migration from the South to Chicago, and, partly as a result of its urging, the African American population of the city tripled during the teens.

The *Defender*, like other papers of the day, presented a vivid and colloquial style in its sports columns. One of the writers, in 1937, reported a tour of the South in which he noted that "country boys who sling gloves, baseballs, heels and whatnot have the spirit if they haven't anything else....I heard they trained the boys on the Three Ms. which translated into good Chicago English means, 'Meat, Meal and Molasses.' Now you can figure out for yourself that when a fighter gets a load of sorghum, salt-pork and cawnbread in his gizzard, he's one tough hombre to appease" (Burley 1937, 14). Of course the Chicago readers hardly needed a transla-tion, but there's a witty contrast between "country boys" and city dwellers.

Explosive growth in transport and communications made Chicago a hub for commerce, both licit and illegal. In 1908, a Boston lawyer pub-lished a dictionary of *Criminal Slang*, and one of its entries was *hinky dink* "Clark Street, Chicago" (Sullivan 1908, 13). *Hinky Dink* first surfaced in written English as a name for Chicago's First Ward. It derived from its boss Michael "Hinky Dink" Kenna (1858–1946), and it appeared in one of George Ade's early stories in which Kenna's agents are stuffing ballot boxes. The narrowing of meaning to Clark Street must have come early; in 1929, at 2112 North Clark Street, the St. Valentine's Day Massacre took place in which gunmen employed by Al Capone executed six members (and a by-stander) of the North Side gang. The carnage left its indelible mark on Chicago as the realm of gangsters.

Clout is what Hinky Dink Kenna had: the political power to sway elec-tions, oversee civic improvements, and allocate jobs. *Clout* is a Chicago word now used nationally for that kind of power (though an isolated ex-ample from 1868 suggests it may have originated in New York). *Stuffing ballot boxes* was not an expression invented in Chicago, but it was long the practice (and an expression used) there. Politicians could *steam-roller* (1912) their slates of candidates and control public life through clout.

Other early Chicago words included *play-by-play* 'running account of a sporting event (1905),' *nifty* 'joke, witty remark (1918),' *gangway* 'passage-way between apartment buildings' (Pederson 1971b, 166), *prairie* 'vacant lot (1938).' The *Loop* for the part of the center city surrounded by public transport came into use when the lines were built in 1890.

Chicago did not set out to influence the language, but it did so through vast investments in public and private works. The Illinois and Michigan Canal reversed the flow of the Chicago River and made trade and trans-port possible between the city and the Mississippi valley. A "corridor" of dialect similarities extends northern features southwestward toward St. Louis even today. The Great Lakes Naval Training Center was established to make sailors of young men who had never seen an ocean and came from all over the midland. Religious institutions (some of them established in the East) came to Chicago and its suburbs: the Women's Christian Tem-perance Union (1871); the Theosophical Society in America (1875); the

Chicago Evangelism Society (1886; later called the Moody Bible Institute); and Hebrew Theological College (1922, "which filled the Midwest with an Americanized version of the ancient faith" [Grossman 2004, 441]). The AM radio station WGN (1924) broadcast Chicago voices over much of North America. The Merchandise Mart (1930) was, when built, the largest building in the world and served both the wholesale and retail trade. All of these increased the swirling movement of population that Tocqueville had seen as so characteristic of America a century earlier. Chicago by drawing so many from such distant places—whether for visits or residence—contributed to the leveling of American English.

These language changes did not take place by themselves. Scott, Foresman, a Chicago publisher, recognized that money was to be made in schoolbooks. Their earliest texts were designed to assist the teaching of Latin, but the firm soon discovered that English books would be better sellers. Among their earliest publications in the field were *A Brief English Grammar* (Scott and Buck 1907), *A Handbook of English for Engineers* (Sypherd 1913), and *A Handbook of American Speech* (Lewis 1916). As author for the last of these they discovered a professor at a private college in upstate New York, where, as seen from Chicago, excellent English might be found. He warned: "Simple speech defects, however, like those of pronunciation, enunciation, dialect, lisping, etc., should be corrected as early as the intelligence of the child permits—the earlier the better" (Lewis 1916, 2). Among the company's most influential publications was *The Thorndike-Century Junior Dictionary* (Thorndike 1935), accompanied by a small pamphlet *Building the Dictionary Habit: A Handbook of Teaching Helps* (Dolch 1935). The title drew on two famous authorities: Edward L. Thorndike, an educational psychologist at Teachers College, Columbia University, who had published lists showing the words most frequently encountered in children's literature; and the *Century Dictionary*, the most voluminous American dictionary ever produced. The success of this campaign was that Scott, Foresman put several dictionaries in every classroom rather than just one in a school library. It also fostered the idea that the dictionary was an authority, and that expressions not included or discountenanced were not properly English.

In 1911, the National Council of Teachers of English was founded in Chicago, and one of its first presidents was Fred Newton Scott, a native of Indiana. Earlier, Scott had written severely about the nitpicking usage choices adopted at the end of the nineteenth century in the admissions examination for Harvard College. In "What the West Wants in Preparatory English," Scott favored eloquence over correctness, and he pointed out that many eminences used the very expressions that Harvard had chosen to filter out unworthy applicants (Scott 1909). Speaking to the NCTE in 1915, Scott presented a far more democratic view of English. (As most of his audience would have recognized, Hoosiers were residents of Indiana; Wolverines of Michigan; Badgers of Wisconsin; and Suckers of Illinois.)

> The aristocratic period has passed and we are now on a thoroughly democratic basis. Hoosier and Wolverine and Badger and Sucker may hold up their heads when they use their native vowels, and the Southerners, who have always been justly proud of their beautiful speech, need no longer take the trouble even to defend it. (Scott 1926, 7–8)

Scott's view of history shocked purists across the nation. Surely Chicagoese could not be viewed as an admirable variety of the language. Surely the "aristocratic period" was something to be dreamed for the future and not a phase through which English in America had already passed. Tocqueville would have been pleased by Scott's speech.

America's late entry into World War I brought transformations to the culture of the Midwest. In many places from Minnesota southward to Missouri, Germans had established prosperous farms and villages, and they supported many institutions where the German language was used—for instance, newspapers and churches. "Americanization" campaigns made these prosperous citizens the target of suspicion and abuse, and many states attempted to eradicate German, and other languages, from the country. Telephone operators were instructed to cut off conversations in languages other than English; shopkeepers suffered boycotts; churches were told that only English might be used in worship services. In 1923, the Illinois legislature adopted a statute: "The official language of the State of Illinois shall be known as the 'American' language" (chap. 127, par. 177, sec. 1). The result was to marginalize the languages of recent immigrants and to cast aside the idea that "English" was in some way connected to Great Britain.

The process shown so clearly in *The Jungle* was now rapidly, and often unfairly, accelerated. Both Presidents Theodore Roosevelt and Wilson spoke sharply against "hyphenated Americans." In 1915, Roosevelt declared: "There is no room in this country for hyphenated Americanism." Wilson was even more emphatic: "Any man who carries a hyphen about with him carries a dagger that he is ready to plunge into the vitals of this Republic whenever he gets ready." Such sentiments led to a policy that changed America in the twentieth century. Founded in 1894, the Immigration Restriction League gained adherents across the country by urging that the numbers of people coming to the United States be sharply reduced. One goal, based on the race theories popular at the time, was to increase migration from northern and western Europe and limit it from southern and eastern Europe. Swedes and English were welcome; Italians and Polish were not. In 1917, Congress enacted a quota system to further these objectives, and the Immigration Act of 1924 consolidated existing laws (for instance, on Asians) and introduced new limits and lower quotas. The effect was to cut off the communities of Chicago from their homelands, making it very difficult indeed for the neighborhoods (and the institutions built around language and religion) to survive as linguistically distinct enclaves.

The *Chicago Daily Tribune* editorialized about the need for Americanization. "Enfranchised aliens"—that is, voters of various nationalities—might control politicians who would attempt to represent them. Some cities, Chicago among them, made it too easy for immigrants to become citizens, and the requirements already in place (for instance, being literate in some language) needed to be made more stringent. One editorial read:

> The percentage of downright disloyalty among aliens may be small. We believe it is, but it is a curious nation which has any percentage of avowed disloyalty in its enfranchised citizens, with these citizens carrying their disloyalty into elections and maintaining it defiantly in communities. (April 5, 1918, 6)

Foreign-language newspapers were under pressure to accept censorship or close. All languages other than English were viewed with fear and suspicion, despite the fact (as Sinclair had shown in *The Jungle*) multilingualism was on the rise and English more and more the language of public life. Attempts to purge the language of German loanwords were not very successful, but the fact they were proposed shows how much Chicagoans wanted to rid themselves of reminders of their diverse community. *Liberty cabbage* did not displace *sauerkraut* but some hoped that it would (*Chicago Daily Tribune*, October 15, 1918, 14).

Not everyone was stampeded in the waves of fear that swept the city. Mary McDowell, who had gotten her start as a kindergarten teacher at

Hull House and then led the University of Chicago Settlement, told the Americanization committee in Washington that its efforts were "tinkering" and "stuff." *Stuff* 'ideas of little value' was strong language from a devout Methodist and member of the Women's Christian Temperance Union. The men who raised fears "have never been near an immigrant in their lives and know nothing about them." She continued:

> We can't make a man who works ten to fourteen hours a day in a factory English in fifteen minute noon lessons.... We can't crush the foreign languages out or the foreigners will not understand what we are trying to tell them about this country. (*Chicago Daily Tribune*, June 6, 1918, 10)

McDowell had a history of speaking truth to power—she had supported packinghouse workers who had struck in 1904 and 1921—and she was active in investigating and improving the working conditions for children and women. Still, she was unable to change the direction of Chicago life away from compulsory Americanization (even though voluntary Americanization was working well).

Vigilantes made Americanism a special goal, and efforts were directed at thwarting "the reds." According to one estimate, of the 276 foreign-language newspapers published in the city during World War I, 260 were "highly loyal to our country and our government" (Loomis 1920, 26). The ones that were not needed to be closed. The use of *our* in "our country and our government" made vivid whose country it was, and the anarchists, the communists, and the radicals did not belong. Lyrics of songs promoted by these groups were intended to, and probably did, cause alarm in the business community that funded the study. Chicago's local efforts along these lines were part of the wave of raids and deportations that followed the war.

With alarming speed, Americans fastened onto the idea that one language—English—and one kind of English needed to prevail if division were to be avoided. In addition to discouraging the use of languages other than English, those declaring their ownership of "our country and our government" set out on the task of enforcing "good English." In Chicago, this "good English" was no longer to be sought in Boston or New York but right at home. The "rich middle-west r's" were staunchly maintained against the substitution of vowels in words like *fur* and *first* adopted by the elite of southeastern England, Boston, and New York.

The issue was wonderfully illustrated in a story by a writer, then resident in Chicago, who had attended Oxford University in 1928 as a Rhodes scholar. In it, the Iowan scholar waits anxiously for his name to be called by the principal of his Oxford college. As it begins, the American realizes that the English youth answer the call of their names with "Heah": "The Iowa Rhodes scholar noticed that they use the kind of 'r' that he called 'Eastern.'" As his name approaches on the roster, he is increasingly disturbed:

> He could change his pronunciation. People had done it before. But it was nasty business, he realized. His teacher in freshman composition had been brought up in Iowa and had got her master's degree at the State University, and then after one summer session at Columbia in New York City she had come back with a full-fledged Eastern accent. How people had razzed her behind her back and recounted incidents where she had forgotten for the moment. (Read 2002, 326–27)

The story is not quite resolved but the reader knows how the scholar will answer. If he were to say "Heah," he would be a "traitor." He concludes: "I am an American, and I know I love the Middle West, my prairie."

A letter writer to the *Tribune* in 1936 declared: "…so far as pronunciation is concerned, in my opinion least, the midwesterners speak better English than do other English speaking peoples" (R. W. 1936, 12). A columnist ridiculed people who spoke of "dear old Hahvahd" (*Tribune*, February 27, 1940, 10). Another writer, in 1942, was even more assertive of the great value of the English of Chicago: "The English spoken in the west and middle west is the purest in pronunciation…" (Hartwell 1942, 16). The example raised in support of this proposition was the sound of *r*: "The accepted standard is patently western. 'R' is audible but is not a 'burr-r-r.'"

Chicagoans did not need to travel abroad to learn how to pronounce, nor did they need to be "eastern." In George Ade's fiction, variety was celebrated. In one story, subsequently chosen by a historian of English to illustrate Chicago pronunciation, Ade represented a clerk and a messenger. Returning to the office after an extended errand, the messenger says: "W'y, t'e four-eyed nobs dat sent me out on t' Sout' Side" (Krapp 1919, 198). Unlike the messenger, the clerk does not substitute [t] for [θ] (as in *the* and *South*) nor [d] for [ð] (in *that*). These had become shibboleths of lower-class speech. But Ade also presented usages that were typical of

Chicago English then as well as today: for instance, the collapse of the eastern distinction between the first consonant of *why* and *Wye* or *which* and *which*. The messenger, Ade noted, uses [s] in final position where other varieties use [z] (in "Where 'ce at" for "Where's he at." (This trait remains a marker of proud Chicago speech in the twenty-first century in the celebration of its professional football team, "da bears," in which the final sound of *bears* is [s].) While the substitution of [t] in *South* and [d] in *that* was largely suppressed by purists, the other two features continue, especially the consonantal [r] after vowels and at the ends of words.

By the time a survey of Chicago English was conducted in 1962–63, only elderly and bilingual persons still substituted [t] for [θ] and [d] for [ð]. (One Irish American was an exception to this statement.) African Americans spoke as their white neighbors did, for the most part, but the omission of [r] after vowels was found only in two young African Americans (out of twenty-seven) and was a feature scattered among words (Pederson 1964, 40–41). In what would later become a distinctive feature of African American English, the pronunciation [I] (as in *tip*) rather than [ɛ] (as in *bet*) before nasal consonants, African Americans had the former sound in *ten* but the latter in *since* (Pederson 1964, 66). From these examples, and others, it may be fairly stated that English in Chicago was far more uniform in 1950 than it was in 1900.

Chicago English became more uniform for the two reasons that Leonard Bloomfield suggested in 1935: "universal schooling by semi-educated teachers, and wide reading" (107). This scornful evaluation missed two important facts about Chicago English. The first is that teachers were likely to come from bilingual households and thus to speak a more prestigious variety of English than their monolingual counterparts.[1] Not having the stylistic range drifting toward informal and nonstandard varieties, these "semi-educated" teachers presented a bookish and formal kind of English. Bloomfield's second cause of the English he investigated was "wide reading." According to one contributor to the *Chicago Tribune*, Midwesterners spoke better English because of the conventions of written English: "They, more than others, seem to pronounce most words as they are spelled" (R. W. 1936, 12).

The effect of spelling appears in the treatment of vowels in unstressed syllables. In many kinds of English, these unstressed vowels are given the

---

1. This principle was at work in the English of the western Highlands of Scotland, where emerging bilingualism in the late eighteenth century gave rise to a "better" English than was to be found in the monolingual Lowlands.

value of [ə] (as in the first syllable of *about*). This sound can be heard in some pronunciations of the final vowel in *shadow* or *Missouri*. In Chicago, however, these pronunciations were seldom employed among the educated. Instead, the spelling led to what seemed to outsiders like fussily correct speech: *shadow* and *mushroom* with [o] and *Missouri* with [i] as the final vowel (Pederson 1964, 36–37). Deriving their authority from spelling, purists urged that the second consonant of *diphtheria* be [f] rather than [p]. One such person declared that there were no "silent letters" in the following words: *Arctic, artistically, authoritatively, auxiliary, cruel, factory, facts, February, geometry, government, laboratory, library, pumpkin,* and *recognize* (Bartlett 1934, D6). This statement was untrue. Many of these words had long established and respectable pronunciations that did not slavishly follow the spelling—for instance, *Arctic, factory, facts,* and *February* were often pronounced as if spelled *Artic, factry, faks,* and *Febyewary.* Having been silent for at least three hundred years, the [l] in *calm* and the [t] in *often* began to creep back into spoken English. Chicago, at least among the book-learned and semieducated, wanted no truck with pronunciations that departed much from the spelling.

Sometimes spelling might mislead the unwary, so people bent on improvement should not, in the words of this purist, "take their own word for it." Words like *archipelago* and *debut* should not be pronounced as spelled, and all that the linguistically anxious could do was to read over lists of such misleading words and memorize their correct pronunciation. (They would discover that the first consonant in *archipelago* was [k] and that the final consonant in *debut* was silent.) So confident in the authority of dictionaries was the *Chicago Tribune* that it set out to challenge spellings recorded in them and thus alter English. Beginning early in 1934, the newspaper introduced an ever increasing list of words that would thenceforth appear in its pages in a more rationalized spelling. These spellings were not, for the most part, intended to impose pronunciation on readers; there were only a small number in which sounds played a part (like *drouth* "drought"). Instead, the list shows the removal of letters thought to be superfluous: *catalog* 'catalogue,' *crum* 'crumb,' *etiquet* 'etiquette,' *heven* 'heaven,' *iland* 'island,' *jaz* 'jazz,' *sofomore* 'sophomore,' *rime* 'rhyme,' *tarif* 'tarriff.' The paper was especially concerned about spellings with *ph* and so recommended *fantom* "phantom" and *philosofy* "philosophy."

Seeking endorsements from scholars, the *Tribune* sought out eminences to recommend its innovations. The chair of Greek at the University of

Chicago, a self-defined "conservative and classicist," found the list "reasonable." The president of Northwestern University thought the "movement" should be carried even further. Carl Darling Buck, the philologist who published the survey of languages in Chicago in 1903, agreed: the *Tribune* list "does not go very far," he said (*Chicago Daily Tribune*, January 29, 1934, 3). The paper continued to add to the list and to require the spellings in its copy. Frequent words were added as time went on: for example, *altho* 'although,' *tho* 'though,' *thoro* 'thorough,' *thru* 'through.' In 1949, the list was augmented yet again: "The TRIBUNE cannot be arbitrarily drastic, but it can be continuously consistent, and thereby maintain its leadership as a proponent of sane spelling without incurring the accusation of iconoclasm" (*Chicago Daily Tribune*, July 3, 1949, 3).

None of these "reforms" had any consequential effect on the system of English spelling, but the fact they were attempted reveals the sense of linguistic independence that prevailed in Chicago in the first half of the twentieth century.

Opinion leaders asserted ownership of their English, and to do so they needed to take pride in their own distinctiveness. One step was to distinguish what rightfully belonged to Chicago and what did not. In this effort, they promoted the idea that the pronunciation of the name of the city was a shibboleth. Chicagoans pronounced their city *Chickawgo* [ɔ] and outsiders *Chickahgo* [ɑ]. As a descriptive statement, this claim was untrue (and remains untrue), but it became a symbolic gesture separating insiders from outsiders. Among the earliest claims for this myth was an article in the *Chicago Tribune* in 1940. Having described the difference, the writer pointed out that local preferences should take precedence, and "in the case of Chicago its four million inhabitants can't be wrong." The [ɑ] pronunciation belongs to "certain pundits" of Boston and the inhabitants of Oxford who allege that "the genuine Chicagoan is merely speaking a middle west dialect, and that his vulgar phonetics are not according to the classic rules of English." Such claims are ridiculous, the paper declared: "Our pronunciation is the softest and most agreeable arrangement of sounds that can be obtained from the word. So remember: 'a' as in 'hawg' proves that you are a regular Chicagoan and dawggone proud of it" (*Chicago Daily Tribune*, February 27, 1940, 10; see also Cresswell 1985).

Within the city, neighborhood distinctiveness took a linguistic turn, and nowhere was this aspect of English more evident than in the usage of gangs. A pioneering sociological study produced the following significant conclusion:

The isolated life of gangland leads to the development of a distinctive universe of discourse. The gang acquires its own language. (Thrasher 1963, 190)

Gangs, and the neighborhoods that supported them, were internally cohesive and used English to maintain that cohesiveness. The most dominant gang in the 1920s was the Union Sicilione, but it was not limited in its membership to Sicilians or even Italians. Like nearly half of the gangs, it was made up of mixed nationalities (Thrasher 1963, 130), and it entered into folklore as *The Outfit*. Throughout Chicago, gangsters had nicknames that became well known to newspaper readers, and it is significant that all of them were English nicknames, including: Big Jim Colosimo, Scarface Al Capone, Jake "Greasy Thumb" Guzik, Frank the Enforcer Nitti, George Clarence "Bugs" Moran, Earl "Hymie" Weiss, Murray "The Camel" Humphries. Unlike his East Coast counterparts in the La Cosa Nostra, Capone did not make heritage a requisite for membership in his Outfit, but he did demand absolute loyalty and punished those who fell short.

Gangsters were no different from other Chicagoans in their pride in their language. Here is Big Tim Murphy:

"I talk back-of-the-yards English," he said and in the forcible way in which Big Tim talked this picturesque lingo, he needed no interpreter to make himself understood. "Racket," "bum rap," and "lamster" are among a number of expressions with which he is said to have enriched the language. (Burns 1931, 246)

Murphy did not enrich English with *lamster* 'fugitive' or the other expressions attributed to him here. But the idea that a gangster would "enrich" English by introducing criminal argot into it emerged from the same impulse that motivated more elevated Chicago expressions.

Sneak thieves participated in the effort to uplift Chicago English. While there was a long history of coded language through which criminals could identify each other, pickpockets and others dependent upon respectable society needed to disguise themselves with language. In one report, two thieves managed to present themselves, while under close observation by the police, as professors by discussing arcane academic subjects and thus misleading the detectives who had observed them (Sutherland 1965, 20). The verb *con* in a sentence like "She conned the mark so he happily turned over all his money" derives from *confidence* (< *confidence game*), and among the earliest written evidence for *con* came from two Chicago writers, George Ade and Theodore Dreiser. *Con men* and other *grifters* 'swindlers' were constantly on the move, so it is difficult to identify just what was distinctive of Chicago in their usage. The secret argot of criminals affected English only as accounts of them reached a wider public through reporting and fiction. A well-dressed man might be a *cannon* 'pickpocket' but he endeavored through dress and language to be entirely respectable (Maurer 1940).

A typical example of underworld English rising to reach a wider public appeared in a report of Edward "Spike" O'Donnell, an ex-con and "hard guy." With a roll of $9,700 in his pocket he lifted his son Patsy to his shoulders so the tyke could have a better view of a parade. Confident of his street smarts, O'Donnell declared later: "I didn't think there was a cannon in Chicago who could work me." But he was wrong and his roll was lifted. Police found it amazing that O'Donnell reported the theft to them:

> "I ain't squawking. You know I wouldn't do that," he reminded Lieut. Grafton.
>
> "But my wife's all broke up about this and I thought maybe if the 'cannons' found out how bad she felt about it and got to thinking what a dirty trick it was to rob a man at such an occasion, they might slip a little of it back."
>
> The police are skeptical of Spike's theory. (*Chicago Daily Tribune*, May 13, 1924, 1)

Here *cannon* entered the world of respectable English through the medium of the newspaper.

Chicago's word of the half century was *jazz*. In 1915, the *Chicago Tribune* printed one of the first uses of *jazz* to describe music. The story concocts a conversation between a husband ("the worm") and his wife in a nightclub. The wife wants to fox-trot, and the husband complains that he is unable to dance. Suddenly there is a *blue note* from a saxophone:

> The Worm had turned—turned to fox trotting. And the "blues" had done it. The "jazz" had put pep into the legs that had scrambled too long for the 5:15. (*Chicago Daily Tribune*, July 11, B8)

One of the two accompanying satirical illustrations shows an awkward-looking white couple, the worm scratching his head in perplexity. The other depicts a handsomely dressed African American with a polka-dotted tie and a suit with wide lapels; he looks heavenward as the notes pour from the mouth of his instrument. The word became rapidly familiar (sometimes spelled *jas* or *jass*).

As the *Tribune* article attests, most of the pioneers of jazz were African American, but in 1915 Johnny Stein brought north from New Orleans a group of white musicians calling themselves "Stein's Dixie Jass Band." Shortly renamed "The Original Dixieland Jazz Band," the group made the first jazz recording in 1917: "Dixie Jass Band One Step." The popularity of this style of music fueled both sheet music and record publishing in Chicago, and the most prominent figures in popular music came from Chicago (like Benny Goodman) or spent time in the music scene there (Louis Armstrong, Bessie Smith, Jelly Roll Morton). Sheet music published there achieved national acclaim—for instance, "Livery Stable Blues" (Chicago: Roger Graham, 1917). Record labels like Okeh and Chess spread the Chicago sound internationally, and persons with no firsthand experience of African American culture began to collect *race records* (Grossman, Keating, and Reiff 2004, 433–34) and to imitate both musical and linguistic performances found on them.

Songs, and the recordings made from them, became powerful vehicles for spreading Chicago English. *Skiffle*, *jive*, *boogie-woogie*, and *scat* are all styles that emerged from the Chicago music scene. In 1926, Jimmy O'Bryant produced "Chicago Skiffle" for Paramount, "The Popular Race Record" (*Chicago Defender*, March 4, 1926, 7). In 1928 Cow Cow Davenport recorded "State Street Jive," and Lil Hardin Armstrong and Louis Armstrong "Don't Jive Me." In the same year, Pinetop Smith recorded "Pine Top's Boogie Woogie" for Vocalion. In the early 1930s, Cab Calloway introduced "The Scat Song" (recorded 1932), and *scat* became a verb for the verbal improvisation found there:

When your sweetie tells you everything'll be okay,
Just skeep-beep de bob-bop beep bop bo-dope skeetie-at-de-op-de day!

Like these other performers, Calloway soon found his way to New York with its larger audience, more prosperous publishers, and opportunities for national exposure. Yet Chicago remained a testing ground for musicians moving north from New Orleans, Memphis, Kansas City, and St. Louis.

In 1933, Chicago opened the Century of Progress exposition. Though there was a small replica of Fort Dearborn, the place that gave rise to the idea of a centennial, everything else looked to the future: huge modernistic buildings, illumination with miles of neon tubing, celebration of science as the foundation for progress. The promotion materials for the exposition declared:

> Chicago is not simply the metropolis of the Middle West; it is bound to the entire civilized world by a thousand ties of commerce and finance and ideas and kinship. It is the superlative product of the forces that have moved the world during its lifetime, and it is the clearest prophecy of the future of mankind. (*Official* 1932, 7)

What Chicago believed about itself, it believed about English. Chicago English showed the promise of the future.

None of these enthusiastic Chicagoans were prepared for what would happen next. Railroad tracks divided neighborhoods that were often at war with each other. The construction of limited-access highways destroyed the neighborhoods and widened the gaps between them. Suburbanization split the city along lines of social class; prosperous Lithuanians, for instance, moved away and left poor ones behind. Redlining led to the rapid decline of communities when banks declined to make loans for home improvement or for new homeowners.

Linguistic surveys taken in the 1960s revealed that Chicago English was more uniform than it had been before, and it was more uniform than it would be later as racial conflict tore apart the fabric of the city.

9 Los Angeles, 1950–2000

WRITING IN 1956, the novelist Saul Bellow declared "that in Los Angeles all the loose objects in the country were collected, as if America had been tilted and everything that wasn't tightly screwed down had slid into Southern California" (1964, 14–15). Prejudicial as this observation may be, it speaks to the nontraditional lifestyles Southern California has welcomed.

To take one example, early in the twentieth century, gays and lesbians from across the nation found refuge along the Pacific shore in a homosexual colony centered in Long Beach. In 1914, an investigative journalist reported the existence of a "society of queers" given to lavish parties, cross-dressing, and participation from every origin and social class. These parties included, according to the reporter, "some of the wealthy and prominent men of the city, politicians, prominent business men, and even prominent churchmen" (Ullman 1995, 599). Terms now well-known, with specific meanings for this community, have their first documentation in the reporter's notes: *chicken, go down on,* and *queer*. What was forbidden elsewhere in America was tolerated in Southern California.[1]

In 1940, 190,774 people (10 percent of the total) had been born abroad: 37,143 in Mexico, 32,868 in the Soviet Union, 29,828 in English Canada, 23,818 in Scotland and England. In the census of 1950, the population of Los Angeles County was just short of two million, but only 27 percent of the respondents were born in California. States contributing more than 50,000 to this mix included northern states: New York, Pennsylvania, Illinois, Iowa. In addition, the great drought of the 1930s had brought westward many migrants from the most severely afflicted regions, particularly Texas. Oklahoma and Arkansas were important states of origin too (41,405 and 30,032 respectively). The last of these new Californians were known as *Oakies* (1918) and *Arkies* (1927), two terms that to this day are often derogatory.

Los Angeles had long fostered a mythical view of its origins with pious Franciscans and manly grandees moving northward from Mexico, and the series of movies and television programs devoted to the exploits of Zorro promoted this view. This legendary history, however, was mostly fabricated by boosters and real-estate speculators, and it became increasingly irrelevant in the second half of the twentieth century as the city struggled to discover itself.

By 1950, Los Angeles was prospering in the defense industries created during World War II and the successive developments in *aerospace* (a word first attested in 1958). These sources of employment pulled in workers from recent arrivals and drew others to the attractive climate and high-paying jobs of what became known as the Southland. All of these varied origins, both in the United States and abroad, produced a linguistic and cultural mix even more diverse than that found in New York and Chicago in earlier days.

In the half century after 1950, Los Angeles County was new every morning. The total population increased from 1.97 million to 9.50 million with

---

1. In this era, oral sex aroused outrage as great from lawmakers as same-sex relations, and in 1915 the California legislature provided harsh penalties for anyone convicted of engaging in fellatio or cunnilingus. Soon after it had been litigated, the State Supreme Court vacated the law on the grounds that *fellatio* and *cunnilingus* were not English words—because they were not found in dictionaries—and thus the law violated the state constitutional requirement, passed as part of anti-Spanish fervor, that laws be written in English (Ulmann 1995, 594n). Legalistic reasoning was thus applied in a way that declared California more tolerant than eastern states and more welcoming to people who were not tightly screwed down to puritanical rules of conduct.

migrants taking up residence at an astonishing rate. According to the 2000 census, more than half of the respondents used a language other than English at home. For most Angelinos, English was an additional language, not a mother tongue.

In his 1948 novella, Evelyn Waugh began his satire of the Los Angeles funeral industry in a colony of expatriate Englishmen who do their best to uphold the traditions of their homeland. One worries that another is letting down the side by wearing a belt rather than *braces* 'suspenders,' and another is given to appearing in an Inverness cape and deerstalker on wet days. Their English has a prewar flavor that emphasizes just how anachronistic they were in Southern California: "I should be toddling," says a member of this set on preparing to depart (Waugh 1948, 11). American voices, as Waugh represented them, reflect the usual prejudices of the English scribbling class about the sad fate of their language in America, where sentences begin with "I reckon" and "I guess." Like most such English observers, Waugh had a tin ear for English in America. For him *pass the buck* (53) meant 'to make a payment' rather than 'to shift responsibility elsewhere.' He put into American mouths sentences that the most persnickety English purists (and some American ones too) would find objectionable: for instance, "What did your Loved One pass on from?" (55). A sentence like that one was sure to raise a laugh in Britain.

With a populous colony of British actors and writers like those in Waugh's novel, Los Angeles had some yearning for British English, particularly in the entertainment industry. Such respect for stage voices was long-standing in the American theater. Many of the popular actors of the nineteenth-century American theater were British: Junius Brutus Booth (father of the assassin) and Laura Keene became leading figures of the American stage and influenced a taste for English-inflected voices. Any serious attempt to domesticate stage voices to something more homespun in serious drama met with resistance.

With the export of American films, an English purist warned that California English would lead innocent Britons to "the matricide of their mother tongue." He called it *lingua californica*: "It has devastated Europe. The subtitles have created a wilderness and called it prose" (Knox 1930, 187–88). If the language of words seen on film was so pernicious, how effective would the voices of Americans be in the new wave of *talkies*? This Englishman attacked this kind of speech by calling it *cinemaese*.

One response to such slurs on English was the decision by the Hollywood studios to foster what was called *Transatlantic English*. This artificial dialect contained some elements of the British prestige standard—particularly the loss of the consonant *r* in words like *fear* and *farm* and the character of the vowel in *bath* and *grass*. Just a few exchanges of dialogue in a 1930s comedy reveal that the transatlantic actress will wed the leading man and the American-sounding one will end as the unwed girl-next-door. British voices were disappearing from films just at the time of Waugh's postwar visit, but the legacy of voice coaching persisted in lending prestige to actual (or pseudo-) British English, particularly for Shakespearean performances. But after 1950, even American actors who had established successful careers using transatlantic began to perform with more American voices. Not long after the 1950s, the practice of performing in this artificial standard ceased, or nearly so (Elliott 2000). By the 1980s this dialect was used only by marginal characters in films: "Transatlantic is used when producers wish to suggest that characters are removed from reality or are removed in time or space" (Hobbs 1986, 4). In *Star Wars* (1977), for instance, Alec Guinness, a classically trained British actor, played Jedi master Obi-Wan Kenobi, powerful primarily because of wisdom, although he is still capable of engaging in physical combat.

So by 1950, in films set in America, the decision was made to abandon synthetic voices for local ones, but it was not immediately transparent just what might replace transatlantic. What was Los Angeles English?

Among long-settled citizens of Los Angeles, the origins of the city are traced not to the friars and grandees but to Iowa. Long Beach, the port district, has been known as the "seaport of Iowa." For many, Los Angeles English is merely a subdialect of Iowa and is seen to be bland, unremarkable, and Caucasian. This opinion, still widely held today, expresses the idea of Los Angeles as an Anglo-American paradise in which there is no dialect but a form of expression as clear as glass. Everyone can single out a New Yorker, in this view; no one would notice anything local about Los Angeles. To an outsider, this opinion seems delusional, and even insiders acknowledge that there is more to Los Angeles English than Iowa.

Los Angeles is an important center for English in America because it has created (and marketed) versions of how people talk. National and international export of films required that the "dialects" employed in them be widely intelligible. But there remained the choice of the kind of English to employ and the ways in which subordinate kinds of English would be articulated.

Ideology and English did not emerge in some natural way but were both constructed to project a set of "American" values. In this effort, no one was more influential than Walt Disney, the head of Disney Studios, who migrated from the Midwest to Los Angeles in 1923. A successful producer of animated and live-action films, Disney set out to influence America by his ownership of children's imaginations. Many well-established stories were rewritten and reillustrated in a Disney version, including *Winnie the Pooh* and *Alice in Wonderland.* This process was recognized early and led to terms describing it: *disneyesque* (1939), *disneyfied* (1947), *disneyification* (1959), and *disneyfy* (1965). While other Hollywood executives saw the emergence of television as a threat to the film business, Disney immediately grasped its potential to market entertainment and products of all sorts across the nation. On Christmas 1950, Disney made his debut in national television with a program called *One Day in Wonderland.*

In 1955, Disney opened Disneyland just south of Los Angeles, the first of the theme parks that would subsequently open around the world. Language for the park was carefully devised by *imagineers* (< *imagination + engineers*), and managers were designated *leads,* subordinates acted in *roles,* and the paying visitors were known as *guests.* All sorts of theatrical terminology was used in the park, and the workers were designated as *on stage* whether their roles were ticket taker, security guard, or costumed character. What Disney saw as "good English" was required for employment, and part of the prerequisites included the ability to speak in a "standard" style.

From 1957 to 1959, Disney studios produced for television *Zorro,* drawing on a tradition of film versions of early Los Angeles. The masked hero was played by Guy Williams, born Armando Joseph Catalano, but not readily identifiable as Latino by his speech. His nemesis, Sergeant Garcia, was a rotund and comic figure whose dialogue was spoken in exaggeratedly accented Spanish. (The actor who played him was a Texan with the birth name "Wimberly Calvin Goodman.") With no great subtlety, the programs illustrated that heroes speak a standard kind of English and those who oppose them use accented speech. The ideology in this early series has continued with remarkable vitality to this day. In fully animated films from Disney, there are vivid contrasts between heroes and villains (as might be expected in the fantasy worlds represented), and there is a striking correlation between virtue and unaccented speech. About 20 percent of the English-speaking characters are villainous; some 40 percent of characters employing accented English are villains. Late in the century African American voices began to appear in Disney films but never once in the twentieth century was such a voice assigned to a human being. All such voices belonged to animals (Lippi-Green 1997, 87–98).

If foreign-accented speech was threatening, foreign languages seemed terrifying in the world Los Angeles created for voices.

In *The Godfather* (1972), Francis Ford Coppola presented a story of gang warfare in post–World War II New York. In one crucial scene, Michael, the man who will succeed his father as the principal gangster of the city, meets with two men whose interests are opposed to those of his family, one a police captain and the other a rival named Virgil "The Turk" Sollozzo. Apologizing to the Irish police officer, Sollozzo speaks to Michael in Italian, and his words are translated into English as subtitles. After a brief interruption when Michael seeks permission to go to the restroom (and returns with a gun hidden there for his use), Sollozzo resumes speaking Italian but this time the words are not translated. After a carefully timed pause in which the audience imagines what has been said, Michael kills both men by shooting them in the face.

For Michael to speak in Italian is to demonstrate that he is not merely the assimilated and decorated veteran of the opening scene of the film in which he has distanced himself from his family and from his Italian heritage. The plot shows his descent into the criminal world of his father, and the fact of his speaking in what (until that point) has been a foreign language belonging to the previous generation is a stage in the process. That this scene culminates in a double murder dramatizes in a linguistic way Michael's deepening embrace of the criminal world.

This small episode resulted from careful thought about the language to use in the film. Here is the editor, Walter Murch, in conversation with Michael Ondaatje:

M[URCH]: Another element in that scene is Francis's use of Italian without subtitles. It's very bold, even today, to have an extended scene between two main characters in an English-language film speaking another language with no translation. As a result you're paying much more attention to *how* things are said and the body language being used and you're perceiving things in a very different way. You're listening to the *sound* of the language, not the meaning.

O[NDAATJE]: What was the word you used last night? Not aphasic but...

M: Yes, that's it: aphasic. You don't know what they're saying, so the only way to understand what that scene is about is to watch *how* they say it, through the tone of the voice and their body language. The sound exercises the mind in much more complex ways than appear on

the surface of the scene, which is otherwise just a dialogue scene between three people. The use of unsubtitled Italian is making you pay
attention to sound, setting you up for what is about to happen.
(Ondaatje 2002, 121–22)

Aphasia is a speech disorder usually resulting from some damage to the
brain (often in a stroke). By using this word to describe the artful use of
bilingualism in *The Godfather*, Murch imagines that the audience has been
shut out of the meaning of language while still attentive to its sound. Un-
translated language is a threat to our ability to understand.

Multilingualism can be troubling to the monolingual speakers of Los Angeles English, and so the entertainment industry has generally skirted the issues
it raises. That an esteemed film editor compares the use of Italian to a language
disorder is a remarkable admission. It is not the actors who are suffering from
aphasia; it is the audience. Viewers are suddenly denied intelligibility and
hence shut out of the bilingual world of the film.

Fantasy in television and movies nearly always presents Los Angeles as far
less culturally diverse than it actually is. The 1990s television serial *Beverly
Hills 90210* follows a cast of students from high school to college. All are
white, and all are coping with growing up in English-speaking homes. The
2000 census data for the ZIP code 90210 showed a far different cultural picture from the one presented in the programs. In 90210, there were 21,495
houses, and of these 8,449 employed a language other than English as the
household language. Nearly a third of the residents were born outside the
United States, and the most frequently used language after English was Farsi.
The producers of the program created a fiction by simply ignoring the facts of
life in that ZIP code.

As in *The Godfather*, Hollywood has constructed multilingualism as a
problem, usually insoluble, rather than a normal feature of everyday life.
As part of a series of films known as *film noir*, Ridley Scott's *Blade Runner*
(released in 1982), a science-fiction film, imagines Los Angeles as a social
and economic horror city in 2019. Part of the social collapse represented
in it involves multilingualism.

The most important character in *Blade Runner*, from the perspective of
language in America, is a police officer named Gaff, a nickname derived in
the mind of the scriptwriter as a version of *gaffe* 'a mistake.' As the character evolved during the preparation for filming, some of Gaff's characteristics were based on the casting choice of Edward James Olmos, a Mexican

American actor born in East Los Angeles. Here's how Olmos saw the character developing:

> First I asked Ridley [Scott] if I could embellish the character, make him more interesting to the audience. Ridley respected me enough as an artist to trust me with building up an entire history for Gaff. So the backstory I came up with was that Gaff was primarily Mexican-Japanese, and that his lineage in America stretched back at least five generations. Gaff was quite proud of that, as well as the sense of his past culture. (Sammon 1996, 113)

Gaff, Olmos explained, was a talented linguist with fluency in ten languages. When he first speaks in the film, he employs "a nearly indecipherable tongue," identified in the 1981 version of the script as "Cityspeak." The writers saw it as a "gutter language." The word *Cityspeak* echoes *Newspeak*, the language of totalitarian society in George Orwell's *Nineteen Eighty-Four* (1948). Both are damaged human languages, drained of their community-forming powers.

To develop the idea of *Cityspeak*, Olmos took extraordinary steps:

> My first idea was to put a mixture of genuine Spanish, French, Chinese, German, Hungarian, and Japanese into Cityspeak. Then I went to the Berlitz School of Languages in Los Angeles, translated all these different bits and pieces of Gaff's original dialogue into fragments of foreign tongues, and learned to properly pronounce them. I also added some translated dialogue I'd made up myself. All that was a bitch and a half, but it really added to Gaff's character. (Sammon 1996, 115)

A painstaking translation of Gaff's Cityspeak has, in addition to some of the languages mentioned in Olmos's recollection, characteristics of code-switching, the difficult-to-predict intermixture of English with other tongues (Sammon 1996, 116). In Olmos's imagination, Gaff is not a recent immigrant but a man of American ancestry (and proud of it), employing languages other than English.

Blade Runner is a nightmare with many voices drowning out English. In a 1988 futuring exercise called "California 2000," the epilogue holds up to horrified examination the possibility of "the *Blade Runner* scenario: the fusion of individual cultures into a demotic polyglotism ominous with unresolved hostilities" (Los Angeles 2000 Committee 1988, quoted in Rieff 1991, 133).

Hollywood not only markets ideas about language; it markets language itself. If audiences can no longer react to the menace of particular foreigners, they can be scared by the terrors of "demotic polyglotism."

While moviegoers may occasionally wish to be frightened by predictions of an alarming future, they are far more interested in romantic comedy in which young people overcome obstacles (including those raised by parents) to find bliss. In seeking a setting for youthful romance, Los Angeles producers discovered and marketed *beach culture* and the characters who inhabited it. *Gidget*, the film of 1959, was the first of many productions intertwining surfing and romantic life at the edge of the water in Southern California. (*Gidget* is a blend of *girl* and *midget*. The young woman who was the model for Gidget, Kathy Kohner, was fourteen when her father wrote the novel upon which the film is based.)

Language was central to the wholesome image created for these productions.

Publicized by the films, the novel on which these films were founded gave rise to vocabulary that spread across the country: for example, *barfy* as in "My English comp teacher . . . that barfy-looking character" (*OED*, s.v. *barfy*). Another innovative usage from *Gidget* is *bitchin* 'excellent,' a reversal of the long-established meaning of 'unpleasant, despicable': "It was a bitchen day too. The sun was out and all that, even though it was near the end of November" (*OED*, s.v. *bitching*).

Formerly seen as an outlaw pursuit, beach culture popularized surfing and the vocabulary involved in it: *curl* 'breaking crest of a wave' (1962); *drop-knee* 'a kind of turn' (1967); *hang-time* 'duration of surfing' (1969); *gnarly* 'challenging, unpleasant' (1977); *hot dog, big gun* (1963), and *boogie-board* 'types of surfboard' (1976); *spin out* 'loss of control when the keel of the board pops out of the water' (1961). *Surfer* shifted from beach culture to the world of electronics in *channel surfer* and *surf the Internet*. While surfing was not invented in Los Angeles, Hollywood created and popularized much of the language involved with it.

Creative works like these do not grow solely out of some historical sense of American culture. Instead, they show the power of the entertainment industry to create new language for new circumstances. The novel upon which the *Gidget* films were based was written by a refugee from Hitler, Frederick Kohner, who arrived in Los Angeles in the 1930s not knowing much English. Insofar as there is a literary ancestry for Gidget, it is Mark Twain's Huckleberry Finn. At the end of Twain's novel, Huck lights out for the territory, and the territory turns out to be Los Angeles. The first actress to play Gidget was Sandra Dee, as wholesome a blonde Californian as might have been found. Like Kohner, she arrived in Los Angeles to create the American dream girl, and no one thought any the less of her that she had been born as Alexandra Zuck in Bayonne, New Jersey. Both Twain and Kohner imagined a youth culture and gave it a language. Hollywood was the medium by which the vision reached back across America and beyond.

Kohner's representation of the English of the beach culture was strongly influenced by his teenage daughter, and in the next generation Frank Zappa based an influential song on his daughter, Moon Unit, who was also fourteen at the time her father composed the song "Valley Girl" in 1982. At the outset, *Valspeak* (a blend of San Fernando *Valley* and *–speak*) was known to the wider world only through Moon Unit's monologue that appears as background to the song. Zappa, a political conservative, intended to lampoon this way of speaking, but his daughter's words had exactly the opposite effect and led to an enormous popularity for her kind of English and the images associated with it. (Zappa attempted to undo what he had done, and sued the makers of the 1983 film *Valley Girl*. His suit was unsuccessful.)

The speed at which Valspeak was developed resulted from the growth of information technologies unimaginable before 1950. Almost immediately "everyone" knew of this new kind of English thanks to the frequent broadcasting of "Valley Girl" on radio stations across the land.

The first extended narrative involving the Valley culture appeared in a draft film script just months after Zappa's song gained popularity. Here is the opening scene:

> An area that has numerous fast food restaurants. We FOCUS on this same group of teenaged girls. They seem to embody all the attributes of the famous "Valley Girl." JULIE RICHMAN, 15, is a pretty blonde, squeakily cute clean. At her side is her best friend, STACEY GARRISON, 15, the ultimate Valley girl. She's pretty and brunette. She dresses and is coiffed to perfection. SUZI BRENT, 15, fits right in with this pattern. The last girl friend is LORYN LICHTER, 15 going on 25. She's got a body that would arouse the terminally limp. MOVING IN on their conversation, we hear what every girl talks about and how.

stacey
Barf out. Gag me. How could you?
suzi
For sure!
julie
I'd be freakinggg out!
loryn
It's totally outrageous! I don't want to like start a family. Like I'd get
puffed out to the max and all, for sure. I'd be scarfin' up everything
in sight. I don't know, like...I'd be sooo fat and all. Like, what'd
happen to my zits? They can get so grody. Besides, it's like totally
gnarly birth control. (Lane and Crawford 1982, 3)

Setting the scene for what is to follow, the film introduces young women
whose way of speaking defines them. Unlike Gidget, who was presented
as an innocent, these girls are sexually active and deeply materialistic. The
Valspeak term for them is *airheads*. Like many of the expressions associated with this culture *airhead* drew on actual adolescent usage. (The first
written example of *airhead* so far noticed is from 1972.)

As with many teenagers in Hollywood films, these girls have a different
value system from their parents, and in *Valley Girl* the comedic contrast is
shown in language. The parents speak in 1960s *hippie*—an expression
shortened from *hipster* and the center of a variety of expressions associated
with this culture: *hippiedom, hippieland, hippiness*. (Linguistically, *hippie*
and its derivatives descend from the 1950s *beatnik* culture—another mani-
festation of California linguistic innovation.)

In a later scene in the draft script for *Valley Girl*, the young women are
ashamed of the way their parents talk.

Julie squirms at the parental restraint.
mr. richman
(continuing)
We understand where you're coming from, Julie. Believe me, I can dig
that scene.
Julie now squirms at her parents' archaic jargon. Stacey stifles a giggle.
(Lane and Crawford 1982, 12)

All of this imaginary dialogue is founded on creative use of stereotypes
just like those of earlier dialect humor. The difference is that Hollywood

has made it seem attractive to speak in the most up-to-date of these ways, Valspeak.

And Hollywood had the power to market this kind of English around the world. As a result, copycat concepts have appeared, based on the Valley Girl image, in such diverse places as Israel, Brazil, and England. In California, Valspeak merged with *surfer dude* slang in presenting a unified image of beach culture and suburban privilege into the twenty-first century.

In addition to Zappa's song and *Valley Girl*, 1982 saw no fewer than four short books devoted to the ways of Valspeak, all written by adults and all acknowledging the assistance of teenaged informants—for instance "Tiffany T. of Encino" (Corey and Westermark 1982). All of them connected surfing to the culture of the shopping mall, and all asserted its vitality and authenticity. One guide answered the question "Where Val Parents Came From":

> Val kids have always been there, but Val parents come from like Cleveland or Scranton or Tulsa. And they're wandering around the Valley mumbling, "Who am I," "Where am I," "Where am I going," and "Where can I get a good Maine lobster?" (Posserello 1982, 31)

Insightfully, the author detects that parents are anxious about rootlessness, but their children are not. These books are no more reliable as reports of the language of teenaged Los Angeles girls than their antecedent "dialect" books, but in creating (if not capturing) a linguistic image for Southern California they have had remarkably widespread influence. One of them was written by a speech correctionist (recently the coauthor of a work on the relation of dental appliances and noise to intelligibility), and she included Valspeak spectrograms made at the phonetics laboratory at UCLA. With the idea that parents would like to persuade teenage daughters to erase Valspeak from their English, she even included information for getting in contact with a speech pathologist in their neighborhood. She herself attracted clients among the wealthy in Beverly Hills who paid handsomely to have their daughters Valspeak eliminated (Glass and Liebmann-Smith 1982, 63; Pond 1982).

While these books were not used as manuals of instruction in places distant from Los Angeles, they did capture practices of teenage English that were found elsewhere. Here's a specimen sentence: "Like. Omigod! I mean like way totally wicked dude, y'know" (Glass and Liebmann-Smith 1982, 33). *Like* as a frequent connective binding words and sentences together is mentioned by all of these "guides." High-rising intonation (or *uptalk*) on declarative sentences—a verbal strategy designed to elicit attention and perhaps agreement—did not begin in Valspeak but it was very much part of the image: "Val girls talk like they're surprised a lot…and they're always asking questions?" (Posserello 1982, 17). Valspeak was revived in the 1995 film *Clueless*, based on Jane Austen's *Emma*, and Amy Heckerling (the writer and director) immersed herself in the world of teenage girls to bring the dialect up to date.

With the financial success of these productions, Hollywood determined to continue creating mythical high-school settings shot on location in Los Angeles. From 1997 to 2003, the television program *Buffy the Vampire Slayer* presented yet another version of the youth culture of Southern California. In these programs, Los Angeles English was even more central to the creativity of the series and its appeal. Script writers in their thirties and older were creating slang for high school students, and real high school students across the nation picked it up and used it. One of the writers, Jane Espenson, had studied metaphor in the graduate linguistics program at the University of California at Berkeley and thus was better prepared than the proponents of Valspeak to make complicated use of word and phrase-making in English (Adams 2003, vii–xii). Like all successful fabricators, she used familiar materials but deployed them in new ways. Blends are common in the *Buffyverse* (*Buffy* + *universe*), as are suffixes applied in novel ways: *angsty* 'depressing' (based on the root of *anguish*), *hotness* 'sexual attractiveness' (from *hot* + *ness*), *wiggage* 'confusion' (derived from *wig/wigged out* 'agitated'). The lexicographer of *Buffiness* believes that the innovation likely to endure from being made popular by the program is *much* 'often' as used to modify the previous word: "Morbid much?"; "Having issues much?" (Adams 2003).

The evolution of Los Angeles English from Gidget to Buffy shows, among other things, the expenditure of creative energy, not only in recording but also in inventing a part of the vernacular.

Los Angeles was also a major player in the "Summer of Love" in 1967, though the movement's epicenter was in San Francisco. A huge crowd assembled for a *be-in* in Griffith Park in July came to an unfortunate conclusion, captured in this headline: "Melee Erupts as Hells Angel Hits Officer at Hippie Love-in" (McCurdy and Houston 1967). Both *be-in* and *love-in* are first attested in 1967. They were formed on the pattern of *teach-in* (1965), a gathering for the earnest discussion of ideas. A sense of the language of this movement can be given in the following opening of a business story in the *Los Angeles Times*:

> Trade follows the fads. On the one hand stand the hippies, suppliers of psychedelic art, tribal crafts, drug religions, acid rock, love-ins, be-ins, underground newspapers and flowers. On the other hand stand the voracious teenyboppers, curious college kids, swinging singles, gimmicky housewives, and panicky over-30s, who fear that Life may be passing them by. The hippies are supplying something, the straight world is demanding something, and in the middle—guessing—stand a few fearless entrepreneurs. (Wilson 1968, B16)

The ensuing story explains the ways and wares of *head shops*, a term first attested in 1967. A rich vocabulary arose to capture the essence of this movement: *acid trip* (1966), *drop acid* (1966), *groupie* (1967), *hang loose* (1968), *hippiedom* (1967), *psychedelia* (1967), *roach clip* (1966), *Yippie* (< *hippie*, 1968), *bong* 'water pipe for marijuana' (1971). The era revived and adapted older vocabulary, some of it of limited use earlier: *far out*, *groovy*, *raunchy*. All of this "new" English was promptly publicized in popular music and film, so Los Angeles became, once again, the site of language innovation reaching an international audience.

At the same time, California became associated with the *New Age* movement in spirituality and various ego-centered psychological therapies. A California doctor published *I'm OK, You're OK* in 1969 with its emphasis on *Transactional Analysis*. Various treatment centers arose from the Esalen Institute in the north (the *Human Potential* movement) to the Center for Studies of the Person in the south (where *Optimal Development* was implemented). These efforts also produced vocabulary that became widely known beyond California: *bipolar disorder* (1973), *centered* 'self-assured' (1974), *co-dependent* (1979), *ego-trip* (1969), *get it together* (1970) and *get their shit together* (1976), *holistic medicine* (1960), *meaningful relationship* (1963). The expression *to lay a guilt trip on* seems to have arisen in 1978.

Another powerfully influential kind of English can be attributed to a Los Angeles teen, Raymond Washington. Like most Angelinos, he was a migrant—in this case from Texas. At age fifteen, he founded a street gang known as the *Baby Avenues* as homage to an established gang of older children, the *Avenue Boys*. Two years later, in 1971, the name of Washington's group shifted to the *Avenue Cribs*. (*Crib* 'dwelling, neighborhood' had a long history in criminal slang that emerged at the end of the eighteenth century in London.) With a contemporary, Washington expanded the gang and renamed it the *Westside Crips*, and the name was finally abbreviated as *Crips*.[2] Before Washington was murdered in 1979, the Crips became the overwhelmingly dominant gang in Los Angeles. In response to its growth, other gangs merged under the name *Bloods* (< *Blood* 'a young African American man'). Both emerged from territorial gangs on the south side of Los Angeles to become "money gangs" at war over control of the sale of illegal drugs. These struggles—called *gang-banging* (1969)—are given visual expression in the use of *colors* by the two gangs, blue for the Crips and red for the Bloods.

The Crips and the Bloods would be of no more than local interest if it were not for the fact that "franchises" of the two gangs spread across the country, influencing language in just the way that the dialect of beach culture grew and spread. One dance emerging in the 1970s was the *C-walk* (< *Crip Walk*), usually performed to the musical style that became known as *gangsta rap*. (*Gangsta* in this sense was first noticed in a song title by the performer Ice T in 1988. Another migrant to Los Angeles, Ice T grew up in New Jersey before moving to South Central at age thirteen.) From the *C-Walk* and *gangsta rap* emerged both musical styles and poetic forms including *hip-hop* and *rap*. Performers in these styles achieved widespread and national publicity, particularly the New York performer Tupac Shakur. Bad blood between artists on the two coasts culminated in the drive-by shooting death in Las Vegas of Shakur in 1996. Subsequently, *West Coast G-Funk* (< *gangsta funk*) came to dominate the national market for Los Angeles–based music with the evolution of *hip-hop* (an expression first recorded in New York in 1982).

Expressions associated with the Crips and the Bloods reached across American English to all racial groups: *boo* 'boyfriend or girlfriend' (1988), *dis* (< *disrespect*, 1980), *def* (< *definite*) 'excellent' (1979), *janky* (< ?) 'bad, untrustworthy' (1993), *jump in* 'initiation ceremony in which the candidate for membership is beaten senseless by the established members' (1990), *thugged out* (< *thug*) (1996), *wigger* or *wigga* 'white person who

---

2. The American yearning for etymology can be discerned in efforts to fabricate an origin for the name *Crip*. Some have attempted, unpersuasively, to link it to *cripple*. The *Los Angeles Times* speculated that the name derived from the habit of members of carrying canes or sticks. Expressing the long-cherished belief that words contain secret messages encoded in them, one gang participant declared that *Crip* was an acronym for "Community Revolutionary Inter-Party Service" (Jah and Shah'Keyah 1995, 329). Other similarly fantastic sources include *Cultural Revolution in Progress*, *Community Resources for an Independent People*, and *California Rebels in Power*.

adopts African-American styles and language, often in an exaggerated way' (1988).

The very first dictionaries to explain English words by English definitions were not the *hard-word* dictionaries of the early seventeenth century but collections of criminal slang, the first two of which appeared in England in the 1560s. Some of the expressions first found there persist in modern English—for instance *drawers* 'underpants' and *filch* 'steal.' These compilations of criminal slang show a fascination with new words; for instance, in the sixteenth century the glossarists recorded many words for *pickpocket*—among them *bung-nipper*, *diver*, and *operator*. The criminal world had an elaborate division of labor with such specialists as a *bulker* to jostle a passerby and a *file* to extract the valuable (Coleman 2004).

Los Angeles gangs are no different from their predecessors in articulating identity and social practice through English. In the subculture of *tagging*, a *crew* (itself a very old expression for a criminal gang) sets out to *kill a wall* by decorating it with *graffiti*. Various tools of the *tagging crew* have their own terminology: *stecko* (< a manufacturer of spray paint), *three-fingers* (< width of the sprayed line), *fat cap* (< wide spray nozzle). According to those who attempt to police *taggers*, the *crew* has a special fondness for initialisms: *CSU* 'can't stop us,' *JTB* 'just the best,' and *MWS* 'mobbing with style.' Though *tagging* has a long history, *writers* who produce *masterpieces* in the *sky* (< graffiti executed on particularly hard-to-reach locations) have identified themselves with hip-hop culture. Los Angeles taggers are not different from earlier criminal specialists; they are just like them in their use of language.

What makes the underworld of the Southland so interesting for a history of American English is that the traditional and local can become innovative and national through the power of Hollywood. White Supremacists in California prisons (and on the outside) have their own distinctive use of English. The vocabulary includes well-known racial and anti-Semitic slurs, a national day of founding (September 22), and an apocalyptic work of revelation, *The Turner Diaries* (1978). Just as taggers have enjoyed initialisms, so Supremacists admire *rhyming slang*. (*Rhyming slang* has its origins in mid-nineteenth-century London street life. It consists of a pair of words, the second of which rhymes with the word being encoded. So *have a butcher's* means 'have a look' from the rhyming pair *butcher's hook*.) Though in use in Australia and other places influenced by London English, there is little evidence that rhyming slang has ever been much used in America. Supremacists in Los Angeles employ *charles* 'chap-lain' (< *Charlie Chaplin*), *ocean* 'shave' (< *ocean wave*), *Ophelia* "snitch" (< *rat* < *Ophelia Pratt*), and *slay* 'Jew' (< *slay and slew*). Favored forms of physical assault include *boot party* in which the victim is kicked insensible or killed. This group also employs the expression *my braces are down by my side*. *Braces* 'suspenders' are symbolic garments among Supremacists; red ones symbolize that the wearer has drawn blood. (The terms in this and the previous paragraph come from Flores 1998.)

How was it that British terms (like *braces*) or London rhyming slang came into use among Supremacists in California? The answer lies in the popularity among them of Stanley Kubrick's film *A Clockwork Orange* (1971). Based on a novel by Anthony Burgess, *A Clockwork Orange* depicts futuristic street life in London with an elaborate slang used by the ultra-violent gang members who inhabit it. (Burgess called the fictional dialect *NADSAT* [< Russian *–teen*] and incorporated into it, among other things, rhyming slang.) Among Supremacists, *A Clockwork Orange* has become a cult film inspiring the use of braces and boots as symbolic gear and aspects of linguistic practice as symbolic of group membership.

Cult jargon is no different in the underworld than it is in the world of respectable business. While developments in computer science are associ-ated with companies northward of Los Angeles along the Pacific Coast, the transformation in communicative practices (and names employed in it) developed in Los Angeles when the System Development Corporation (SDC) was formed in Santa Monica in 1955. SDC was the first to develop *software*, a term attested in 1961. Locating expressions in this domain is difficult because, especially recently, terms are created and circulate in *vir-tual* reality—an electronic place with apparent but little actual physical reality. Given the speed at which new expressions are coined and circulate, one can only point to the kinds of word-forming techniques employed without finding it possible to determine with any precision where they come from: *time-sharing* (1953), *mainframe* (1964), *mouse* (1965), *fire-wall* (1974), *internet* (1974), *screen saver* (1982), *cookie* 'packet of data' (1987), *platform* (1987), *spam* (1993), *webcam* (1995). Some of these in-volve abbreviations of one sort or another: *browser* (< *browsing online with selective retrieval*) (1969), and *Fortran* (< *formula translation*) (1956). Most "new terms" have arisen as new senses of existing words; here is a selection from 1982–85: *click* (noun and verb), *desktop, drag, hotlink, laptop, note-book, screen saver*. The prefix *e-* has been especially productive in this domain: *e-book, e-commerce, e-credit, e-mail, e-text*.

Television and moviemaking contributed many new expressions to American English, and these became familiar far beyond Los Angeles. Blends were common: *docudrama < documentary + drama* (1961); *claymation < clay + animation* (1979); *infomercial < information + commercial* (1980). *CinemaScope* (1953) popularized the practice of using uppercase letters in the middle of words, later common in such names as *PowerPoint* (1987). Production techniques also contributed vocabulary that would become widely known: *zoom* (1948), *fade to black* (1956), *roll credits* (1989), *over-the-shoulder shot* (1993).

Entertainment, gangs, Valspeak, and surfer talk seldom made much of multilingualism in their linguistic creativity. Popular music only glancingly touched on it, for instance "Speak English or Die" (1985) with this arresting chorus:

> You always make us wait
> You're the ones we hate
> You can't communicate
> Speak English Or Die

Performed by a group called "Stormtroopers of Death," this song combines hard-core punk with thrash metal, and the album with the same title as the song sold more than a million copies. The performers claimed that they wanted to provoke angry responses, a rhetorical strategy common in popular music with alarmingly antifeminist and even racist overtones.

What has happened in Southern California (and elsewhere) is the rapid assimilation to English of most of the multilingual communities. Hispanics, the largest of these communities, increasingly find that children are only haltingly fluent in Spanish. As the linguist Allan Metcalf observed in the 1970s, increasing numbers of young people were developing "Chicano English," a dialect of English evolving in communities with increasing monolingualism (Metcalf 1979). The early speakers of the dialect did not know much Spanish, but their English dialect expressed solidarity with the Mexican American community. Still spoken today, Chicano English shows strong influences from African American English, and its speakers do not necessarily participate in the changes in English going on among their age-mates in the white community. For instance, among white youth the vowel of *boot* (and similar words) has moved toward the front of the mouth, making *boot* and *bit* near homophones; similarly, the vowel of *sing* may be sounded close to *seen*, and not, as elsewhere in American English, with the vowel of *sin*. In the Mexican community—*Mexican* is the preferred term in Los Angeles and comprehends American-born persons—boys and gang members do not participate in these changes, though women and upwardly mobile persons sometimes do (Fought 2003; Veatch 2005).

Code-switching—the practice of mixing languages in discourse—does not occur in Chicano English since a prerequisite of code-switching is bilingualism. Since the Chicano English speakers are generally monolingual, mixture seldom occurs. Others of the dozens of ethnic communities in Los Angeles make frequent use of code-switching. Here, for instance, is an example of *Vietglish* (< *Vietnamese* + *English*):

> "He nói với me, she thích you a lot."
> "Really, she là ai? Me không biết."
> Translation:
> "He said to me, she likes you a lot."
> "Really, she is? Me not know." (Thanh 2005)

As we have seen, code-switching of this kind can be found from the earliest days of American English. Most of it has no long-term effects on the state of the language, but it is a crucial part of multilingualism and of assimilation.

In their linguistically isolated world, whites became increasingly anxious about the future of English. Foreign languages (and unintelligible mixtures) seemed to be heard everywhere; schools all over the city enrolled students who spoke languages other than English in the home. Print and broadcast media were filled with unfamiliar voices. In 1981, California senator S. I. Hayakawa introduced a proposed English Language Amendment that would incorporate into the U.S. Constitution a provision to make English the "official language" of the country. If adopted, it would have limited education in other languages to transitional programs to encourage the use of English. Bilingual ballots would have been scrapped, and government services in foreign languages would have been curtailed or eliminated. Hearings on the proposal were held in 1984 with heated testimony on both sides (Hatch et al. 1984), and the Subcommittee on the Constitution concluded that the matter was best treated at the state level. Many states adopted statutes or amendments to their state constitutions, if they had not already done so, though many of them had mainly symbolic value with no specific provisions or penalties.

In California, however, matters were taken much more seriously. Most of the proponents of Hayakawa's amendment were based in California, and they made legislative efforts to limit the use of foreign languages in public life. In 1985, for instance, the city council of Monterey Park, a Los Angeles enclave, passed an ordinance making English the "official language" of the community. (The proposal was inspired by the immigration of Chinese people from Taiwan and China.) For the 1986 election, these ideologues put on the ballot Proposition 68, a constitutional amendment not only making English the official language of the state but also including provisions to allow anyone resident or doing business in the state to initiate a cause of action objecting to the use of languages other than English. Giving "standing," the legal term for the right to go to court, to such a broad population would allow persons who heard languages other than English used in a transaction in a store, for instance, to sue to prevent any repetition of that conversation. The campaign on behalf of Proposition 68 emphasized the idea that a single language was a unifying force and that to be an American was to use English in public life. The patriotic and symbolic values of the amendment persuaded many people that the proposal would benefit the community.

To the surprise of many, Proposition 68 passed overwhelmingly, 73 percent to 27 percent. Later surveys showed that the only demographic to oppose it were the highly educated, those holding graduate degrees (Dyste 1989). Others favored it, including those born in the United States and those born abroad, all racial categories, and all income levels. Conservatives were more likely to favor it than liberals; white people more than people of color. The well-attested fact that bilingual school programs produce higher test scores than monolingual English teaching—for both first- and second-language pupils—had little effect on the voting.

Proposition 68 seems not to have affected the linguistic ecology of Los Angeles. No lawsuits have been brought under its provisions, probably because proponents of English suspect that any such action would be thrown out on the basis of provisions of the U.S. Constitution. There is no evidence that it has had any effect on the rate of acquisition of English by those who speak other languages. Assimilation to English remains high, particularly if one tracks the language preferences of the very young. English, though frequently in a distinctive form like Chicano English, continues to consolidate and grow.

Nonetheless, the movement to enforce the use of English has not abated. On July 19, 1997, a full-page advertisement appeared in the *Los Angeles Times* with the headline "Reconquista: Mexico's Attempt to Annex the Southwest." (*Reconquista* was a term used in medieval Spain as part of the effort to expel Muslims.) The copy declared that there was a conspiracy to recapture political control of the regions that had been part of Mexico in the early nineteenth century: Arizona, portions of Texas, New Mexico, and much of California. The name for this region, the ad said, was *Aztlán*. The Reconquista movement should be resisted by Californians wishing to retain their freedom and their English. Anxieties about this supposed plot continue in the twenty-first century.

10 Epilogue

WHAT IS THE future of speaking American? Two things we can be sure of in speculating about what comes next.

First, all the ways we now think of as ways of speaking will change beyond recognition. None of the language varieties we have described is still in use. Valley Girl is gone; the dialects of the b'hoys and g'hals of mid-nineteenth-century New York are forgotten. The "Pilgrim" dialect of Plimoth Plantation, the New England theme park, is well intentioned but certainly unlike what the seventeenth-century Bostonians would have spoken.

Second, the new varieties of American English will be shaped from new materials, and they will not necessarily be specific to a time or place as in the past. People, especially young people, pick up voices where they find them, and now, with the Internet offering riches, the voices could be from almost anywhere.

The only way to be sure what will happen next is to wait and see.

References

Adams, Michael. 2003. *Slayer Slang: A Buffy the Vampire Slayer Lexicon*. New York: Oxford University Press.

Ade, George. 1903. *In Babel: Stories of Chicago*. New York: McClure, Phillips & Co.; Albany: J. Munsel.

Ade, George. 1972. *Fables inz Slang* (1899). [New York:] Westvaco Corporation.

Algren, Nelson. 1949. *The Man with the Golden Arm*. Garden City, NY: Doubleday.

Allen, L[ouis] L[eonidas]. 1848. *A Thrilling Sketch of the Life of the Distinguished Chief Okah Tubbee*. New York: [Cameron's Steam Power Presses].

Allen, Paula Gunn. 2003. *Pocahontas: Medicine Woman, Spy, Entrepreneur, Diplomat*. San Francisco: Harper-Collins.

Alleyne, Warren, and Henry Fraser. 1988. *The Barbados-Carolina Connection*. London: Macmillan Caribbean.

Allsopp, Richard. 1996. *Dictionary of Caribbean English Usage*. Oxford: Oxford University Press.

"An American." [1775?]. *The Yankies War Hoop*. London: G. King.

Anghiera, Pietro Martire d'. 1516. *De orbe nouo decades*. [Alcalá de Henares]: Arnaldi Guillelmi.

Arnold, Theodore. [1748.] *Grammatica Anglicana Concentrata*. Philadelphia: Gotthard Armbruster.

Axtell, James. 2001. "Babel of Tongues: Communicating with the Indians in Eastern North America." In Gray and Fiering, 15–60.

Babbitt, E. H. 1896. "The English Language of the Lower Classes in New York City and Vicinity." *Dialect Notes* 9:457–64.

Bailey, Richard W. 2003. *Rogue Scholar: The Sinister Life and Celebrated Death of Edward H. Rulloff.* Ann Arbor: University of Michigan Press.

Bailey, Richard W. 2006. "Standardizing the Heartland." In *Language Variation in the American Midwest,* ed. Thomas E. Murray and Beth Lee Simon, 165–78. Amsterdam: John Benjamins.

Baird, Keith E., and Mary A. Twining. 1991. "Names and Naming in the Sea Islands." In *Sea Island Roots: African Presence in the Carolinas and Georgia,* ed. Mary A. Twining and Keith E. Baird, 37–55. Trenton, NJ: African World Press. A slightly altered version of this essay appears in *The Crucible of Carolina: Essays in the Development of Gullah Language and Culture,* ed. Michael Montgomery (Athens: University of Georgia Press, 1994).

Baker, Benjamin A. 1848. *A Glance at New York.* New York: Samuel French.

Baldwin, Leland. D. 1941. *The Keelboat Age on Western Waters.* Pittsburgh: University of Pittsburgh Press.

Baranowski, Macier. 2007. *Phonological Variation and Change in the Dialect of Charleston, South Carolina.* Durham: Duke University Press for the American Dialect Society.

Bartlett, Helen. 1934. "Correct Use of Words Is major Etiquet [*sic*] Factor." *Chicago Tribune,* March 11, D6.

Bartlett, John Russell. 1859. *Dictionary of Americanisms.* Boston: Little, Brown.

Bartram, John. 1751. *Observations on the Inhabitants, Climate…and other Matters worthy of Notice.* London: J. Whiston and B. White.

Bellow, Saul. 1964. *Seize the Day* (1956). New York: Viking Press.

Best, Mark, Duncan B. Neuhauser, and Lee Slavin. 2004. "Cotton Mather, you dog, damn you! I'l inoculate you with this; with a pox on you": Smallpox Inoculation, Boston, 1721." *Quality and Safety in Health Care* 13:82–83. [The words in the title are not historically accurate.]

Bible, The. 1782. Philadelphia: Robert Aitken.

Bloomfield, Leonard. 1935. "The Stressed Vowels of American English." *Language* 11:97–116.

Boewe, Charles. 2000. "Henry Muhlenberg." *American Biography Online,* February. http://www.anb.org.proxy.lib.mich.edu/articles/13/13-0192.html.

Booker, Karen M., Charles M. Hudson, and Robert I. Rankin. 1992. "Place Name Identification and Multilingualism in the Sixteenth-Century Southeast." *Ethnohistory* 39:399–451.

Booth, Mary L. 1867. *History of the City of New York.* New York: W. R. C. Clark.

"Borealis." 1836. "English Language in America." *Southern Literary Messenger* 2:110–11.

Bötte, Gerd-J. 1989. *The First Century of German Language Printing in the United States of America.* 2 vols. Göttingen: Niedersächsische Staats- und Universitätsbibliothek.

Boyer, Paul, and Stephen Nissenbaum, eds. 1977. *The Salem Witchcraft Papers.* New York: Da Capo Press. http://etext.virginia.edu/salem/witchcraft/texts/transcripts.html (viewed March 2008).

Breslaw, Elaine G. 1996. *Tituba, Reluctant Witch of Salem.* New York: New York University Press.

Bright, William. 2004. *Native American Placenames of the United States.* Norman: University of Oklahoma Press.

Brinsley, John. 1622. *A Consolation for Our Grammar Schooles.* London: Printed by Richard Field for Thomas Man, dwelling in Pater noster Row, at the signe of the Talbot.

[Bristed, Charles Astor.] 1852. *The Upper Ten Thousand: Sketches of American Society.* London: J. W. Parker and Son.

Bristed, Charles Astor. 1855. "The English Language in America." In *Cambridge Essays, contributed by Members of the University,* 57–78. London: John W. Parker.

Brougham, John. [1855?]. *Po-ca-hon-tas*. New York: Samuel French.

Brown, Edward Monroe. 1916. *The Book of Boston*. Boston: Book of Boston Company.

Brown, Samuel R. 1817. *The Western Gazetteer; or Emigrant's Directory*. Auburn, NY: H. C. Southwick.

Browne, Junius Henri. 1868. *The Great Metropolis: A Mirror of New York*. Hartford: American Publishing Company.

Bryant, Cullen. 1941. "Dictionary of the New York Dialect of the English Tongue." *American Speech* 16:157–58.

Bryant, William Cullen. 1920. "Bryant's Index Expurgatorius" (ca. 1870). In *History of Journalism in the United States* by George Henry Payne, 386–87. New York: D. Appleton and Company.

Buck, Carl Darling. 1903. "A Sketch of the Linguistic Conditions of Chicago." In *The University of Chicago Decentennial Publications*, 1st series, 6:97–114.

Buntline, Ned [pseud. of Edward Zane Carroll Judson]. 1849. *The Mysteries and Miseries of New York: A Story of Real Life*. New York: Burgess & Garrett.

Buntline, Ned [pseud. of Edward Zane Carroll Judson]. 1850. *The G'hals of New York: A Novel*. New York: DeWitt and Davenport.

Burdett, James S. 1884. *Burdett's Negro Dialect Recitations and Readings*. New York: Excelsior Publishing House.

Burley, Dan. 1937. "Talkin' Out Loud." *Chicago Defender*, March 27, 14.

Burns, Walter Noble. 1931. *The One-Way Ride: The Red Trail of Chicago Gangland from Prohibition to Jake Lingle*. Garden City, NY: Doubleday, Doran & Company.

Cahan, Abraham. 1970. *Yekl and The Imported Bridegroom, and other Stories of the New York Ghetto* (1896). New York: Dover.

Campbell, Helen. 1895. *Darkness and Daylight; or, Lights and Shadows of New York Life*. Hartford: Hartford Publishing Company.

Carey, T. J. 1884. *Brudder Gardner's Stump Speeches and Comic Lectures*. New York: Excelsior Publishing House.

Carver, Craig M. 1987. *American Regional Dialects: A Word Geography*. Ann Arbor: University of Michigan Press.

Cassidy, Frederic G., and Joan Houston Hall. 1985–. *Dictionary of American Regional English*. 4 vols. to date. Cambridge, MA: Belknap Press of Harvard University Press.

Cassidy, Frederic G., and Robert B. LePage. 1980. *Dictionary of Jamaican English*. Cambridge: Cambridge University Press.

Cecil, Thomas. 1635. *A Relation of Maryland: Together, Vvith a Map of the Countrey, the Conditions of Plantation, His Majesties Charter to the Lord Baltimore, Translated Into English*. London.

Charles I. 1625. *A Proclamation for Settling the Plantation of Virginia*. London: Bonham Norton and Iohn Bull.

Chickering, Jesse. 1848. *Immigration into the United States*. Boston: Little and Brown.

Clark, Charles E. 1991. "Boston and the Nurturing of Newspapers: Dimensions of the Cradle, 1690–1741." *New England Quarterly* 64:243–71.

Cody, Sherwin. 1903. *The Art of Writing and Speaking the English Language*. Chicago: The Old Greek Press.

Coleman, Julie. 2004. *A History of Cant and Slang Dictionaries*. 2 vols. Oxford: Oxford University Press.

Coles, Felice Anne. 1997. "Solidarity Cues in New Orleans English." In *Language Variety in the South Revisited*, ed. Cynthia Bernstein, Thomas Nunnally, and Robin Sabino, 219–24. Tuscaloosa: University of Alabama Press.

Collymore, Frank. A. 1957. *A Glossary of Words and Phrases of the Barbadian Dialect*. Bridgetown: Barbados Advocate Company.

Cooper, George. 1891. *Cooper's Yankee, Italian and Hebrew Dialect Readings and Recitations*. New York: Wehman Bros.

Corey, Mary, and Victoria Westermark. 1982. *Fer Shurr! How to be a Valley Girl—Totally*. New York: Bantam.

Craigie, William A., and James R. Hulbert. 1938–44. A *Dictionary of American English on Historical Principles*. Chicago: University of Chicago Press.

Crane, Stephen. 1991. *Maggie: A Girl of the Streets* (1896). New York: Signet Classics.

Cresswell, Thomas J. 1985. "The Great Vowel Shift in Chicago." In *Festschrift in Honor of Virgil J. Vogel*, 176–89. DeKalb: Illinois Name Society.

Crété, Liliane. 1978. *Daily Life in Louisiana, 1815–1830*. Trans. Patrick Gregory. Baton Rouge: Louisiana State University Press.

Crystal, David. 2009. *Just a Phrase: My Life in Language*. New York: Routledge.

[Curry, Daniel.] 1853. *New-York: A Historical Sketch of the Rise and Progress of the Metropolitan City of America*. New-York: Carlton & Phillips.

Darby, William. 1817. *A Geographical Description of the State of Louisiana*. New York: James Olstead.

Davies, Mark. 2010–. The Corpus of Historical American English (COHA): 400+ million words, 1810–2009. Available online at http://corpus.byu.edu/coha (viewed September 30).

Debow, J. D. B. 1848. Review of Chickering 1848. *Debow's Review* (New Orleans). 5.3: 243–49.

DeCamp, David. 1967. "African Day-Names in Jamaica." *Language* 43:139–49.

Dillard, J. L. 1972. *Black English: Its History and Usage in the United States*. New York: Random House.

Doblin, Helga, and William A. Starna, trans. and eds. 1994. *The Journals of Christian Daniel Claus and Conrad Weiser: A Journey to Onondaga, 1750*. Philadelphia: American Philosophical Society.

Dolch, Edward W. 1935. *Building the Dictionary Habit: A Handbook of Teaching Helps*. Chicago: Scott, Foresman.

Dow, George F. 1911–78. *Records and Files of the Quarterly Courts of Essex County, Massachusetts*. Salem: Essex Institute.

Dreiser, Theodore. 1961. *Sister Carrie* (1900). New York: Signet.

Dreiser, Theodore. 1985. *Selected Magazine Articles of Theodore Dreiser: Life and Art in the American 1890s*. Ed. Yoshinobu Hakutani. Rutherford: Fairleigh Dickinson University Press.

Dreschsel, Emanuel J. 1997. *Mobilian Jargon: Linguistic and Sociohistorical Aspects of a Native American Pidgin*. Oxford: Clarendon Press.

Dubbs, Joseph Henry. 1903. *History of Franklin and Marshall College*. Lancaster: Franklin and Marshall Alumni Association.

Duden, Gottfried. 1980. *Report on a Journey to the Western States of North America*. Trans. James W. Goodrich et al. Columbia: State Historical Society of Missouri.

Dunaway, Wayland F. 1944. *The Scotch-Irish of Colonial Pennsylvania*. Chapel Hill: University of North Carolina Press.

Dunne, Finley Peter. 1913. "Mr. Dooley on Slang." *Kansas City Star*, August 3, 7C.

Dwight, Margaret Van Horn. 1991. *A Journey to Ohio in 1810, as Recorded in the Journal of Margaret Van Horn Dwight*. Ed. Max Farrand. Lincoln: University of Nebraska Press.

Dyste, Connie. 1989. "Proposition 63: The California English Language Amendment." *Applied Linguistics* 10:313–30.

Easterby, J. H., ed. 1958. *The Journal of the Commons House of Assembly, September 10, 1746–June 13, 1747*. Columbia: South Carolina Archives Department.

Eden, Richard, trans. 1555. *The Decades of the New Worlde or West India*. London: Guilhelmi Powell.

Edgar, Walter. 1998. *South Carolina: A History*. Columbia: University of South Carolina Press.

Eggleston, Edward. 1871. *The Hoosier Schoolmaster*. New York: O. Judd.

Eliot, John. 1660. *A Further Account of the Progress of the Gospel amongst the Indians in New England*. London: John Macock.

Elliott, Nancy C. 2000. "A Sociolinguistic Study of Rhoticity in American Film Speech from the 1930s to the 1970s." Ph.D. dissertation, Indiana University.

Everett, Edward. 1825. *An Oration Delivered at Concord, April the Nineteenth 1825*. Boston: Cummings, Hilliard and Company.

Faithful Picture of the Political Situation in New Orleans: At the Close of the Last and the Beginning of the Present Year, 1807. 1809. Boston: Reprinted from the New-Orleans Edition.

Farrell, James T. 1993. *Studs Lonigan* (1932–35). Urbana: University of Illinois Press.

Flores, Russell D. 1998. *Gang Slanging: A Collection of Words and Phrases Used by Gang Members*. San Clemente, CA: LawTech Publishing.

Fogelman, Aaron Spencer. 1996. *Hopeful Journeys: German Immigration, Settlement, and Political Culture in Colonial America, 1717–1775*. Philadelphia: University of Pennsylvania Press.

Foley, William E. 1989. *The Genesis of Missouri: From Wilderness Outpost to Statehood*. Columbia: University of Missouri Press.

Forde, C. Daryll. 1956. *Efik Traders of Old Calabar: The Diary of Antera Duke*. London: Oxford University Press.

Forney, John W. 1873–81. *Anecdotes of Public Men*. 2 vols. New York: Harper & Brothers.

[Foster, George G.] 1849. *New York in Slices*. New York: W. F. Burgess.

Fought, Carmen. 2003. *Chicano English in Context*. New York: Palgrave Macmillan.

Franklin, Benjamin. 1755. "Observations concerning the Increase of Mankind, Peopling of Countries, &c." *Gentleman's Magazine* 25:483–85.

Fraser, Timothy C. 1996. "The Dialects of the Middle West." In *Focus on the U. S. A.*, ed. Edgar W. Schneider, 81–102. Amsterdam: John Benjamins.

Friebert, Stuart, and David Young, eds. 1995. *Models of the Universe: An Anthology of the Prose Poem*. Oberlin: Oberlin College Press.

Garden, Alexander, and Thomas Fleet. 1741. *Regeneration, And the Testimony of the Spirit: Being the Substance of Two Sermons Lately Preached In the Parish Church of St. Philip, Charles-town, In South-Carolina*. Boston: re-printed by Tho. Fleet.

Garland, Hamlin. 1894. *Crumbling Idols*. Chicago: Stone and Kimball.

Germantown Academy. 1760. *Certain Agreements and Concessions...for Erecting and Establishing a School House and School in Germantown*. Germantown: Christopher Saur.

Gill, Alexander. 1972. *Logonomia Anglica* (1619). Ed. Bror Danielsson and Arvid Gabrielson. 2 vols. Stockholm: Anmqvist & Wiksel.

Glass, Lillian, with Richard Liebmann-Smith. 1982. *How to Deprogram Your Valley Girl.* New York: Workman Publishing.

Goddard, Ives. 1977. "Some Early Examples of American Indian Pidgin English from New England." *International Journal of American Linguistics* 43:37–41.

Goddard, Ives. 1988. "David Zeisberger." In *Handbook of North American Indians,* ed. Wilcumb E. Washburn, 4:698–99. Washington, DC: Smithsonian Institution.

Goddard, Ives. 1994. "Two Mashpee Petitions from 1752 (in Massachusett) and 1753 (in English)." In *American Indian Linguistics and Ethnography in Honor of Laurence C. Thompson,* 397–416. Missoula: University of Montana.

Goddard, Ives. 1997. "The True History of the Word *Squaw.*" http://www.nmnh.si.edu/anthro/goddard/ (viewed May 2006).

Goddard, Ives. 2001. "The Use of Pidgins and Creoles on the East Coast of North American." In Gray and Fiering, 61–73.

Goddard, Ives, and Kathleen J. Bragdon, eds. 1988. *Native Writings in Massachusett.* 2 vols. Philadelphia: Memoirs of the American Philosophical Society.

Gookin, Daniel. 1792. *Historical Collections of the Indians in New England.* Boston: Belknap and Hall.

Gray, Edward G., and Norman Fiering, eds. 2001. *The Language Encounter in the Americas, 1492–1800.* New York: Berghahn Books.

Grovinius, Johannes Fredericus, and John Clayton. 1739. *Flora Virginica, Exhibens Plantas.* Leiden: Lugduni Batavorum.

Grossman, James R., Ann Durkin Keating, and Janice L. Reiff, eds. 2004. *Encyclopedia of Chicago.* Chicago: University of Chicago Press.

Grund, Peter. 2007. "From Tongue to Text: The Transmission of the Salem Witchcraft Examination Records." *American Speech* 82:119–50.

Grund, Peter, Marja Kytö, and Matti Rissanen. 2004. "Editing the Salem Witchcraft Records: An Exploration of a Linguistic Treasury." *American Speech* 79:146–66.

Hagy, James William. 1993. *This Happy Land: The Jews of Colonial and Antebellum Charleston.* Tuscaloosa: University of Alabama Press.

[Hamilton, Thomas.] 1833. *Men and Manners in America.* Philadelphia: Carey, Lea & Blanchard.

Hamor, Ralph. 1615. *A True Discourse of the Present Estate of Virginia.* London: Iohn Beale.

Hannibal, Julius Caesar [pseud. of William H. Levinson]. 1857. *Black Diamonds.* New York: A. Ranney.

Harriot, Thomas. 1590. *A Brief and True Report of the New Found Land of Virginia.* 2nd ed. London: [Robinson].

Hartwell, E. E. 1942. "Middle Western Speech." *Chicago Daily Tribune,* December 20, 16.

Hatch, Orrin G., et al. 1986. The English Language Amendment (S. J. Res. 187), June 12, 1984. Washington, DC: Government Printing Office.

Hatcher, John. 1977. *Plague, Population, and the English Economy, 1348–1530.* London: Macmillan.

Heckewelder, J. G. E. 1820. *A Narrative of the Mission of the United Brethren among the Delaware and Mohegan Indians.* Philadelphia: McCarty and Davis.

Hiestand, Sarah Willard. 1906. "Slovenly Speaking of English." *The Nation,* January 25, 72–73.

Hobbs, Robert L. 1986. *Teach Yourself Transatlantic: Theatre Speech for Actors.* Palo Alto: Mayfield Publishing Company.

Holley, Horace. 1818. ALS to Mary Austin Holley (March 6). Unpublished letter held by the Clements Library, University of Michigan (Holley Papers 12).

Holloway, Charles. 1997. "Loss of Linguistic and Cultural Awareness among Speakers of a Dying Spanish Dialect." *Hispanic Linguistics* 9:203–21.

Holloway, Joseph E., and Winifred K. Vasa. 1993. *The African Heritage of American English.* Bloomington: Indiana University Press.

Hooker, Edward. 1897. *Diary of Edward Hooker, 1805–1808.* Ed. J. Franklin Jameson. Annual Report of the American Historical Association for the Year. Washington, DC: Government Printing Office.

Horn, James. 1994. *Adapting to a New World: English Society in the Seventeenth-Century Chesapeake.* Chapel Hill: University of North Carolina Press.

Howells, William Dean. 1896. "New York Low Life in Fiction." *New York World*, July 25, 19.

Howells, William Dean. 1906. "Our Daily Speech." *Harper's Bazaar*, January, 930–34.

Hughes, Griffith. 1750. *The Natural History of Barbados.* London: By the Author.

Humphreys, David. 1730. *An Historical Account of the Incorporated Society for the Propagation of the Gospel in Foreign Parts.* London: Joseph Downing.

Humphreys, David. 1815. *The Yankey in England: A Drama in Five Acts.* Boston: n.p.

Hutchins, Joseph. 1806. *A Sermon Preached… on the Opening of Franklin College.* Philadelphia: Daniel Humphries.

[Ingraham, Joseph H.] 1835. *The Southwest.* 2 vols. New York: Harper.

Jah, Yusuf, and Sister Shah'Keyah. 1995. *Uprising: Crips and Bloods Tell the Story of America's Youth in the Crossfire.* New York: Scribner.

James, Henry. 1906–7. "The Speech of American Women." *Harper's Bazaar* 40:979–82, 1003–6; 41:17–21, 113–17.

Johnson, George Lloyd. 1997. *The Frontier in the Colonial South: South Carolina Backcountry, 1736–1800.* Westport, CT: Greenwood.

Johnston, Gideon. 1946. *Carolina Chronicle: The Papers of Commissary Gideon Johnston, 1707–1716.* Berkeley and Los Angeles: University of California Press.

Jones-Jackson, Patricia. 1987. *When Roots Die: Endangered Traditions in the Sea Islands.* Athens: University of Georgia Press.

Jortner, Maura. 2005. "Playing 'America' on Nineteenth-Century Stages; or, Jonathan in England and Jonathan at Home." Ph.D. dissertation, University of Pittsburgh.

Joynes, Edward S. 1887. "Discussion: 'Charleston's Provincialisms.'" *PMLA* 3:xix–xx.

Kalm, Peter. 1964. *Peter Kalm's Travels in North America: The English Version of 1770.* Rev. Adolph B. Benson (1934). New York: Dover Publications.

Kamensky, Jane. 1997. *Governing the Tongue: The Politics of Speech in Early New England.* New York: Oxford University Press.

Kautzsch, Alexander. 2002. *The Historical Evolution of Early African American English: An Empirical Comparison of Early Sources.* Berlin: Mouton de Gruyter.

Kingsbury, Susan Myra, ed. 1906. *The Records of the Virginia Company of London.* Washington, DC: Government Printing Office.

Kliger, Hannah, and Rakhmiel Peltz. 2002. "Yiddish in New York." In *The Multilingual Apple: Languages in New York City*, ed. Ofelia García and Joshua A. Fishman, 93–116. Berlin: Mouton de Gruyter.

[Knight, Henry C.] 1824. *Letters from the South and West; by Arthur Singleton, Esq.* Boston: Richardson and Lord.

Knight, Sarah Kemble. 1992. *The Journal of Madame Knight.* Ed. George Parker Winship (1920). Bedford, MA: Applewood Press.

Knox, E. V. 1930. "Cinema English." *Living Age* 338 (April 1): 187–89.

Krapp, George Philip. 1919. *The Pronunciation of Standard English in America.* New York: Oxford University Press.

Krapp, George Philip. 1960. *The English Language in America* (1925). 2 vols. New York: Frederick Ungar.

Kretzschmar, William A.. Jr., Virginia G. McDavid, Theodore K. Lerud, and Ellen Johnson. 1993. *Handbook of the Linguistic Atlas of the Middle and South Atlantic States.* Chicago: University of Chicago Press.

Kupperman, Karen Orndahl. 2000. *Indians & English: Facing Off in Early America.* Ithaca: Cornell University Press.

Kupperman, Karen Orndahl. 2004. "Alexander Whitaker (1585–1617)." In Matthew and Harrison.

Kurath, Hans. 1949. *A Word Geography of the Eastern United States.* Ann Arbor: University of Michigan Press.

Kurath, Hans, and Guy S. Lowman, Jr. 1970. *The Dialectal Structure of Southern England: Phonological Evidence.* University: University of Alabama Press.

Kurath, Hans, and Raven I. McDavid, Jr. 1961. *The Pronunciation of English in the Atlantic States.* Ann Arbor: University of Michigan Press.

Kytö, Merja. 2004. "The Emergence of American English: Evidence from Seventeenth-Century Records in New England." In *Legacies of Colonial English: Studies in Transported Dialects,* ed. Raymond Hickey, 121–57. Cambridge: Cambridge University Press.

Labbé, Dolores Egger. 1998. "'The Encouragement of Foreigners': A Multicultural Population in a New Land." In *The Louisiana Purchase and Its Aftermath, 1800–1830,* ed. Dolores Egger Labbé, 537–46. Lafayette: Center for Louisiana Studies, University of Southwestern Louisiana.

Labov, William. 1966. *The Social Stratification of English in New York City.* Washington, DC: Center for Applied Linguistics.

Lane, Andrew, and Wayne Crawford. 1982. "Valley Girl." Revised draft. Los Angeles: Valley 9000 Prod. Co. Unpublished typescript, Margaret Herrick Library, Academy of Motion Picture Arts and Sciences, Beverly Hills.

Lardner, Ring. 1916. *You Know Me Al: A Busher's Letters.* New York: Charles Scribner's Sons.

Larsen, Cedric. 1937. "The Drinkers Dictionary." *American Speech* 12:87–92.

Lass, Roger. 1999. "Phonology and Morphology." In *The Cambridge History of the English Language,* ed. Roger Lass, 56–186. Cambridge: Cambridge University Press.

Latrobe, Benjamin Henry Boneval. 1951. *Impressions Respecting New Orleans: Diaries and Sketches, 1818–1820.* Ed. Samuel Wilson, Jr. New York: Columbia University Press.

Laurens, Henry. 1968–2003. *The Papers of Henry Laurens.* Ed. Philip M. Hamer. 16 vols. Columbia: South Carolina Historical Society.

Le Jau, Frances. 1956. *Carolina Chronicle, 1706–1717.* Ed. Frank J. Klinkberg. Berkeley: University of California Press.

[Leacock, John.] 1776. *The Fall of British Tyranny.* Philadelphia: Stykner and Cist.

Lee, David S. 1999. "Lutheran Clergymen, German Patriots, Twenty Sedges, a Pennsylvania College, a Yellow Oak, and a Small Turtle: What's in a Name?" *Bulletin of the Chicago Herpetological Society* 24:25–31.

Legaré, Hugh Swinton, and Mary Swinton Legaré Bullen. 1846. *Writings of Hugh Swinton Legaré.* Charleston: Burges & James.

Lepore, Jill. 1994. "Dead Men Tell No Tales: John Sassamon and the Fatal Consequences of Literacy." *American Quarterly* 46.4:479-512.

Lewis, Calvin Leslie. 1916. *A Handbook of American Speech.* Chicago: Scott Foresman and Co.

Lighter, Jonathan E. 1994–. *Historical Dictionary of American Slang.* New York: Random House.

Lippi-Green, Rosina. 1997. *English with an Accent: Language, Ideology, and Discrimination in the United States.* New York: Routledge.

Lipski, John M. 1990. *The Language of the "Isleños": Vestigial Spanish in Louisiana.* Baton Rouge: Louisiana State University Press.

"Lithuanian Girls of Chicago." 1908. *Chicago Daily Tribune,* March 8, F1.

Littlefield, Daniel F., Jr. 1988. *The Life of Ohah Tubbe.* Lincoln: University of Nebraska Press.

[Littleton, Edward]. 1689. *The Groans of the Plantations; or, a True Account of their Grievous and Extreme Sufferings by the Heavy Imposition upon Sugar.* London: M. Clark.

Lockridge, Kenneth A. 1981. "Literacy in Early America, 1650–1800." In *Literacy and Social Development in the West: A Reader,* ed. Harvey J. Graff, 183–200. Cambridge: Cambridge University Press.

Logan, James. 1838. *Notes of A Journey through Canada, the United States of America, and the West Indies.* Edinburgh: Fraser and Co.

Long, John. 1791. *Voyages and Travels of an Indian Interpreter and Trader.* London: printed for the author.

Loomis, Frank D. 1920. *Americanization in Chicago: A Report of a Survey.* Chicago: Chicago Community Trust.

Los Angeles 2000 Committee. 1988. *LA 2000: A City for the Future.* Los Angeles: Los Angeles 2000 Committee.

Macafee, C. I., ed. 1996. *A Concise Ulster Dictionary.* Oxford: Oxford University Press.

Marryat, Frederick. 1839. *A Diary in America, with Remarks on Its Institutions.* London: Longman, Orme, Brown, Green & Longmans.

Martineau, Harriet. 2000. *Retrospect of Western Travel* (1838). Ed. Daniel Feller. Armonk, NY: M. E. Sharpe.

Mather, Cotton. 1721. *Some Account of What is Said of Inoculating or Transplanting the Small-Pox.* Boston: Zabdiel Boylston.

Mather, Cotton. 1972. *The Angel of Bethesda.* Ed. Gordon W. Jones. Barre, MA: American Antiquarian Society.

Mathews, M. M. 1926. "Humphrey's Glossary." *Dialect Notes* 5.9: 375–82.

Matsell, George W. 1859. *Vocabulum; or, the Rogue's Lexicon.* New York: G. W. Matsell & Co.

Matthew, H. C. G., and Brian Harrison, eds. 2004. *The Oxford Dictionary of National Biography.* Oxford: Oxford University Press.

Maurer, David W. 1940. *The Big Con: The Story of the Confidence Man.* Indianapolis: Bobbs-Merrill.

McCurdy, Jack, and Paul Houston. 1967. "Melee Erupts as Hells Angel Hits Officer at Hippie Love-in." *Los Angeles Times,* July 24, 1.

McDavid, Raven I., Jr. 1979. "The Position of the Charleston Dialect" (1955). In *Dialects in Culture: Essays in General Dialectology,* ed. William A. Kretzschmar, 272–87. University: University of Alabama Press.

McDavid, Raven I., Jr., and Theodore Lerud. 1984. "German Relics in the English of South Carolina." In *Dialectology, Linguistics, Literature: Festschrift for Carroll E. Reed*, ed. Wolfgang W. Moelleken, 133–49. Göttingen: Kümmerle Verlag.

McDowell, W. L. 1955. *Journals of the Commissioners of the Indian Trade, September 20, 1710– August 29, 1718*. Columbia: South Carolina Archives Department.

McFarlane, Anthony. 1992. *The British in the Americas, 1480–1815*. London: Longman.

Meaders, Daniel. 1993. *Eighteenth-Century White Slaves: Fugitive Notices*. Westport, CT: Greenwood Press.

Mereness, Newton D., ed. 1916. *Travels in the American Colonies*. New York: Macmillan.

Message from the President of the United States, Transmitting a Report of the Secretary of State. 1811. February 5. Washington, DC: R. C. Weightman.

Metcalf, Alan A. 1979. *Chicano English*. Arlington, VA: Center for Applied Linguistics.

Molina, Alonso. 1555. *Aqui Comiença un Vocabulario en la Lengua Castellana y Mexicana*. Mexico City: Juan Pablos.

Molina, Alonso. 1880. *Vocabulario de la Lengua Mexicana* (1571). Facsimile ed. Leipzig: Teubner.

Monroe, B. S. 1896. "The Pronunciation of English in the State of New York." *Dialect Notes* 1:445–46.

Morel, John. 1771. "A Letter on the Expressing of a Fine Oil from Bene." *Transactions of the American Philosophical Society* 1:239–40.

Morton, Thomas. 2000. *New English Canaan by Thomas Morton of "Merrymount": Text and Notes* (1637). Ed. Jack Dempsey. Scituate, MA: Digital Scanning.

Muhlenberg, Gotthilf Heinrich Ernst (= Henry). 1784–1813. Writings on Botany and Natural History. . Mss.580.M89.xxx. American Philosophical Library, Philadelphia.

Muhlenberg, Henry, and Benedict J. Schipper. 1812. *English-German & German English Dictionary*. Lancaster: William Hamilton.

[Murdoch, John.] 1795. *The Triumphs of Love; or, Happy Reconciliation*. Philadelphia: R. Folwell.

[Nairne, Thomas.] 1710. *A Letter from South Carolina*. London: A. Baldwin.

Nairne, Thomas. 1988. *Nairne's Muskhogean Journals: The 1708 Expedition to the Mississippi River*. Jackson: University Press of Mississippi.

Nash, Gary B. 2002. *First City: Philadelphia and the Forging of Historical Memory*. Philadelphia: University of Pennsylvania Press.

Nichols, Thomas L. 1844. *Forty Years of American Life*. 2 vols. London: John Maxwell and Company.

[Norman, Benjamin Moore.] 1845. *Norman's New Orleans and Environs*. New Orleans: B. M. Norman.

Nützliche Anweisung oder Beyhülfe vor de Teutschen um Englishc zu lernen. 1751. Philadelphia: Christoph Saur.

"Observations in Several Voyages and Travels in America." 1746. *London Magazine* 15:321–30.

Official Book of the Fair. 1932. Chicago: Century of Progress, Inc.

Ondaatje, Michael. 2002. *The Conversations: Walter Murch and the Art of Editing Film* (1997). New York: Borzoi Books.

Orbeck, Anders. 1927. *Early New England Pronunciation*. Ann Arbor: George Wahr.

Oxford English Dictionary, 3rd online ed. 2000–. Oxford: Oxford University Press. www.oed.com.

Over 1000 *Mistakes Corrected*. 1856. New York: Garrett & Company.

Peck, George W. 1883. *Peck's Bad Boy and His Pa*. Chicago: Belford, Clarke & Co.

Pederson, Lee A. 1964. "Terms of Abuse for Some Chicago Social Groups." *Publication of the American Dialect Society* 42:26–48.

Pederson, Lee A. 1971a. "An Approach to Urban Word Geography." *American Speech* 46:73–68.

Pederson, Lee A. 1971b. "Chicago Words: The Regional Vocabulary." *American Speech* 46:163–92.

A Perfect Description of Virginia. 1649. London: Richard Wodenoth.

Perkins, Benjamin. 1806. *A Letter to a Friend in London: On Certain Improprieties of Expression used by some of the Society of Friends*. [Philadelphia]: Kimber, Konrad and Co.

Phyfe, W. H. P. 1905. *Ten Thousand Words often Mispronounced*. New York: G. P. Putnam's Sons.

Pinckney, Eliza Lucas. 1972. *The Letterbook of Eliza Lucas Pinckney, 1739–1762*. Ed. Elise Pinckney. Chapel Hill: University of North Carolina Press.

Pitot, James. 1979. *Observations on the Colony of Louisiana from 1796 to 1802*. Trans. Henry C. Pitot. Baton Rouge: Louisiana State University Press.

Pond, Mimi. 1982. *The Valley Girls' Guide to Life*. New York: Dell.

Posserello, Jodie Ann. 1982. *The Totally Awesome Val Guide*. Los Angeles: Price/Stern/Sloan.

[Pöstl, Karl Anton.] 1828. *The Americans as They Are; Described in A Tour through the Valley of the Mississippi*. London: Hurst, Chance and Co.

Preston, Dennis R. 2004. "Language Attitudes to Speech." In *Language in the USA: Themes for the Twenty-first Century*, ed. Edward Finegan and John R. Rickford, 480–92. Cambridge: Cambridge University Press.

Primer, Sylvester. 1887. "Charleston Provincialisms." *PMLA* 3:84–99.

Primer, Sylvester. 1889. "The Huguenot Element in Charleston's Pronunciation." *PMLA* 4:214–44.

R. W. 1936. "Pronunciation." *Chicago Daily Tribune*, January 11, 12.

Ralph, Julian. 1897. "The Language of Tenement Folk." *Harper's Weekly*, January 23, 90.

Ranney, H. M. 1849. *An Account of the Terrific and Fatal Riot at the New York Astor Place Opera House*. New York: H. M. Ranney.

Rawson, Edward, ed. 1660. *The Book of the General Lavves and Libertyes concerning the Inhabitants of Massachusetts*. Boston: Samuel Green.

Rawson, Edward, ed. 1672. *The General Laws and Liberties of the Massachusetts Colony*. Boston: John Usher.

Read, Allen Walker. 1934. "The Philological Society of New York." *American Speech* 9:131–36.

Read, Allen Walker. 1939. "The Speech of Negroes in Colonial America." *Journal of Negro History* 24:247–58.

Read, Allen Walker. 2002. *Milestones in the History of English in America*. Durham: Duke University Press.

A Relation of Maryland. 1635. London: William Peasley.

Rieff, David. 1991. *Los Angeles: Capital of the Third World*. New York: Simon & Schuster.

Robbins, Katharine Knowles. 1918. "The Work of the American Speech Committee of the Chicago Woman's Club and Notes upon Its School Survey." *English Journal* 7:163–76.

Robin, Claude-Charles. 1807. *Voyages dans l'intérieur de la Louisiane, de la Floride occidentale, et dans les isles de la Martinque et Saint-Domingue*. Paris: F. Buisson.

Rockefeller, John D. 1913. *Random Reminiscences of Men And Events*. Garden City, NY: Doubleday.

Rogers, George C., Jr., and C. James Taylor. 1994. *A South Carolina Chronology*. Columbia: University of South Carolina Press.

Rosenthal, Bernard, et al. 2008. *Records of the Salem Witch Hunt*. Cambridge: Cambridge University Press.

Rountree, Helen C. 2005. *Pocahontas, Powhatan, Opechancanough: Three Indian Lives Changed by Jamestown*. Charlottesville: University of Virginia Press.

Rush, Benjamin, and I. Daniel Rupp. 1875. *An Account of the Manners of the German Inhabitants of Pennsylvania*. Philadelphia: S. P. Town.

Salmon, Vivian. 1996. *Language and Society in Early Modern England*. Amsterdam: John Benjamins.

Sammon, Paul M. 1996. *Future Noir: The Making of "Blade Runner"*. New York: Harper Prism.

Schele de Vere, Maximilian. 1872. *Americanisms: The English of the New World*. New York: Charles Scribner and Company.

Schepp, James W. 1894. *Shepp's New York City Illustrated*. Chicago: Globe Bible Publishing Company.

Schöpf, Johann David. 1787. *Materia Medica Americana*. Erlangae: Palmii.

Schultz, John A. 2000. "Thomas Mayhew, Jr." In *American National Biography*. New York: Oxford University Press.

Scott, Fred Newton. 1909. "What the West Wants in Preparatory English." *School Review* 17:10–20.

Scott, Fred Newton. 1926. *The Standard of American Speech and Other Papers*. Boston: Allyn and Bacon.

Scott, Fred Newton, and Gertrude Buck. 1907. *A Brief English Grammar*. Chicago: Scott, Foresman and Co.

Shurtleff, Nathaniel, ed. 1855. *Records of the Colony of New Plymouth in New England*. Boston: William White.

Sinclair, Upton. 2003. *The Jungle*. Ed. Clare Virginia Eby. New York: Norton.

Slave Narratives. 2000. Selected and with notes by William L. Andrews and Henry Louis Gates, Jr. New York: Library of America.

Sloan, Hans. 1707–25. *A Voyage to the Islands Madera, Barbados, Nieves, St. Christophers, and Jamaica*. London: Printed by B. M. for the Author.

Smith, Dwight L., ed. 1958. "Nine Letters of Nathaniel Dike on the Western Country, 1816–1818." *Ohio Historical Quarterly* 67:189–220.

Smith, John. 1612. *A Map of Virginia*. Oxford: Joseph Barnes.

Smith, John. 1624. *A Generall Historie of Virginia*. London: Michael Sparkes.

Smith, John. 1986. *The Complete Works of Captain John Smith (1580–1631)*. Ed. Philip L. Barbour. 3 vols. Chapel Hill: University of North Carolina Press.

Smith, Mark Hale. 1868. *Sunshine and Shadow in New York*. Hartford: J. B. Burr.

St. George, Robert. 1984. "'Heated' Speech and Literacy in Seventeenth-Century New England." In *Seventeenth-Century New England*, ed. David D. Hall and David Grayson Allen, 275–322. Boston: Colonial Society of Massachusetts.

Standley, Fred S. 2000. "Hiacoomes." In *American National Biography*. New York: Oxford University Press.

Stone, William L. 1865. *The Life and Times of Sir William Johnson, Bart*. 2 vols. Albany: J. Munsell.

Strachey, William. 1999. *A Dictionary of Powatan* (1849). Southampton, PA: Evolution Publishing.

Studer, Gerald C. 1967. *Christopher Dock: Colonial Schoolmaster.* Scottdale, PA: Herald Press.

Sullivan, Joseph M. 1908. *Criminal Slang.* Boston: Wayland D. Russell; Chicago: Detective Publishing Company.

Sutherland, Edward. 1965. *The Professional Thief* (1937). Chicago: University of Chicago Press.

[Sutterfield, L. H.] 1945. *A Leter by Dr. Benjamin Rush, Describing the Consecration of the German College at Lancaster in June* 1787. Lancaster: Franklin and Marshall College.

Sypherd, Wilbur Owen. 1913. *A Handbook of English for Engineers.* Chicago: Scott Foresman and Co.

Tabbert, Russell. 1991. *A Dictionary of Alaskan English.* Juneau: Denali Press.

Thanh, Nguyan Nhon. 2005. "What are you speaking? Hey, it's just Vietglish." April 29. http://www.nguoi-viet.com/absolutenm/anmviewer.asp?a=22829&z=47 (viewed September 2010).

Thomas, Philip Drennon. 1999. "John Bartram." In *American National Biography*, ed. John A. Garraty and Mark C. Carnes, 2:296–97. New York: Oxford University Press.

Thorndike, Edward L. 1935. *The Thorndike-Century Junior Dictionary.* Chicago: Scott, Foresman.

Thorowgood, Thomas. 1650. *Ievves in America, or, Probabilities that the Americans are of that Race.* London: W. H. for Thomas Slater.

Thrasher, Frederic M. 1963. *The Gang: A Study of 1,313 Gangs in Chicago* (1927). Abridged ed. Chicago: University of Chicago Press.

Tilton, Robert S. 2004. "John Rolfe (1585–1622)." In Matthew and Harrison.

"Titles of Office, Rank, Respect." 1865. *Godey's Lady's Book* 70 (March): 276.

Tocqueville, Alexis de. 2000. *Democracy in America.* Trans. Harvey C. Mansfield and Delba Winthrop. Chicago: University of Chicago Press.

Tregle, Joseph. G. 1999. *Louisiana in the Age of Jackson: A Clash of Cultures and Personalities.* Baton Rouge: Louisiana State University Press.

Trollope, Frances. 1832. *Domestic Manners of the Americans.* London: Whittaker, Treacher, & Co.

Trollope, Frances. 1984. *Domestic Manners of the Americans* (1839). London: Century Publishing.

Trumbull, J. Hammond, ed. 1850. *The Public Records of Connecticut.* Hartford: Brown & Parsons.

Tryon, Thomas. [1684]. *Friendly Advice to the Gentlemen Planters in the East and West Indies.* London: A. Sowle.

Turner, Lorenzo Dow. 1974. *Africanisms in the Gullah Dialect* (1949). Ann Arbor: University of Michigan Press.

Ullman, Sharon R. 1995. "'The Twentieth Century Way': Female Impersonation and Sexual Practice in Turn-of-the-Century America." *Journal of the History of Sexuality* 5:573–600.

Vaughan, Alden T. 2004. "Pocahontas (c1596–1617)." In Matthew and Harrison.

Veatch, Thomas. 2005. *Los Angeles Chicano English.* http://tomveatch.com/Veatch1991/node111.html (viewed September 2010).

Verhoeven, W. M. 2005. "'A Colony of *Aliens*': Germans and the German-Language Press in Colonial and Revolutionary America." In *Periodical Literature in Eighteenth-Century America*, ed. Mark L. Kamrath and Sharon M. Harris, 75–102. Knoxville: University of Tennessee Press.

Vulgarities of Speech Corrected. 1829. London: F. C. Westley.

[Washburn, William Tucker.] 1869. *Fair Harvard: A Story of American College Life.* New York: G. P. Putnam and Son.

Washington, George. 1931–44. *The Writings of George Washington.* 39 vols. Washington, DC: Government Printing Office.

Watson, John Fanning. 1830. *Annals of Philadelphia.* Philadelphia: E. L. Carey and A. Hart.

Waugh, Evelyn. 1948. *The Loved One: An Anglo-American Tragedy.* Boston: Little, Brown.

Wax, Darold D. 1968. "A Philadelphia Surgeon on a Slaving Voyage to Africa, 1749–1751." *Pennsylvania Magazine of History and Biography* 92:465–93.

Weiser, Conrad. 1757. *Translation of a German Letter, Wrote by Conrad Weiser, Esq; Interpreter, on Indian Affairs, for the Province of Pennsylvania.* Philadelphia: n.p.

Wesley, John. 1988. *The Works of John Wesley.* Ed. W. Reginald Ward and Richard P. Heitzenrater. Nashville: Abingdon Press.

White, Andrew, and Edwin A. Dalyrymple. 1874. *Relatio Itineris in Marylandiam.* Trans. J. H. Converse. Baltimore: J. Murphy.

White, Andrew. 1995. *Voyage to Maryland* (1633). Trans. Barbara Lawatsch-Boomgaarden with Josef Ijsewijn. Wacaunda, IL: Bolchsazy-Carducci Publishers.

Whitefield, George. 1741. *A Continuation of the Reverend Mr. Whitefield's Journal.* Boston: G. Rogers and D. Fowle.

Whitman, Walt. 1964. "New Orleans in 1848" (1887). In *Prose Works 1892,* ed. Floyd Stovall, 2:604–7. New York: New York University Press.

Whitman, Walt. 1982. *Complete Poetry and Collected Prose.* New York: Library of America.

Whitney, William Dwight. 1874. *Oriental and Linguistic Studies, Second Series.* New York: Charles Scribner's Sons.

Williams, Roger. 1997. *A Key into the Language of America* (1643). Bedford, MA: Applewood Books.

Wilson, Jane. 1968. "Commerce in Hippieland." *Los Angeles Times,* January 28, B16.

Winthrop, John. 1645. *A Declaration of Former Passages and Proceedings betwixt the English and the Narrowgansets.* Boston: Stephen Day.

Wirth-Nesher, Hana. 2006. *Call it English: The Languages of Jewish-American Literature.* Princeton: Princeton University Press.

Wood, Peter H. 1974. *Black Majority: Negroes in Colonial South Carolina from 1670 through the Stono Rebellion.* New York: Norton.

Woolley, Lisa. 2000. *American Voices of the Chicago Renaissance.* DeKalb: Northern Illinois University Press.

Wright, Laura. 2001. "Third-Person Singular Present-tense *-s, -th,* and Zero, 1575–1648." *American Speech* 76:236–58.

Wyatt, Edith. 1903. *True Love: A Comedy of the Affections.* New York: McClure, Phillips & Co.

Index